Discover the Secret to
Raising Impressive Kids

The
Question
Based
Parent

Thomas A. Freese

Published by:

QBS Publishing, Inc.
P.O. Box 922933
Atlanta, Georgia 30010-2933

www.thequestionbasedparent.com

Cover and book design by Craig Moonshower

ISBN: 978-1-891892-80-6
Printed in Canada
1st printing 2007

...to Laura

Acknowledgements

Many people have influenced the writing of *The Question Based Parent*, some without even knowing it. When it comes to raising children, all we ever have to go on is the cumulative knowledge that we ourselves learn through our own trials and tribulations, along with the wisdom we glean from the experiences of others.

I am forever grateful to my wife Laura who has given me great insight about people in general, and more specifically, about how to be a father. Together, we are blessed to have two lovely daughters, Sarah and Mary Claire, who fortunately have inherited many of their mother's best qualities. Although this book was never intended to be a biography of our immediate family, I thank both of my girls for playing a starring role in my life and for allowing me to write about them.

A special note of gratitude must go to my Executive Assistant, Robin Decker, who is a pleasure to work with and has an amazing way of making sure that everything in my work life is moving in the right direction. I also wish to acknowledge my colleague and friend, Alan Rohrer, for his contributions to content as the book was taking shape.

Regarding design, layout, and the finished product, much appreciation goes to Craig Moonshower, whose graphical capabilities, professionalism, and friendship have vaulted him to the top of my list. I also wish to thank Emily Gilreath for keeping a keen eye on grammar, and also for her editing contributions to this, my fourth book. Don't worry, Emily, even if this book doesn't sell a million copies, we can still be friends.

I also wish to express my gratitude to Mark Reed, Richard Sites, Jim Hardee, Mark Selleck, Scott Whitney, John Patinella, Mitch Little, Jim Claffey, and Don Speese, all fellow parents, who were instrumental in motivating me to get this project get off the ground. Thank you for encouraging me to take my question-based thought process to the next level.

Lastly, I wish to acknowledge our friends, neighbors, and extended family for helping us to preserve a sense of balance in our lives and to maintain the proper perspective on what's really important.

Table of Contents

Introduction

I never intended to be a sales trainer. If someone had told me back in college, that I would write and publish four books on *anything*, I would have said they were crazy. Now, some years later, I run a sales consulting firm that is hired to train some of the most sophisticated sales organizations all over the world. Life is funny.

Similarly, before my wife Laura and I had two daughters, I didn't have a great deal of perspective regarding what parenting might be like, either. Truthfully, nothing can adequately prepare you for the awesome responsibility of raising a child. The Lamaze classes my wife and I attended while she was pregnant only taught us how to pop 'em out. "Does this thing' come with an owner's manual?" I remember thinking, just after the doctor spanked my newborn for the very first time. As you know, there is no instruction manual for how to raise a child. For most parents, it's trial by fire.

Somewhere along the way, my professional career as a business person intersected with the responsibilities associated with being a parent, and it turns out that the job function of a professional salesperson and the role of a parent have a lot in common. Consequently, I have learned a great deal about the human side of parenting by teaching people how to sell. I have also learned a lot about selling and training through my ongoing experiences of being a parent.

The most significant contribution of my professional career has been the creation and development of a strategic sales methodology called Question Based Selling. After investing the first seventeen years of my business experience in the trenches of sales and management, I jumped out of the corporate world and founded QBS Research, Inc. Our philosophy for being successful is very simply based on communication style, conversational dynamics, and the premise that the questions you choose to ask, and *how* you ask them, is oftentimes more important than what you could ever *say*.

Ever since I started training people on the QBS Methodology, I have received countless letters, emails, and personal notes from people in all walks of life telling me that in addition to QBS increasing their business effectiveness, the same techniques that work with customers have also dramatically improved the way they now interact with their family, friends, neighbors, spouse, and yes, even their children. After hearing this feedback virtually every week for the past ten years, it became clear that it was time to put the wheels in motion to complete this project.

For me, *The Question Based Parent* has grown into an evolving mission field, where this book gives me an opportunity to make a contribution that I hope will have an immediate impact on the way you interact with your children. More importantly, I believe that the concepts outlined in this book will change the way your kids interact with you. At some point, the bigger-picture question needs to be asked: Are you doing things as a parent that will create the desired long-term results in the way your children conduct themselves, or are you just a combatant in the ongoing battle to make it through the day?

I am the proud father of two very impressive daughters, Sarah and Mary Claire. While my natural sense of pride would like to think that they are indeed the beneficiaries of good genetics, it must be noted that children are incapable of parenting themselves. Therefore, some credit must be attributed to the environment in which they were raised, as well as the training they have received thus far. Have we done everything correctly as parents? Clearly, the answer to that question is no. Trust me when I tell you that we have stumbled upon numerous bumps in the road, in addition to encountering a few sizable potholes along the way. Fortunately, I believe that most of the lessons we learn from the school of hard knocks ultimately make us better people, and better parents. The parental lessons that my wife Laura and I have learned have also made the document you now hold in your hands a better book.

The Question Based Parent was written to put some methodology to the madness in our quest to become more effective parents, and to raise impressive kids. In our favor is the fact that human nature is often very predictable. There is no doubt that children are going to test your patience on a regular basis. Pushing parents to the limit is part of the job description of every son or daughter. Ever so slowly, however, you will begin to realize that while the struggle between parent and child hasn't changed significantly since we were young, your perspective on what is fair and reasonable has probably changed dramatically now that you are the parent.

That's because you no longer think like a child. Instead, you are now responsible for your family's health, welfare, and future direction, and the weight of every dilemma will ultimately rest on your shoulders. But, your kids are still kids, and they will never buy into the idea that spanking can actually 'hurt' a parent much worse than it hurts the child. Likewise, their youthful perspective doesn't allow them to comprehend the logic behind basic principles like the need for good manners, disciplinary consequences, or your desire for mutual respect.

But, suppose there was a way to reduce the number of daily squabbles that can so easily interrupt an otherwise happy morning or soothing bedtime routine. What if it were possible to be in closer touch with your kids, to the point where they come to you asking for guidance, as opposed to just having parental advice heaped upon them? What if bouts of contention within the family could be replaced by feelings of contentment, thereby fostering a more open and more communicative household environment?

There is no magic formula that will completely eliminate the ongoing struggle between parents and children, as you learn to coexist with your kids under the same roof. No one ever promised that parenting was going to be easy, or that you and I would inherently possess the skills required to be a successful mother or father. Trying to be the *best* parent in the world has never been my objective. If there is such a person, I would certainly love to meet them. In the meantime, the goal of this book is very simple. We have a responsibility to our children be the best parents *that we can be*, which includes setting reasonable boundaries, making decisions that benefit the overall well-being and development of our kids as they mature into adulthood, and administering consequences when our children exhibit momentary lapses in good judgment.

It is in our nature to care for others, and as parents, it is natural to care deeply about our children. We want to share our hopes and dreams with the people we love most, and we want those people to openly share their thoughts, feelings, and concerns back with us. Every parent wants to end up with confident, well-behaved, respectful and appreciative offspring. Now, wouldn't that be impressive? To achieve this goal, however, there is some responsibility on your part to be an effective communicator. No doubt you already recognize that or you wouldn't have made the investment to read this book. From here, my goal is simply to give you the tools and insight needed to be successful, so you can fulfill your destiny as a question-based parent.

Chapter 1

The Psychology of Questions vs. Statements

Isn't it strange that you must register for a specific fishing license in order to catch a trout, but you can raise as many kids as you want without any training whatsoever?
—Thomas A. Freese

For seven consecutive years, I taught the first-grade Sunday school class at our church. Teaching first-graders was perfect for me, because it's that magical time when kids transition from a playtime atmosphere in the kindergarten nursery, to more of a structured environment where young children can actually start absorbing the lesson of the day. It was also a good training ground for what I do now, as it isn't any more or less difficult to grab and hold the attention of a six-year-old, than it is to deliver "live" seminar material to a room full of twenty-year business veterans.

Then a couple years ago, my wife Laura and I were asked to lead a parenting Sunday school class at a different church. I intentionally use the word lead instead of teach, because the goal of the class was simply to facilitate discussion among a group of fellow parents who were all dealing with the many challenges associated with raising respectful children. Both Laura and I were excited about the opportunity to lead an adult parenting class, hoping that we would, in fact, pick up some valuable pointers along the way.

We ended up sharing the duties with two other couples, where each couple assumed the leadership role for a month of Sundays, as a way to foster some consistency with regard to the topics being discussed from week to week. That created an easy transition where the on-deck couple would take the leadership reins the following month, and it was understood that whoever was teaching was at liberty to choose whatever topics they wished to discuss.

Mid-year into this experience, Laura and I finished off our month and then handed the leadership baton to the next couple on the schedule. Let's call them Robert and Leslie. As we learned more about people in the class, we discovered that Robert and Leslie both were psychologists with doctoral degrees, both of whom were renowned in their respective areas of expertise. We affectionately called them Dr. Robert and Dr. Leslie. How ironic, we thought, that "experts" in the field of psychology were struggling with many of the same parenting issues as the rest of us. I remember that they had two energetic boys who I believe were four and five years old at the time.

One Sunday morning, Robert started the morning off with an opening prayer, as was customary. He then passed around copies of a one-page document he had reproduced, which was often the jumping-off point for class discussion, as many of the lessons we covered started with a Xeroxed worksheet of some kind. This particular document happened to be a photocopy of an article that Robert authored, which if memory serves me, had subsequently been printed in a local newspaper. The essence of his article was to characterize the five "keys" to raising good children.

With the slight self-conscious glow that comes from pride of authorship, Robert then proceeded to lead our parenting Sunday school class that day by reviewing each of his five points in some detail.

I don't remember anything about his first point. It might have been about child safety or creating a nurturing environment, but for some reason, I tuned out the whole discussion. I know that sounds rude, but if we are being totally honest, Robert's second point flew over my head just as quickly as the first. Perhaps I was distracted by something, or maybe I was just having a bad morning. It may have been that the first two points in his article seemed overly obvious to me, which would explain why it was so easy for my mind to drift. Then, Dr. Robert dropped an absolute bombshell when he introduced point number three, where his third piece of advice to parents started with a heading (in bold type) that read, "Use Statements, not Questions."

Wait a minute! Did I just hear someone say that one of the keys to successful parenting was to use more statements, as opposed to asking questions? Having invested the bulk of my professional career developing a sales methodology called Question Based Selling, I instantly perked up in my seat. Suddenly, the conversation had come around to my area of expertise, as QBS is a methodology that very specifically teaches people how to more effectively interact using question-based communication techniques. As you can imagine, I was suddenly very interested in his perspective on 'punctuation.'

"If you want kids to respect your authority as a parent," Dr. Robert explained, "then it is your responsibility to *tell* them what to do, as opposed to asking." One of the examples Robert cited was the typical bedtime routine where parents often struggle with getting children into bed on time.

"You shouldn't ask a child if they want to go to bed," he said. "Just tell them it's time to go to bed." Likewise, "Parents shouldn't be asking their children to finish their homework. You decide what you want your child to do," he said, "and then use statements to convey your request in an authoritative manner."

After listening carefully to his rationale, my hand shot up in the air. Imagine that, I was about to inquire about why using statements would be better than asking questions. Robert acknowledged my query, and I had the floor.

One important side note to this story: Before I wrote *The Question Based Parent*, most of the good people in our church and community had no idea where I worked or what I did for a living. Some people probably were aware that my career path had something to do with sales, but I don't use the fact that I have published three business books as a calling card within my church. I was just an interested participant who wanted to ask Dr. Robert a question about point number three.

"Robert," I said, "I am very curious about your thoughts on this subject because I have a different perspective with regard to questions vs. statements, and I would like to get your feedback on my thought process as it relates to what you just presented."

"Sure, go ahead," Robert invited.

I explained that my philosophy toward communication is based on the belief that many of the fundamentals regarding human nature apply whether you are dealing with a seventy-six-year-old senior citizen, a forty-six year old business person, or a six-year-old child. With some things, human nature is just human nature. Working in my office, for example, I have a full-time assistant (Robin) who coordinates my calendar, plans upcoming events, and manages the daily operations of our training and consulting practice. Robin is terrific and I often need her to do something for me. But, it would never occur to me to summon her help by saying, "Robin, go make 100 copies of this document!" To me, that sounds harsh, like a command, which seems unappreciative and disrespectful. Therefore, I would much rather deliver my request using words like, "Robin, could you please make 100 copies of this document?" I might even add, "Is there any way you could have this ready before my 2:00pm appointment?"

Robin does not question my authority as her boss, and because she is so competent and capable, I try not to take her for granted. Having asked for her assistance, if for some reason my requested 100 copies won't be ready by 2:00pm, she will tell me and we then put our heads together to figure out the best workaround. Otherwise, she makes it happen. Generally speaking, when I make a reasonable request, Robin finds a way to get it done. By the way, when she needs something from me, I, too, would much rather be asked than told. Much of this is just common courtesy.

If we relate this philosophy back to parenting, it would never occur to me to point my finger and say to one of my daughters, "Pick up your shoes," or, "I want you to go to bed." Instead, I would be much more inclined to ask, "Sarah, would you please pick up your shoes?" Or, instead of just telling my kids to turn off the lights and go to bed, I would be more likely to say something like, "Girls, could you please wrap up what you're doing and head upstairs for bed?" I summed up my comments to Robert by suggesting, "To me, putting a parental request in the form of a question is a much more respectful way for parents to communicate requests to our children, and it is also a much more effective means of achieving the desired result."

Sounds pretty good, huh?

"Well, that's wrong," Dr. Robert replied.

"Wrong?" I asked, surprised as to the starkness of his response.

"Yes," he insisted. Robert took the position that conveying our desires in the form of a question sends a mixed message to the child, which ultimately erodes your authority as a parent. Basically, his thinking was that asking a child to do something gives them the ability to refuse the request; in which case, your authority as a parent would be reduced to a level lower than before you asked. He seemed very attached to the idea that telling kids what to do somehow substantiates and reaffirms a parent's authority within the household.

Our exchange about item number three in the article ended with Robert saying, "Asking instead of telling causes children to wonder who the authority figure is within the household." I am paraphrasing but he basically explained, "If you use questions, your authority will start to erode and continue to weaken over time."

The discussion moved on to the fourth "key" to raising successful children, and I tuned back out.

Quietly, I leaned over to my wife Laura, who was sitting on my immediate left, and asked, "Do our kids have any problem knowing who the authority figures are within our household?"

"No, honey," she said. "I think that's pretty clear to both of them."

Mutual Respect is a Two-Way Street

You might be surprised to hear me say this, but relying solely on parental authority to control your children is highly over-rated. In fact, one of the chief complaints we heard on a weekly basis while leading this parenting class, that I suspect, reflects a common frustration among parents in all corners of the globe, was the concern that, "My children don't listen to me." Parents are constantly saying, "I have to say the same thing three or four times before my kids will respond."

What's the definition of insanity? Some people say it's the practice of doing the same things over and over and then expecting a different result. To parents who deal with this problem of selective hearing, I must pose a simple question. If making declarations to your children is not working, would you be open to making a few small adjustments in your own behavior, to see if your kids respond better to someone who is question-based, as opposed to the old statement-based approach?

While it may be true that parents have the "right" to tell kids what to do, perhaps part of this discussion needs to focus on the longer term outlook of what kind of relationship you want to have with your children down the road. Consider this: While a parent may have the power and authority to dictate just about anything to a child who is very young, you will not be able to *force* your children to respect you as they get older.

Keep in mind that having control over our children is not the goal. Granted, there are certain rules we want our kids to follow and there are definitely responsibilities we want them to fulfill. As caring parents, we want our kids to do their best whether they are playing a sport or doing chores. We also want them to diligently complete their schoolwork and we hope that they will be kind and charitable toward others. As well, there is a universal feeling among parents that we also want our children to have respect for us as their parents, and for all adults.

Let's face it. Most of us parents have high expectations in this regard. After all, we were taught to respect our parents, and, in an odd twist of fate, we want our kids to do the same! When children are young, you can even force the issue, requiring your kids to say, "Yes, sir," or "Yes, ma'am," at the end of every sentence. But, I can assure you that things will change as your children age and grow increasingly more independent.

During the early years of childhood, it's pretty clear that children are dependent on their parents for virtually everything. From the 'bottle stage' through preschool, a child relies on his parents for the basics like food and shelter, clothes and toys, not to mention a hand to hold while walking across a busy parking lot. At some point, however, a budding sense of independence will begin to develop within every child, and your kids will start to think for themselves, at which point they will begin to make their own assessments and decisions.

For some parents, a child's independence is a double-edged sword.

"Look at how much Johnny can do," a proud parent proclaims, "and he is only four years old!"

"Susie is extremely smart," another parent contends, "and she's already learning Latin in Kindergarten." The competition is underway.

"Aaron has you both beat," a third parent comments, "He is learning logarithms in preschool."

Seriously, what happened to singing songs like, "I've Been Working on the Railroad," or learning to jump rope, or just coloring? Most kids are going to learn at their own pace, and while it's natural for some to progress faster than others, I would urge you to be careful just how hard you push your children.

There's an old saying in sales, that, "The harder you choose to push someone, the more that other person will want to push back." If you're a science buff, this is a simple lesson in physics. Increased force on one side of a relationship tends to create greater resistance on the other. Said differently, the more force you apply, the more likely it is that the other person in the relationship will want to rebel. Interestingly, this science analogy applies to my offspring as well as yours. It also applies to the relationships you have with your spouse, co-workers, friends, and neighbors. We all want to have solid relationships with people we care about and love, but even in these special relationships, no one wants to be pushed or manipulated by force.

Younger children tend to offer little resistance. Sure, infants and toddlers can make a fuss great enough to test the level of anyone's patience, but most parents are still able to use their authority to manipulate the behavior and activities of a totally dependent child. As the years roll by and the child begins to experience a growing sense of independence, however, the parent-child relationship will begin to change. One of those changes has to do with the type of punctuation you use at the end of your sentences. As your kids grow up, outright commands will rapidly become less and less effective parenting tools.

The diagram on the following page further illustrates this point, showing that your parental authority will progressively decrease over time as a child matures. A parent will never have more control over the location, schedule, or activities of a child than in the first year after a new baby arrives home from the hospital. Once the child passes through these early stages of development, however, the line representing your child's independence begins to escalate, and at some point in the future, the child's autonomy will ultimately surpass your ability to exercise parental power as a primary means of controlling them. This maturity cycle is a predictable phenomenon that characterizes how the nature of the relationship between parent and child evolves over time.

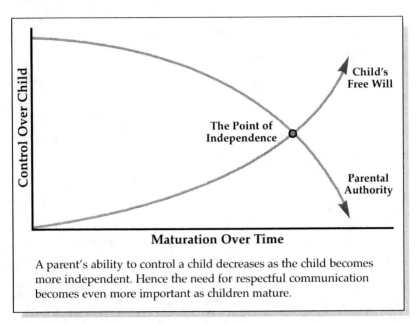

A parent's ability to control a child decreases as the child becomes more independent. Hence the need for respectful communication becomes even more important as children mature.

When will your child reach this point of independence? No one can predict the answer to this question with absolute certainty because every child is different. Suffice it to say that your young son or daughter will soon discover that they are no longer willing to be controlled, and it will begin to happen at some point between the age where they are first allowed to ride a bicycle on a street without supervision and when they finish high school and officially jump out of the nest.

The kicker is, children in our increasingly progressive society are becoming more independent much earlier in the development cycle, which catches many parents off guard. You can see evidence of this at virtually any school, church, or public swimming pool, where kids are increasingly emboldened to talk back to traditional authority figures like teachers, lifeguards, baby sitters, and parents. Unfortunately, many of these authority figures, when faced with a rebellious child, will smart-mouth right back, which tends to escalate the already undesirable behavior.

What is the point of this discussion? As your child's thought process becomes increasingly more independent, it is this author's belief that your ability to control their behavior solely through the use of parental authority will greatly diminish. That's one of the reasons why response statements like, "Because I said so," tend to carry significantly less weight with a young adult than a younger child. At some point, it will occur to the child who is on the receiving end of this logic to think, "Who cares what you say? I want to be my own person."

I am not suggesting that your children, at some point in the future, will totally disregard everything you say. In fact, many of us are still impacted to this day by input we receive from *our* own parents. But, it has become very clear that a parent's ability to have a positive influence on a child in their later stages of development requires a certain level of dignity and mutual respect, to be effective as apposed to just handing out orders. The operative phrase here is *mutual respect*.

Here's what I believe. Children should absolutely respect the moral authority of their parents. This has been a fundamental tenet of our natural order since the beginning of time. If you can be held responsible for your child's behavior and decision making until they reach the age of majority, parents *should* have the moral authority to establish a reasonable set of rules within the household and then expect kids to operate within the boundaries that have been established. But, as young people approach and then pass this point of independence, a child's respect for parental authority is something that must now be earned, rather than claimed.

It should be noted that how receptive a child might be toward their parent's advice during the tumultuous teenage years has a lot to do with the expectations you set for your children when they are much younger, and the resulting consequences of their actions when the line gets crossed. The statement-based parent, for example, who feels powerful and all-mighty because they have complete command over a five-year-old, will likely be brought to their knees in frustration when that same child reaches their early teens and realizes that the phrase, "Because I said so," doesn't carry the same weight it used to.

One of the primary themes throughout this book is the idea that how you interact with your children in the short-term will have a lasting impact on how they choose to interact with you down the road. Do you want your kids to respect you as they grow into young adulthood? Of course, every parent wants this. Then, you might want to put some thought into showing your children a little respect along the way. I am not suggesting that you completely jettison your authority as a parent, just that there are lots of ways to foster a sense of cooperation and camaraderie within the household other than using brute force.

Mutual respect is the key. If you want cooperation from your kids over the long term, then I am here to tell you that you must earn their respect. "But, Tom, I am the parent. They *have to* respect me!" That may be true for a few years, while your kids are young and dependent on you for everything. But, I can promise that the inherent obligation to respect the 'hand that feeds them' will gradually diminish as your children learn how to fend for themselves.

Mutual respect is a commodity that should be earned anyway. If you think about it, we work every day to earn the respect of our friends, neighbors, colleagues, coworkers, and customers. And, I would guess that you have all experienced the lesson where taking someone for granted is one of the quickest ways to lose their respect, and damage the relationship. But, then we adopt, become guardians for, or have children of our own flesh and blood. We take on this awesome responsibility with the intrinsic promise to give these kids the best of ourselves, and the only thing most parents want in return is a little cooperation and appreciation, which starts with one simple word—respect.

What can we as parents do to earn a child's respect? Frankly, there are lots of ways. Let's start with the idea of setting a good example. Ask yourself, are you the kind of person you want your children to grow up to become? Would you like your children to smoke? How frequently would you like them to drink alcohol, if at all? Would you like it if they chose to eat right and exercise regularly? Do you want them to work hard, be involved in community activities, or attend church on a regular basis? Trust me, your kids are watching closely, and the mother and father are their primary role models. So, what behaviors are you demonstrating to your kids on a daily basis?

Along these same lines, how do you want your children (in the future) to talk to your grandchildren? Do you want them to be harsh and dictatorial, or respectful and kindhearted? Most parents I know would consciously choose the later. But then something goes haywire during the normal course of a day, and one of your kids treads on your very last nerve. Suddenly, all bets are off as your rational goals for your family are superseded by the heat of the moment, and you regrettably transform into the socialist dictator you wouldn't necessarily choose to be. Rational goal-oriented parenting is difficult indeed.

It's also worth noting that authority can be an addictive drug. If issuing authoritative commands, like telling your kids to "Pick up your shoes," or, "Go upstairs and do your homework," makes you feel important and powerful, then you may be in for a rude awakening in the not-too-distant future. This type of statement-based discourse can be very demeaning to a child. It essentially communicates that you have unrestricted power over them, without regard to what they think or how they might feel. Now ask yourself, is being demeaning to your children an example you want to set for them? If so, being disrespectful to your kids is one of the quickest ways to cause a child to be disrespectful in return. "You get what you give," is what my wife Laura says.

One of the premise concepts we teach in Question Based Selling is the notion that 'telling is not selling.' Customers actually like to make purchase decisions, but most do *not* want to be dictated to by a salesperson regarding what to buy. As it turns out, most children don't want to be dictated to by their parents, either. "Do this...," then, "Do that!" Why? "Because I said so." Just like if you were stuck reporting to a boss who was overly commanding, this position of parental authority is likely to be short-lived.

Fortunately for parents, and for our children, there is an alternative to being dictatorial. The cool part is, you don't have to throw away all of your experience to successfully implement this new approach. All you have to do is deliver your request in the form of a polite question. This doesn't subvert your power or authority over the household. When I ask my assistant Robin, "Would you please make a photo copy of this contract," she knows I'm the boss, even through my request wasn't communicated in the form of a command. There's no need to worry because your kids also know (all too well) who's in charge. You just don't have to throw it in their face every time you make a simple request like, "Would you please pick up your shoes?" or, "Is this a good time to get started on your homework?"

Be careful, though. This is not a magic pill. Just asking questions won't ensure perfect behavior from your children. There is much more to be said on the issue of *what* questions to ask and *how* to ask them, which explains why this book has ten chapters. Be assured, however, that we will deal with topics like responsibility, motivation, discipline, listening, and how to successfully negotiate with a child.

For now, let's just say that if you are going to implement a question-based approach, then you must be ready to pause and listen to the responses you receive to the questions being asked. Herein lies one of the most important secrets to effective parental communication—if you are willing to communicate in a way that is respectful to your children, as opposed to being dictatorial, you then have the moral authority to expect a reciprocal level of mutual respect in return.

Avoid Questions that Shame Your Child

Are you aware that most of the major cities in the United States are full of counselors—marriage counselors and family counselors? When they are in session, what do you suppose these counselors spend most of their time talking with clients about? The answer is communication. Ineffective communication is by far the leading cause of broken relationships and troubled homes in America. And, in many cases, the situation involves good people who are struggling to find a way to more effectively communicate with their spouse, their friends, their business associates, their coworkers, and also their children.

The question-based parent is in a strong position to break down many of the barriers that can otherwise obstruct effective communication. Talking from the heart, for example, is easy if the other person is *open* to hearing what you have to say. Likewise, listening attentively isn't that difficult provided that people you care about are willing to openly share their thoughts, feelings, and concerns. What can you do to cause people in your life to be more open to listening, or more willing to share? Well, just because a parent wants to ask a bunch of questions, doesn't necessarily mean you will accomplish these objectives.

In fact, asking ineffective questions can actually be a destructive influence within your relationships. This needs to be pointed out before we dive too deeply into the technique discussion. Would you agree that there is a fine line between asking appropriate questions and making someone feel pressured, as if they were on the receiving end of an interrogation? We see this a lot in parent-child relationships, where questions are too often being used as conversational weapons, as opposed to productive communication tools.

Some of you might be thinking, "I don't use conversational weapons on my children." And maybe you don't. But, I bet your parents used them on you, and I would be willing to bet that most of us have been guilty on occasion of using them on our children, as well. Let me give you a few examples that might sound familiar.

The worst questions are those intended to shame a child into recognizing the extent of their mistake. Let me set the stage. Little Johnny is playing outside when suddenly, he hears the bellowing voice of his mother calling, "Johnny, you come inside this instant." Being summoned by a parent to come "this instant" is usually a bad sign for any child.

With hands on hips, mom fires her weapon, by saying, "What on earth were you thinking when you trampled Mrs. Smith's flowers?" Often without waiting for an answer to the first question, the mother then pulls the trigger on the second barrel, saying, "Do you realize the trouble you've caused?"

Most parents have lots more ammunition where that came from. "Well, mister? What do have to say for yourself?" These shame-inducing questions are often followed by a wounding statement or two, which only serves to give the parent an opportunity to reload and fire again. "What's the matter with you? I can't believe that you could be so thoughtless. Someone of your age should know better! What am I going to do with you?"

For a child, there is no adequate way to respond to a question like, "What's the matter with you?" Or, when a parent, in the midst of a tirade, asks a question like, "Do you think I was born yesterday?", they are generally not looking for a thoughtful response. Instead, the parent who delivers this type of rhetorical barb is demonstrating to the child how upset they are, and they are using the closest weapon available to make their point.

If we step back from the heat of the moment, let me ask, what do you suppose the asker of these questions is trying to accomplish? Does this parent really want her child to feel stupid or incompetent? If that's the goal, then mission accomplished. When questions are used to shame a child, even though the parent doesn't actually utter the words, the child hears, "What's the matter with you...you incompetent loser?" Like the finely honed blade of a ninja's sword, this type of verbal weaponry can leave lasting scars on parent-child relations.

That's why I don't ask my kids questions like, "What do you have to say for yourself?" There's no reasonable way for a child to thoughtfully respond to this type of rhetorical question. Another perennial favorite that parents love to ask is, "Do you think money grows on trees?" Most of the time, the person asking the question isn't soliciting input anyway. They're probably just venting, in which case, most children will quickly clam up and tune out.

Ironically, the same questions that can be damaging to a relationship can also be valuable conversational tools, if the parent is earnestly seeking information. Especially when dealing with a behavioral issue, my two daughters understand that their opinions do matter to their mother and I. There are usually two sides to every story, and in the event of a problem, the very first thing I want to know is what happened. I'm not suggesting that my kids won't be held accountable for their actions if they are indeed responsible. I am just saying that the first thing a question-based parent wants to know is what the child was thinking, especially if something they did caused an undesirable outcome.

The key to asking effective questions is to make sure you give the child an opportunity to deliver a reasonable response. There is no point in getting upset until you know the facts, anyway. Consequently, it would be easy for me to start by asking, "Can you tell me what happened?" Notice that the phrase, "Can you tell me..." has a built-in subtlety that is intentionally neutral in an effort to be non-threatening. Technically, the answer to my question is either, "Yes, I can tell you," or "No, I cannot." Most of the time, however, what I get is the child's perspective on what occurred.

You might wonder, why bother with subtlety? If the parent is supposed to be the authority figure within the household, why not just get in the child's face and demand that they share the details with you? Actually, that is one alternative. But, it comes back to the issue of mutual respect. You see, if someone does not want to share information with you, then it doesn't matter what questions you ask—you probably won't get the full story. On the other hand, if your children are willing to open up and share the details of what happened, then you (as a parent) won't have to fight with your kids to have productive conversations.

After gathering the initial facts about what occurred, the second thing I want to know is, "What were you thinking?" There's no point in using a harsh or accusatory tone. That just puts up communication barriers. Honestly, I really do want to know what my child was thinking. Especially when it looks like a consequence might be forthcoming, it's important to know whether you are dealing with an accident, a momentary lapse in judgment, or malicious intent. To me, there's a big different between accidentally stepping in some flowers, and stomping on them for sport.

Avoiding rhetorical questions whose only purpose is to shame your children isn't always easy, especially if they have clearly stepped out-of-bounds and tensions are running high. Fortunately, you can easily control this by making the following commitment to yourself: *I will only ask questions to gather information that I don't already have, confirm a perspective that isn't necessarily certain, or fashion an opinion that hasn't already been formed. Otherwise, there's no point in asking.*

What if a Child Doesn't Comply?

One could argue that children are defiant by nature. But, then, so are most adults. Have you ever attended a meeting of volunteers in your church or at your kid's school? With independent thinkers, securing a consensus on even the simplest of things can sometimes become a torturous task.

This natural defiance is one of the reasons parents default to making dictatorial statements, rather than asking questions. Statements seem so much more authoritative, especially to the insecure parent. They think asking a child, for example, "Would you please pick up your shoes?", leaves the door open for that child to respond by saying, "No, thanks, I would rather leave my shoes in the middle of the kitchen floor."

Dr. Robert pointed this out to me that fateful day in Sunday school. "Asking questions is fine, until the child refuses to comply," he said. "At that point, you have relinquished your parental authority."

Not so fast, Mr. Psychology. My view of the question-based parent is not about winning and losing. Being question-based is more about identifying and implementing communication techniques that will help to foster a more open, loving, and caring foundation for learning how to coexist within the household as parent and child. In fact, every time you ask a thoughtful question, you show the other person that you are genuinely interested in their perspective or opinion. Do children appreciate it when a parent gets down to their level and becomes truly interested in their thoughts, feelings, and concerns? I submit that the answer is a resounding, *YES*. In fact, do you realize that the chief complaint most marriage and family counselors hear on a daily basis stems from the fact that someone close to them is uninterested in their opinions or their point of view?

Personally, I don't worry about my kids being defiant. In addition to demonstrating respect for children, questions ironically put parents in a unique position of strength. For example, if one of my kids wanted to test the waters by saying, "No Dad, I would rather just leave my shoes sitting in the middle of the floor," that would be a very interesting day at the Freese house. You would not see me get upset. Just the opposite, as you will hear me encourage parents throughout this book to say what you mean, and mean what you say. I would probably just fire a shot across the bow, by asking, "Are you still planning watch some television after dinner, or have a friend over on the weekend?"

"Yes," my daughter would say.

"Then, please pick up your shoes from the kitchen floor."

What Does a Sales Trainer Know about Parenting?

By now, you are starting to get a sense for my philosophy on dealing with people, especially as we focus on how communication can affect the relationship between parent and child. I do not intend in this book to discount the reality of psychiatric dysfunction. Admittedly, I am not a therapist, and therefore, will gladly defer to the experts with regard to eating disorders, anxiety, severe emotional trauma, ADHD, or depression. But, come on! Every child who demonstrates some behavioral exuberance does not need to be diagnosed with Attention Deficit Disorder (ADD), or be put on a 'calming' drug like Ritalin. I have seen plenty of cases where the parents should be the ones on Ritalin.

In sales, I learned a long time ago that you cannot pressure customers into purchasing a product or service. Why not? It's because people don't want to be pressured, manipulated, or otherwise controlled. Again, the harder you push, the harder other people will tend to push back. Let me ask you this: How does a salesperson in today's day and age force you to buy something you don't want? The answer is, they can't! Fortunately, the professional world is rapidly adapting to this reality as companies realize that selling is less about brute force, and more about effective communication skills. From my perspective *sales* is not a dirty word, but rather a high integrity profession that involves communicating with customers in ways that will ultimately help them accomplish their goals and objectives.

As my daughters reached the point where they were old enough to communicate, I discovered that many of the same principles that pertain in the business environment also applied right here at home. That's not because we run our home like a business, because we don't. Rather, it's because many of the same interpersonal skills and common decencies that characterize effective interaction make just as much sense whether you are dealing with a customer, a colleague, or one of your own children.

Put it this way, if dealing with your customers (or your children) on an ongoing basis is a daily battle, then I can tell you with some certainty that you are already losing the war. Conflict creates a win/lose scenario which will erode the foundation of any relationship over time. Effective communication is not about defeating another person, anyway. The truth is, if one person in a relationship loses, it's likely that both will lose. Fortunately for us parents, the goal when raising children is to create win/win scenarios, where positive behavior from the child fosters a sense of trust and respect back to the parent. In turn, the respect you show your kids will hopefully instill a sense of trust and confidence that will naturally cause them to gravitate toward more desirable behavior.

There are lots of interesting parallels between my business philosophy and the role of a question-based parent, whose job it is to oversee the family unit. In fact, one of the most rewarding pieces of feedback I have now heard almost every week since I wrote my first book ten years ago, occurs when people tell me or send a note saying, "Hey Tom, in addition to helping me become significantly more successful in my dealings with customers, your approach has also greatly improved the way I communicate with my spouse and children." Bingo! Caring about people is not something that gets turned off at the end of the business day.

Like I said earlier, human nature is human nature, whether you are dealing with a seventy-six-year-old senior citizen, or a six-year-old child. Fortunately for us, the characteristics of human nature that we will focus on in this book are also relatively easy to predict, which is why the same question-based communication techniques that have been perfected in Question Based Selling, are now being made available to empower and benefit you, the question-based parent.

Chapter 2

Train Up a Child

"Train up a child in the way he should go: and when he is old, he will not depart from it."
— Proverbs 22:6 (KJV)

It may be a shortcoming on my part, but I don't want to have to fight with my kids in order to get them out of a swimming pool when it's time to go. I want to ask them once, and then have them choose to get out on their own accord. But, you have probably witnessed the scene yourself on many summer afternoons, where pool decks are loaded with parents pleading with their kids to get out of the pool. "Come on Jimmy. Don't make me ask you again. We need to go home! Jimmy? What's the matter with you? Jimmy! You'd better get out right now!"

Fortunately for everyone involved, this type of "pool pleading" doesn't happen at the Freese house. When it's time to wrap up the fun, Laura or I will purse our lips and deliver one of our patented "Wee-hoo" whistles, which both of our children can hear up to 200 yards away. Upon hearing this whistle signal, our girls will turn from whatever they're doing and make eye contact with us. A quick "come here" signal with the index finger lets them know to tell their friends, "Gotta go," and out of the pool they come. It's like an old parlor trick, and we often have other parents asking, "How do get your kids to be so cooperative?"

The truth is, my children aren't any more or less cooperative than anyone else's kids. Together, we have just developed a very clear understanding that if it is going to be a challenge to drag them out of a swimming pool, then they will probably forfeit their opportunity to get in the water next time. This understanding didn't happen by magic or by accident. It happened because my two daughters happen to be the beneficiaries of parents who believe in the fundamentals of good training. Have we ever been challenged by a strong-willed child with a different perspective? The answer is yes. But I can tell you that it only happened once on the pool issue as my youngest daughter quickly discovered that getting out of the pool upon request was much more enjoyable than sitting on the sidelines and watching everyone else have fun.

A parent's job is easy if you are dealing with a totally independent, completely self-sufficient, and fully cooperative child. These types of kids don't require a whole lot of guidance, and when they do, they are fully receptive and amenable to receiving direction and cooperating with a parent's suggestions. In this environment, parent and child work together as a true team. I wouldn't trade my kids for anything, but I can tell you that this level of parental nirvana is a scenario with which I am unfamiliar.

If I were a betting man, I would guess that your kids (like mine) are not always as self-motivated or autonomous as we want them to be. Hence the challenge that any parent who desires the best for their children faces on a daily basis. How do you foster a sense of teamwork and cooperation with a child who is trying to forge their own identity and doesn't necessarily want to be under the scrutiny or tutelage of a parent or guardian?

The need for training has existed since the beginning of time. But for some reason, it has become politically incorrect to talk about raising a child in terms of training. I'm not sure why our culture has adopted an aversion to the idea of proper training. You wouldn't want a physical examination from an untrained doctor, would you? Every four years at the Olympic Games, gold medals are awarded to the most highly trained athletes in their respective sports. These athletes didn't get there by chance. I bet you wouldn't even schedule a haircut with someone who wasn't appropriately trained. Yet, for some reason, very little attention is paid to the need to train children in "the way he/she should go," and there is even less focus on how to train mothers and fathers to be effective trainers of children.

Note that I am not talking about teaching your kids how to fetch or perform tricks like a dog rolling over. What I am saying is you basically have eighteen years or so to teach your kids how to become responsible, self-reliant adults who will hopefully contribute a net positive to those with whom they interact. While 18 years may sound like a long ramp up, you might as well chop off the first few years when you are doting on your totally-dependent newborns and toddlers, and also the last few years when you are ripping your hair out over having to deal with the stubbornness that often accompanies adolescence. It's the between time where we will have the opportunity and responsibility as parents to train our children in the ways of the world, and the ways to get along in this world. More specifically, it is our responsibility to teach children that there is an upside for doing things that are mutually beneficial, and a downside for behaving in ways that are detrimental to themselves or others.

How do you want your kids to behave in school or in church? Do you want them to wear a bicycle helmet, even when you're not looking? Do you want them to buckle their seatbelt and continue to drive safely long after they get their initial drivers' license? Do you want your kids to say "No" to drugs, and be a role model to others? Do you want them to have personal goals and learn to think before they act, or would you rather they just blurt out whatever happens to be on their little minds?

Even if your children are naturally good kids, you still have a responsibility to prepare them for when it comes time to step out into the real world. Unfortunately for us parents, this is not a parental to-do item that just gets checked off the list. Rather, managing your child's perspective and expectations is an ongoing objective that should remain high on every parent's priority list. It is not realistic to expect young people to somehow learn the most important lessons in life without any guidance from their parents.

Interestingly, some of the most valuable learning opportunities present themselves during the normal course of the family routine. For example, when Laura and I came home a couple of weeks ago from our usual Saturday evening date, no one had cleaned up the kitchen after dinner. The responsible party should have been our oldest daughter Sarah, who was supposed to be babysitting her sister, too. Since this wasn't the first time the kitchen was in disarray when we arrived home, we summoned Sarah and asked, "Why was the kitchen not cleaned after dinner?" By the way, one of the perks of being the oldest is that she can earn money to babysit when we go out. But, babysitting in our house includes more than just hanging out and watching television. Babysitting is a responsibility that includes managing the household, which means serving dinner, supervising activities, getting her little sister into bed on time, and cleaning up whatever mess is made.

Well, guess what? In the real world, if you aren't willing to do the job, you don't get paid. Basically, it cost Sarah about twenty dollars that night because putting away a couple pieces of uneaten pizza and putting the box in the recycling bin was not a priority for her that evening. It's a tough lesson, but that's how they learn. Suffice it to say that Sarah made the adjustment and she has been doing an excellent and complete job ever since.

Are we unfair parents, by expecting our kids to come when called, get out of the pool when asked, or be accountable for a job responsibility they committed to take on? I would like to plant the seed on a much larger discussion, by saying that the parent who gives in every time that little Jimmy complains or comes up short is not doing him any favors in the longer term.

Even if your kids come from good genetic stock, there are no guarantees. The Kentucky Derby will never be won by a poorly trained horse, even if it is a thoroughbred. Likewise, a poorly trained child will likely face a litany of ongoing struggles just to survive, not to mention succeed. In fact, trying to shelter a child in a protected cocoon environment for too long may keep them from discovering their full range of potential. Therefore, it only makes sense that we as parents must assume responsibility for teaching and guiding the next generation.

The Good Old Days?

Keep in mind that in previous generations, there was very little negotiation between children and parents. Kids were more like pets. The family down the street, for example, might have two dogs, three kids, and a cat, all of whom needed to be bathed and fed on a regular basis. For recreation, the dogs, kids, and cat were sent outside to play, until some point later in the day when a booming voice would call them all back in. And, they all equally feared the possibility of being whipped with a newspaper or a belt if the owner got upset with them.

The culture was different back then. Parents felt they had the right to deal with their offspring however they wanted and children knew they had better comply or else. In my neighborhood, kids were not asked for their opinions and they rarely got a vote in family decisions. I am not waxing nostalgically to suggest that those were better times. They were just different times.

Unfortunately, the harshness of the old days has caused the pendulum to swing too far the other way over the last twenty years or so, into an era where children are now being given way too much latitude, too much discretion, and an abundance of freedoms. As a result, kids are being spoiled with overindulgence along with a steadily declining sense of responsibility. To me, either end of this spectrum represents an excessive condition that is ultimately destructive to the family unit.

Does that mean we should resign ourselves to being a product of the surrounding culture? I don't think so. Instead, it might be time to take the bull by the horns relative to training up your own children *in the way he (she) should go, so that later in life, they will not depart from it (Proverbs 22:6)*. Of course, this might require a few small adjustments in strategy on the way to becoming a question-based parent, as opposed to being statement-based.

The ability to be question-based is one of the big differences between kids and pets. You see, pets don't respond to questions. If you ask your dog or cat for input, they will just sit there and look at you. Kids, on the other hand, don't necessarily respond that well to dictatorial commands, so issuing orders is hopefully not your planned strategy for building mutual bonds with your children.

Perhaps we should take a closer look at the correlation that exists between responsibility and privileges and spend some time thinking about how best to communicate these values to our children. As you know, every child comes into the world with a clean slate—they are born without any biases, prejudices, or expectations. Somehow along the way, when a child receives too many privileges without being given an appropriate corresponding responsibility, you increase your risk of ending up with an over-indulged child—one who will likely take many of life's blessings for granted. In these cases, it is not unusual for a child's expectations to escalate to a point where they can no longer be satisfied with the status quo. This pattern can be the beginning of a life-long cycle of behavior that creates conflict, inconsistency, and self-doubt. Have you ever noticed how some of the richest people in the world are also the most unhappy, while some of the poorest cultures in the world are filled with joyful people who are celebrating all the time?

Since parents are, in fact, a child's primary reference when it comes to setting and managing expectations, it is my belief that we should be proactive in this regard. We must teach our kids how to become productive contributors within the family, on the way to becoming confident, responsible, dependable members of society. Even if your child was born with thoroughbred genes, he or she still needs proper training if you want him (or her) to develop into a true champion.

Don't be Afraid to Manage Expectations

Handling the many different responsibilities around the household requires a team effort. Although different people each have their unique roles, there is an opportunity for everybody to share in the overall responsibilities, and everyone should be expected to participate. Does that sound old-fashioned? Honestly, some families (including our own) could learn a thing or two from the way things were done back in colonial times, or on a family farm.

Most kids today have it easy. After they finish watching their favorite television show and chatting with friends on the Internet, they play a little Game Boy on the way to their youth soccer game, and then attend a pizza party afterwards to celebrate the end of the season. Following the festivities, the parent is then expected to hurry home because the child wants to finish a Disney movie that was recorded earlier on the digital video recorder.

Meanwhile, parents are running ragged to keep pace. Bobbie has to be driven to his baseball practice three nights a week, Susie has her piano lessons every Wednesday and dance class on Friday afternoon, and little Johnny is getting ready to start karate lessons twice a week. Poor mom has to keep all the uniforms and school clothes clean and ready. Dad has to hurry home from the office to help shuttle the children. Never mind the ever shrinking amount of time parents get to spend together nurturing the bonds of their own relationship as a couple. All bets are off if mom works outside the home, or if this schedule is being thrusted upon a single parent.

Even with all this attention, kids still believe that the world is unfairly stacked against them. More than ever, I am convinced that what seems fair to a child is a simple matter of perspective. "But, Daaaad, that's not fairrrrrr!" has been a common complaint at times in the Freese house. And I have learned through experience that when either of the words 'daaaad" or 'fairrrrrr' are pronounced with three distinctly separate syllables, trouble is definitely brewing.

It has also become clear that it's futile to attempt to counter a child's reasoning with adult logic. Try if you must, but the simple truth is we have become an entitlement society where children continually push to get more privileges, but they don't necessarily want to work for them.

This entitlement phenomenon isn't caused by parental ignorance or maltreatment. Instead, the whole notion of 'getting something for nothing' is what most children experience when they are first brought into the world. A newborn infant, for example, does not have to reciprocate in any way to receive their mother's milk. To them, it just happens magically. The child doesn't know how or why, but for some reason, new parents are more than ready and willing to provide unconditional support for their wonderful little bundles of joy. If, for some reason, the parent is not ready at feeding time, the child frantically whines and complains (otherwise known as crying) until the parent rushes to satisfy their desire. For many months, the conditioned behavior that gets ingrained is a basic one—whenever the child peeps, the parent responds, and they do so until the full extent of the child's desires are completely satisfied. Being a newborn is a privileged existence to be sure.

At some point, however, children start to develop levels of capability where they are no longer totally dependent. A boy or girl progressively learning to do more and more things on their own is a good thing. It's part of the natural order of social development. In fact, your child's development and growing independence can foster a significant sense of accomplishment. Learning to tackle exciting tasks like tying one's shoes or combing one's own hair can make a child feel smart and capable. But, for some reason, kids aren't nearly as eager to develop the same level of independence for those things that seem like work to them.

I remember when my oldest daughter was a toddler; she used to follow me all over the house, wanting to "help" empty the trash cans. To her, retrieving the trash from every room in the house was loads of fun. Helping her dad do something that seemed important probably made her feel very grown-up. At some point, however, she realized that what we were actually doing was taking out the garbage. Suddenly, emptying trash cans all over the house was no longer fun! Sarah still has 'Trash Duty' on her list of weekly responsibilities and it's part of her allowance. But, you can usually tell when it's trash day at the Freese house, because you will probably hear the familiar phrase, "But, Daaaad, that's not fairrrrrr!"

Don't get me wrong, our two daughters are great kids. For the most part, they are respectful toward others and they have a healthy appreciation for what they have, as opposed to focusing on what they don't have. They also understand that privileges are not something to be taken for granted. Rather, the privileges that my daughters enjoy are granted in direct correlation with their willingness to fulfill certain responsibilities. Acquiring this perspective didn't happen by magic, however. It required a few tough lessons.

Let me take you back to the summer of 2002. We had just moved into a new home, and stress levels were running high on all fronts. For kids, moving to a new house in a different neighborhood is both exciting and traumatic at the same time. Our girls loved their new rooms, but they missed their old friends. So, some bumps in the road were certainly to be expected. However, even after a few months, the level of bickering in the house was on the rise, daily attitudes were generally poor, and the family's overall spirit of cooperation had hit an all-time low. For whatever reason, everyone in the house was unhappy, and it was clear that the time had come to take corrective action.

Calling a Family Meeting

One of the things we have done right is that we have periodic family meetings in our house. Family meetings aren't called just for the purpose of resolving issues and problems, however. Sometimes we call a family meeting to plan a busy weekend or plan an upcoming vacation. But, when a problem is brewing in the Freese house, especially one that begins to affect the entire family, we bring our group together to discuss it openly, and very directly.

Furthermore, any one of us can call a family meeting at any time, for any reason. And there are a few ground rules. During these family meetings, everyone has an opportunity to voice their opinion. Even if the topic being discussed is serious, there is never any yelling at a Freese family meeting. If it is inappropriate to yell at your colleagues at the office, then there's no sense yelling at your kids during a family discussion. Everyone gets to be heard, and the intent of the meeting is to formulate the group's input into a plan that will adequately deal with the issue, and then secure agreement from everyone involved.

I can tell you that the most impactful family meeting we ever had was held on a now infamous day back in July, 2002. Something had to be done to reduce the escalating tension, and I believe it is a reasonable parental responsibility to provide this kind of leadership within the household.

Opening the discussion was easy. Since I called the meeting, I simply said, "Girls, we have a problem. Ever since we moved into our new home a couple of months ago, the way everyone is treating each other seems to have deteriorated to an unacceptable level, which from my perspective, cannot continue. I wanted to bring everyone together to see if you are feeling the same way, and also to share some ideas I have for how to address this situation." My kids are perceptive enough to realize that there was a problem, and that I was serious about dealing with it.

"But, before I jump right into my list of concerns," I continued, "does anyone else have any comments, questions, or concerns that you would like to voice?" And here's an important point. The next step is critical—you have to be quiet. Inviting your children to share first is a fantastic strategy. If a problem has been festering within the household, chances are good that your kids are also wrestling with issues or demons of their own that you may not even know about. Asking calmly and then waiting for an answer is the best way to uncover any hidden concerns. You might be surprised to learn that you don't have all the facts, or haven't adequately considered someone else's point of view.

Sarah voiced a concern about her younger sister barging into her bedroom without knocking. Of course, this wasn't the end of the world, but it was a valid concern for a ten-year-old to raise, given that the intent of these get-togethers is to foster open communication. Once it was Mary Claire's turn, she voiced a concern about Sarah bossing her around all the time.

A question-based approach is required to moderate a productive family meeting. For example, after Sarah aired her grievance, I asked, "Can you give me some specific cases where this has happened?" Like most kids, Sarah was well armed with plenty of examples. I subsequently turned to Mary Claire (MC) and asked, "Have you been barging into Sarah's room without knocking, as Sarah described?" Pointing fingers, assigning blame, and assessing punishment is not the goal in these meetings. At this point, I just wanted an accurate picture of what was happening. Luckily, Laura and I have found that our kids are generally very honest in family meetings when everyone is sitting face-to-face and an issue is being discussed.

Next, I asked Mary Claire, "Is there something that you can do differently so that Sarah no longer feels you are barging into her room?" Asking the offending party to suggest a solution works well, too, because you ultimately want them to buy into whatever remedy is going to resolve the problem. After a little back and forth, I closed on a commitment from both girls, saying, "Does everyone agree that these suggestions will eliminate this problem?"

"Thank you, girls," I said. Then I asked Laura, "Do you have any concerns or issues to discuss?" She mentioned a thing or two that needed to be tended to around the house, although nothing major. I clearly had the biggest issue, but I was purposely saving it until everyone else had had a chance to voice their perspectives and be heard.

When it was finally my turn, I wasn't harsh and I refrained from delivering a speech or giving a lecture. Instead, I pulled a one-page document out of a nearby folder and said, "I am concerned about the way we are treating each other in what is supposed to be a loving family environment. And, from my perspective, we have reached a point where something needs to be done. Therefore, I have taken action," I continued, "I have created a document called The Freese Family Rules, that will serve as a contract, or a promise, for how people should treat each other in the Freese house."

It is intentional that the title of this document has a double meaning. You will see what I mean when you read it. The six items outlined in the document are clearly intended to communicate what is expected in terms of being a cooperative part of the family. But the phrase, "Freese House Rules!" is also intended to reflect the pride that comes from being an integral part of a team, much like you might hear students at a pep rally exclaim, "Northview High School Rules!"

I explained, "I will read each of the six points contained in this contract aloud and then ask for your feedback after each point. This document," I continued, "can be openly discussed, challenged, and the wording can be changed to whatever it needs to be, but we will ultimately come to agreement as a family on how everyone in this house is going to treat each other. Then, we will all sign it, and these six items will serve as our guide for acceptable behavior moving forward. Is everyone okay with that?"

(See actual document on next page.)

The very first point in this agreement pretty much sets the tone for the rest of the document, saying, *The people in this house are going to respect each other at all times.* I am always open to listening to another person's point of view, but to me, this item is non-negotiable. If we agree that we do indeed love each other, then the constant bickering needs to stop. So, I paused after reading the first point (in its entirety) and asked, "Does anyone have any changes or suggestions that need to be made to point number one?" Everyone shook their heads, which I took as group confirmation and then moved on to item number two.

The second item in the document builds on the first. I understand that one of the reasons toddlers cry is to get

Freese House Rules!

1.) The people in this house are going to respect each other at all times. Respect includes talking to and treating others like you would want them to talk with and treat you. Respect also includes NOT borrowing someone else's personal possessions without asking, and not grabbing them back if the offense occurs. Failing to be respectful will result in loss of privileges and no excuses will be accepted. If someone else is disrespectful to you, you do not have the right to return the offense.

2.) If you lose control, you lose your vote. Too often, someone ends up in an emotional pile because something has not gone their way. As parents, we are not going to alter our course to keep a child from raising your voice, rolling eyes, crying, or otherwise putting up a fuss. If you have a problem, you may certainly speak calmly about your concern. You may also ask us to consider your feelings. But then, a decision will made and any additional fussiness will result in escalating consequences. If someone chooses to continue displaying dissatisfaction, you will loose full privileges and your vote in family matters until you are able to demonstrate that you can once again be part of a cooperative team. Please note that just shutting off the tears does not reinstate one's privileges.

3.) Privileges are not something that family members will automatically receive. We are fortunate to have many nice things. And, for those who are willing to be a cooperative and loving part of the family, your privileges will remain far and wide. But, please be advised that the State of Georgia only requires parents to provide food, shelter, and public schooling. Everything else is considered a privilege. This includes playing with friends, soft drinks, snacks, computer, television, art projects, telephone, games, receiving a weekly allowance, going out for dinner, staying up to normal bedtime, music, electronic games, sports activities, a driver's license, and anything else that exceeds the State of Georgia's minimum requirement.

4.) Responsibilities. Each person in the family is expected to have certain responsibilities that include weekly tasks, as well as other requests that a parent may ask of the child. Parents will decide what is reasonable. Children may certainly voice their opinion, and parents agree to listen, but once a decision is made, there will be no arguments over participating when asked.

5.) When a child does not like a decision (or agree with a request), there is some tendency to react disrespectfully, with the child raising a fuss by whining, complaining, or otherwise, pleading their case. The parent agrees to listen to the child's opinion if they remain civil and calm, but an unreasonably negative reaction from the child will immediately cause the child's request to be denied. Even if you are right, we cannot reinforce disrespectful behavior.

6.) Listening skills are an important part of being respectful, and listening to parents is an expected behavior. We understand that sometimes you may not have heard and we are willing to repeat. But, ignoring multiple requests will earn an automatic time out, so you can think about how important it is to listen to said parent.

We have too many blessings and opportunities to let argument and fuss get in the way.

Agreed by the following on date _____

_____   _____

_____   _____

attention. In fact, most toddlers learn by the time they are two years old, that throwing a bigger fit tends to command a quicker reaction from their parents. Getting upset to cause the desired reaction is what they learned in infancy, and it's what they know. But, my girls were ten and four at the time, and they needed to understand that *if you lose control, you lose your vote*. There are other ways to communicate besides having a tantrum, and we needed that to be very clear in everyone's mind. It should be noted that some patience may be required when dealing with a child who is learning to communicate their thoughts. That's fine. I have all kinds of time and patience to calmly discuss just about anything. I just don't want my children to use manipulative tactics to try and force me to tolerate bad behavior. Since no one had any questions or concerns about point number two, we moved on.

Honestly, I had some fun with point number three, to the point where I had trouble reading it to the family with a straight face. Nonetheless, I read it out loud: *Privileges are not something that family members will automatically receive. We are fortunate to have many nice things. And, for those who are willing to be a cooperative and loving part of the family, your privileges will remain far and wide. But, please be advised that the State of Georgia only requires parents to provide food, shelter, and public schooling. Everything else is considered a privilege. This includes playing with friends, soft drinks, snacks, computer, television, art projects, telephone, games, receiving a weekly allowance, going out for dinner, staying up to normal bedtime, music, electronic games, sports activities, a driver's license, and anything else that exceeds the State of Georgia's minimum requirement.*

When I finished reading point number three, you could have heard a pin drop in our meeting that day. Even Laura was a little agog over that part about the State of Georgia's minimum requirement. But, that's okay. Kids might as well

learn at a young age that there is no such thing as an entitlement program that offers something for nothing. If our kids
want to maintain their privileges, then there is an expectation that we will receive a certain amount of cooperation in
return. "Does everyone agree with point number three?"

The fourth, fifth, and sixth points deal with having a
certain spirit of cooperation. I don't want to fight with my
kids in order to peacefully coexist. Apparently, it must be
working because so far I am not one of those parents standing
on the pool deck begging their kids to get out of the pool.

After reviewing the entire document and making to a
few minor edits along the way, as the consummate question-
based parent, I asked, "Is there anything else that needs to be
discussed or included in this document?" The group shook
their heads, and then we all signed it, including my four-
year-old. This was her first signature ever, and believe me,
she took it very seriously. You would have thought she was
signing the Declaration of Independence, as careful as she
was. Once it was signed, we hung the Freese Family Rules
on the bulletin board above the kid's book bag lockers, and
it has been hanging there ever since.

The attitudinal shift that occurred after this particular
family meeting was nothing short of miraculous. Suddenly,
both of our daughters were much happier, everyone in the
household was exponentially more cooperative, and the
amount of stress needed to get through the day was greatly
reduced. I had a friend say, "Boy, you must have really
brought the hammer down on those kids." Actually, we
didn't "hammer" anyone. In fact, we did just the opposite.
Rather than threaten our kids with consequences and
punishment for not complying with a dictatorial proclama-
tion, we involved them in the discussion and the decision
making process. If either of my children was unwilling to

agree that we should *respect each other at all times,* then we would have had a more serious problem. Given that everyone did acknowledge that respecting each other was a reasonable expectation, we simply asked for a commitment that this was the way we were going to treat each other from now on.

On occasion, just like in any other family, something happens that causes a flare up, and in the heat of the moment, one of my kids loses control. Instead of raising my voice and waving a finger in my daughter's face, now I simply ask, "Would you please retrieve the house rules from the bulletin board and meet me in the dining room in five minutes?"

"Let's review item number two," I will say. "Can you please read it out loud?" This is never fun for the child, but it's a great way to make your point in a calm and judicious way. The goal is not to embarrass your son or daughter, although losing control of one's emotions can certainly cause embarrassment. That's just part of the learning process. But once we created a mutually agreed upon expectation for what is reasonable behavior in the Freese house, attitudinal adjustments that used to cause all kinds of strife are now relatively easy to manage. My thought (toward the child) is, you must either reset my expectations for what constitutes acceptable behavior, or you need to adjust your behavior to what is mutually acceptable. If neither of those options is going to work, we can simply defer to the State of Georgia's minimum requirement.

The Secret to Happiness

One of the keys to being an effective parent is to say what you mean, and mean what you say. That old saying is the one piece of advice Laura's parents gave us when we first had Sarah. It has worked well for us, but that brings me to one of my pet peeves—idle threats. I'm sure you've heard parents say things they don't mean, like: "Benjamin, if you do that again, you are grounded for the rest of the year." If for some reason the child does cross the line, now the parent has created an even bigger problem. Are they really going to ground a child for an entire year? Probably not. But, when you don't follow through on a threat, you lose credibility with your own child. This has lasting repercussions, as losing your credibility will result in your words meaning less and less down the road. Make idle threats often enough, and you will completely erode your position of authority within the household.

One of the best ways to avoid eroding your authority is to be proactive as a parent. This includes setting clear and appropriate expectations with your children in advance, which is essentially what the Freese House Rules contract was intended to accomplish. What's the alternative for parents—standing in the shadows waiting for your children to make a mistake and then punishing them for their missteps? Of course, being proactive requires a little forethought and planning on your part, but that's one of the benefits that comes from being a question-based parent.

If we step back for a moment and look at the parental role from a broader perspective, I would argue that the happiness of a child has a lot to do with the expectations set by their parents. In fact, one point that we focus a great deal of time attention on in the Question Based Selling methodology, is the idea that the secret to being successful with customers is contained in a simple mathematical formula about setting proper expectations. The formula is: H=R-E. To put this into words, happiness (H) is the net difference between the customer's expectations (E) and reality (R).

Do the math. If a child's expectations escalate to a level far beyond what is reasonable or realistic, then they are very likely to be disappointed with whatever happens, because reality will surely fall far short of their expectations. On the other hand, if a circumstance or situation exceeds a child's expectations, they will probably be very content and happy with the result.

Unfortunately, we parents don't always have control over the realities our kids will face on a daily basis. But we often do have the opportunity to set proper expectations in advance, such that our children will not be disillusioned or disappointed later on. Communicating to a child that there are certain responsibilities, for example, that they are expected to handle around the house is a good illustration. Some people use the word chores, which is a dirty word among kids. Let me explain what I mean.

Have you ever noticed that most parental requests to help around the house are met with varying degrees of resistance from your children? That's because doing chores means doing work, and work takes effort. Parents understand this reaction completely, because as kids, we certainly didn't jump for joy whenever it was time for us to do chores.

Regardless, a team effort is still required in order for a household to properly function, and believe me, there is a job for everyone. But, rather than quarrel with our kids every time we want their involvement, we decided to assign certain responsibilities. That was part of our agreement: *Each person in the family is expected to have certain responsibilities that include weekly tasks, as well as other things that a parent may assign to the child. Parents will decide what is reasonable. Children may certainly voice their opinion, and parents will agree to listen, but once a decision is reached, there will be no arguments over participating when asked.*

When my youngest daughter (Mary Claire) turned four years old, she started setting and clearing the dinner table every night. She also feeds the dog in the morning and is responsible for keeping her room in order. Sarah feeds the dog every evening, does the dishes after dinner, and keeps her room neat, in addition to a few other miscellaneous tasks. On the weekend, both kids get a list of chores that generally take forty-five minutes to an hour to complete, based on whatever mom has decided she needs help doing. Because the expectation has been set that these things all need to happen without fuss, the daily operation at the Freese house usually runs fairly smoothly.

As it turns out, assigning responsibilities around the house can be very empowering to a child. Think about it. Doing something that seems important is a real source of pride and self-esteem for kids. It also signals to them that you respect their abilities and are confident that they will do a good job.

My wife was originally against the idea of assigning chores. "In my house growing up," Laura would say, "we just helped around the house because things needed to be done." If you have children like this who are self-motivated and totally self-reliant, you should consider yourself lucky. In Proverbs 22:6, I interpret the phrase, "Train up a child," to mean that children aren't necessarily always going to be self-directed, and that instilling values like teamwork and responsibility is one of our primary roles as parents.

Like other families, Laura and I encountered a certain amount of initial resistance when first implementing these assigned chores. That's just part of your child's natural inclination to test the waters and find out if you are really serious. Once our expectations for them were clearly communicated, however, a very interesting phenomenon happened. Our kids actually started to appreciate the fact that they were being asked to make a valuable contribution. I remember one night after dinner, I approached the sink to rinse my glass, and Sarah said, "Dad, get away from the sink. That's my turf." Thank you, God!

All Work and No Play

Doing chores around the house is not always fun. Shoot, it's no fun for me either. That's a good lesson for kids to learn because they will have many responsibilities later in life that aren't necessarily "fun." But, if you play your cards right, you can sometimes make chores very fun.

One night in the month, have your kids plan and cook the family dinner. Again, you might encounter some initial resistance, but most children get very excited about this when given the opportunity. It doesn't have to be a complex meal, although it's generally good for them to fix something unique and different that will take them out of their comfort zone. Have them try making melted ham and cheese mini-sandwiches or a simple recipe for baked ziti. Be sure to include a few coordinating side dishes like green beans, potatoes, or a squash casserole, along with steaming hot buttered rolls.

Trying to synchronize the preparation of multiple dishes is what makes this adventure both challenging and rewarding. It will also give your kids a new appreciation for what mom (or dad) has to deal with every night. The first time Sarah took on this challenge, she commented afterward that the food seemed to taste "better" than it usually does. I'm guessing that's because dinner that evening included just a pinch of a secret ingredient known as pride of preparation.

I would not recommend trusting a five-year-old with a

pot of boiling water, just like you would not want to hand a chainsaw to a child who is only eight or ten. Perhaps it goes without saying, but safety should always be one of your primary considerations when assigning responsibilities.

There are lots of things your kids can do around the house that don't require dangerous tools, they just require a little creativity. For example, a couple years ago, my wife's sister came to visit us with her three energetic boys. The word "energetic" is a bit of an understatement. That's okay. I can deal with a pack of enthusiastic boys who were five, eight, and eleven at the time. My two daughters were of comparable ages, five and eleven.

Two days into the visit, boredom started to set in and when all five kids woke up the next morning, everyone was dragging around the house in their pajamas with "nuthin" to do. I remember thinking, "What a waste on such a beautiful spring morning."

"Does anyone want to have a contest?" I asked.

Kids love contests! In his best Eeyore voice from Winnie the Pooh, the oldest boy (Sam) sluggishly inquired, "What kind of contest?"

I ignored the question and encouraged everyone to hurry up, get dressed, and meet me on the back porch in eight minutes.

Needless to say, all five kids were ready and waiting when I pushed open the screen door, holding six bamboo television lap trays.

"Good, everyone's here." I said. "Here are the rules of the contest."

I laid the trays, all hand-painted with various colorful designs, on the ground. "First, I invite you to please select the tray of your choice," I said. Each child scrambled to snatch the one with his or her favorite colors. I took the sixth tray because I like to participate in contests, too.

"We're going to have a weed picking contest," I announced. Since the boys were hockey fans, I continued, "There will be three eight-minute periods. At the end of each period, I will blow the whistle, and there will be judging based on size of weeds found, quantity of weeds picked, and there will be extra points given for uniqueness and style. At the end of the contest, there will be awards. You may spread out and find weeds anywhere in the yard, and awards will be given based on age group."

"Take your marks," I said. Everyone braced themselves, ready to dash over toward the pine straw beds. "Go!"

Let me tell you something. You have never seen five children work so hard to find and pick weeds. "Uncle Tom, look at this one," Evan exclaimed, holding up a super-jumbo sized weed. Of course, Evan's comment only made Sam, Jack, Sarah, and Mary Claire want to work even harder. I, too, picked as fast as I could, not wanting to be shown up by a bunch of youngsters. The weeds in my yard didn't stand a chance that day.

After each period, I blew the whistle, signaling everyone to bring their tray to the compost pile. Standing in front of their respective hauls, each child beamed with satisfaction. "Wow," I said, "You guys have done the job!" The judging then commenced, as we sifted through each child's pile, holding up specific examples of prize weeds. Together, we identified the largest weed, the smallest weed, and the most difficult to find weeds. We also identified the tallest, most colorful, and the most dangerous to pick weeds. If you are the least bit creative, there are lots of ways to compliment a job well done.

After three full periods of weed pick'in, all five children were totally exhausted, as was I. But, they were no longer moping around the house. If you can give your kids a feeling of satisfaction and accomplishment, it will totally change their perspective on almost everything.

The following afternoon, we held the First Annual Freese Weed Picking awards ceremony. From my perspective, a six-pack of cupcakes from the corner grocery was a small price to pay for a weed-free yard. I decorated them myself to represent different categories of excellence. Evan (the middle nephew), won the award for the largest weed. Sam (the oldest nephew) won the award for the most dangerous weed, having uprooted a champion prickle bush without gloves. Ouch! Jack (the youngest nephew) won for quantity, having piled his tray high with teeny-tiny weeds.

Mary Claire (my youngest) won the award for greatest coverage, having traveled from the front yard to the back, and both side yards, to find her prey. Lastly, I presented Sarah (my oldest) with a cupcake neatly decorated on top with four capital letters, representing the leadership award from the governing body: *The International Federation of Weed Pick'in* (IFWP).

Yes, they laughed at my humor, and they ate their "trophies," but they have never forgotten the fun they had doing what most kids would consider the worst chore of all—picking weeds in the yard.

Be Mindful of Age Appropriate

Asking a three-year-old to pick up their own toys can be an important responsibility. What's their reward? How about letting them turn on their own bath? Turning the knob "all by myself" can be a big deal to a toddler.

Most six-year-olds can empty smaller trash cans around

the house, sweep porches, and dust window sills. They can also push a shopping cart, and help bring grocery bags in from the car. There are lots of ways to involve your kids in the responsibilities of the household.

Older kids can do almost anything that you can, like plan and cook dinner, wash the car, vacuum, or mow the grass. Older children will sometimes complain that a younger child is not being asked to do as much. Be sure to tell them they're right. Hey, life is not fair. But rather than brushing off their comment, explain that the older child was not expected to do as much when they were that young either. You might also point out that the older child has greater responsibilities in exchange for a broader range of privileges.

Please note that it may take a child much longer to finish one of their responsibilities around the house than if you just went ahead and addressed it yourself. This can be a difficult thing for parents, but I encourage you to be patient. It may take a few days or weeks for a child to become proficient at setting the table, for example, or loading a dishwasher, taking out trash, or feeding the dog, but I promise that teaching them to always do a quality job is a character builder and an investment that will pay big dividends in the long run.

One more note on this subject. If you ask your child to be responsible for doing the dishes, and they happen to drop a dinner plate on the floor and it breaks, don't fly off the handle and get upset. Breaking a dish is not the end of the world. I wouldn't recommend putting a toddler in charge of washing your Waterford crystal goblets, but accidents are going to happen. Particularly for those parents who constantly strive for perfection, my advice would be to take a deep breath, shrug your shoulders, and then smile. After all, it is much easier to replace a dinner plate than to repair a child's broken heart or restore their self-esteem.

Say Thank You with Your Eyes

If you are going to give your kids specific responsibilities, then you must also be ready to give them kudos for a job well done. Just like you and I, children want to be respected for what they can do, and appreciated for what they have done well.

We parents tend to get upset when kids take the things we do for granted. After all, we work hard to provide for our families, and they should appreciate the fact that they have a roof over their head and food on the table! But, with all the time we spend feeling unappreciated, we sometimes forget to say thank you to one of our kids who has dutifully completed their assigned chores, or fulfilled their homework responsibilities without being asked.

Words of affirmation from parents to children are needed vitamins that nourish the soul. Isn't it odd that parents go to great lengths to teach their kids to say, "Please" and "Thank you," but for some reason, we often forget to say those same words ourselves? We sometimes rationalize these omissions by thinking, "Setting the table is not such a big deal, so I will save my appreciation for larger achievements." I must raise my own hand on this one and plead guilty as charged.

There's an old adage that from modest beginnings come big things. If you knew that your children would be energized to take on more responsibility, with greater enthusiasm than ever before, would you be willing to take a risk and show them your true appreciation for their efforts? This is another small investment on your part that will likely be worth its weight in gold.

There's only one catch. Words alone tend to get stale and may even sound insincere if they are thrown around too casually. As a result, it's easy to take words for granted. Therefore, here's an interesting idea. Try saying, "Thank you," with your face. Raise your eyebrows and let your child see that you are impressed with the initiative they have demonstrated. As an added bonus, let responsibility be rewarded by an unconditional smile, one that supersedes whatever trials and tribulations may have affected you both earlier in the day. Raising your eyebrows and projecting a warm smile doesn't take extra time, nor does it cost any money. Sometimes, the smallest signs of appreciation from a parent can provide all the inspiration a child needs to become a superstar. At the very least, every child wants to know that they are a superstar in your eyes.

Family relationships tend to follow certain patterns where parents who constantly complain about their kids often end up raising children who are always complaining. On the flip side, parents who always seem to be very impressed with good things their children do, are more likely to have impressive kids. I encourage you to make a commitment to play a role in "training" your children to respect authority and embrace responsibility, as those two values are ultimately the cement that bonds a family unit together.

Chapter 3

The Art of Negotiation

My children are great negotiators, like most kids. But, they are usually at a disadvantage because I have better negotiation skills! After having spent many years in my professional career studying the art of negotiation, I know the secret and I'm not afraid to use it.
—Thomas A. Freese

Some parents might start "licking their chops" when they come to this chapter on negotiation, thinking, "Hooray, now I can learn how to get the upper hand on my children." Let me stop you right there. Getting the upper hand on your children is not what this book is about. Instead, this chapter on negotiation is about learning how to peacefully coexist with your kids, and about helping them to understand how to be more cooperative with you.

You should notice that our first objective, *learning how to peacefully coexist with your kids*, is for parents. Maintaining long term relationships is difficult to be sure. I probably don't have to tell you this now that the divorce rate in this country is close to fifty percent. Being mindful of the needs and desires of others is particularly challenging within the family unit where kids are constantly testing their independence against a set of rules and expectations that have been established by parents, with whom they sometimes have a love/loathe relationship.

Laura and I both subscribe to the theory that every ship needs a captain and someone ultimately needs to be in charge of the daily operation at home. In some cases, that leaves me in charge; other times it's Laura, depending on the situation. But, you can't let that sense of power go to your head. I can tell you that your kids and mine don't want to be "commanded" any more than we do. How would you feel if your boss periodically came around the corner and ordered you to do this or do that? It doesn't seem reasonable then, that parents should indiscriminately dictate orders to their children, either. Sure, if a child is in physical danger or the house in on fire, then martial law sets in and commanding an immediate response is absolutely warranted.

In truth, however, the house is rarely on fire. I understand all too well the surge of emotions that a frustrated parent feels upon making a simple request for the third time, especially after having already endured a long day at the office. I also agree that sometimes a ship's captain needs to issue a directive, and that order needs to be obeyed. Still, there is some tendency among moms and dads to leverage their parental power by relying too heavily on the argument, "Do it because I said so!"

If you can pull yourself away from the emotions of the moment, and think about what you really want for your children, let me ask this question. Would you want your kids to be good negotiators when they grow up? I have posed this question to many parents and most are quick to answer with a resounding, "Yes." It's a competitive world out there, and at some point, your kids will have to negotiate their way through a wide range of situations in order to stand up for themselves. In fact, there's a lot of truth to the old adage that says you don't get what you deserve in life; you only get whatever you are able to negotiate.

Now the question is: If you do want your kids to grow up to be good negotiators, are you willing to let them practice on you? If you say yes again, then trumping your kids whenever you want simply by using the phrase, "Because I said so," is an unfair and illogical argument. While brute force may enable you to win the current battle, you may be doing so at the expense of failing to accomplish the larger objective.

While the sometimes argumentative nature of the relationship between parent and child can be a constant source of frustration, helping your kids learn how to effectively negotiate with you can actually present a wonderful opportunity to participate in their intellectual and emotional development. Ironically, helping children understand the finer points of negotiation is one of the easiest ways to minimize the number of arguments in your house—between children and their parents, or between siblings.

Negotiation is a valuable life skill indeed, and one that we actually encourage within our household. I want my kids to learn how to think logically, and I want them to understand that the easiest way to get what they want is to help whoever they are dealing with to also get what they want. That's what a lot of people don't understand. Effective negotiation is not about gaining the advantage in every situation or winning at someone else's expense. Rather, effective negotiators know how to create a win/win scenario where all parties achieve a desirable outcome. Doesn't that sound good? What if your kids had a clear understanding that the best way to satisfy their own desires is to help you accomplish your objectives as well?

Creating a Win/Win Scenario

Much of the interaction between child and parent is defined by the role we parents play as *approver* and *provider*, and the role our children take on as *requesters*. "Mommy, can I go outside and play?" a younger child might ask a parent. Or, "Dad, can I watch some television?" Of course, the nature of these parental requests tends to evolve over time from simple grants of permission given to a younger child, to more complex requests that come from budding teens, who are more likely to assume they no longer need permission now that they are almost mature.

The ultimate resolution for any conflict, or difference in perspective between parents and children, is for both parties to end up getting what they want. This is not to suggest that giving a child everything they want is an effective strategy, because it's not. But in case you haven't already noticed, children are sometimes going to have a different perspective of what is fair and reasonable than their parents. This is just part of the human condition, where a child who has to request permission from their parents is always going to desire more than they are allowed, and the parent is never going to give in to everything a child wants.

My daughter, for example, might ask, "Dad, can I go over to Hannah's house to play?" Frankly, whether or not she is granted permission to visit her friend usually depends on the status of other things. If it's a weekday, I might ask, "Have you finished your homework?" Or, "Is your room picked up?" I may also ask, "How long are you planning to stay?" If the request is made on a Saturday morning, I might inquire, "Have you finished your chores?"

My first instinct in these situations isn't just to grant permission or not. Without knowing where other things stand, there's no way for me to know whether a yes or no would be the appropriate response. That's why it is so important for a negotiator to be question-based. If her room is in order and she is all caught up from school, then why not? "Go have fun, honey!" On the other hand, if she had been putting off a class project or is behind on her responsibilities at home, then, "Going to your friend's house doesn't sound like a good idea."

The goal is to create a *win* for both parties. Ultimately, I want my children to do well in school. I also want them to have good attitudes, be contributing participants in the community, and be loving and supportive members of the family. My daughters, on the other hand, want to talk on the telephone, play with their friends, and enjoy increasing levels of independence. Most of the time, both of our goals can be satisfied, but it usually has a lot to do with the choices each child makes along the way.

What happens if a child is behind on homework because he or she hasn't planned well, and as a result, they are not allowed to play with a friend that day? The answer is, nothing happens. Your child might miss out on a play date. But, hopefully, they will also take a valuable lesson away from this experience. Not always getting what you want is one of the important lessons of life and standing your ground as a parent is one of the best ways for your children to learn it.

I don't mean to sound insensitive, but at the end of the day, negotiation is about making certain trade-offs. Simply put, I am willing to say "yes" to all kinds of privileges like playing with friends, computer games, watching television, or even taking the car keys, in exchange for my kids making good decisions and exhibiting desirable and responsible behavior.

Who controls the amount of privileges my kids actually

receive? The answer to this question may surprise you. They do! Therein lies the secret to how to effectively negotiate with your children. My daughters can get almost anything they want in the Freese house. All they have to do is make sure their mother and I get what we want in exchange.

Promises, Promises

Here's the funny part about negotiating. Most kids are way ahead of their parents when it comes to concocting a deal. They are ready to promise you the moon and the stars if you will just agree to let them have one more cookie, spend five more minutes of computer, or go to the mall. In their sweetest little voices, they will plead and cajole. They'll even use flattery if they think it will further their cause. "Please, Dad. You are the best dad in the whole world. Pretty please?"

Sometimes the answer is going to be, "Sure." If you are like most parents that I know, you love your children dearly, and you want them to experience some of the simple joys of growing up. Sometimes no justification is necessary. That's perfectly fine. In fact, I subscribe to the theory that you have to give a little first, in order to get something in return.

I beg of you, however, not to be one of those parents who bribes their kid with whatever it takes to put a lid on a temper tantrum. (Later in the book, we will devote an entire chapter to the issue of discipline, so stay tuned.) For now, I want to point out that from a pure negotiation perspective, you cannot give into a child's demands in exchange for them to stop exhibiting unacceptable behavior. Think about what they learn from these episodes—that exhibiting poor behavior is the best way to satisfy their desires? For the same reason that governments don't negotiate with terrorists, you cannot let yourself be intimidated by the possibility that your child might commit a hostile act if you don't comply with their demands. I can tell you this, if one of my kids loses control in a public place, they not only move farther from their desired objective, they quickly learn that there will be additional consequences to deal with when we get home.

Another challenge for parents is dealing with future promises. Kids are famous for asking for something now while promising to do something later in exchange, but then things get hectic and they often never end up delivering on those promises. And, it's easy for a busy parent to forget to remind them.

For example, kids make proposals like this one all the time. "Mom, if you let me go to the mall, I will clean my room as soon as I get back." Then they tug on your emotional side, saying, "Please, mom? Everybody else is going to be there."

Off to the mall the child goes. Upon returning from the excursion, she comes home tired and cranky. Having granted the child permission to spend time at the mall, you want her to live up to the agreement you made before she left. Of course, when you confront the issue and ask the adolescent to deliver on her promise, what happens? Emotions rise and the conversation quickly escalates into an ugly confrontation. Sound familiar? Well, this kind of scenario will continue to happen unless you are willing to adjust your negotiation style.

We parents can learn a lot from the business world in these cases. At some point your children will become teenagers and many of them will enter the workforce seeking part-time employment. My first official job outside of the family was bagging groceries at Bell's Grocery Store in Spencerport, New York. From there, I was able to parlay my experience and leapfrog into a higher position as a stockboy at the K-Mart. Who knows, your kids might get a job washing cars, providing babysitting services, or working in a fast-food restaurant. No matter what job they land, I can assure you that your child will not receive a paycheck first, with the agreement that they will do the work at some point in the future. Exactly the opposite happens. If your child does the job, the manager will hand them a paycheck at the end of the week.

This being the case, there's no point in waiting until your kids are sixteen or seventeen years old to begin teaching them the ways of the world. Learning that you must "pay to play" is an extremely valuable lesson. It's the way our entire capitalistic society works. Merrill Lynch doesn't deposit a pile of cash into your account in the hopes that you will do business with them at some point in the future. A Coca-Cola machine doesn't dispense a can of soda, and then hope that customers will remember to put money in the slot. In order to enjoy the reward, you first have to be willing to ante-up and pay the price. Or, in parenting terms, only after a child appropriately fulfills their own responsibilities can they expect something in return.

The underlying logic of this makes total sense to most parents because we have been operating within this philosophy most of our adult lives. But, there is no reason to believe that a child would inherently understand what I call tit-for-tat reasoning. In fact, as I mentioned in the previous chapter, we spend the first few years conditioning our children to believe that the best way to satisfy their needs and generate the desired parental response is for them to make a fuss. This need/response mechanism that exists between infants and their parents isn't going to change anytime soon, because crying is the only method small children have to communicate. However, once your child reaches the age of four or five, where they have the mental capacity and the physical ability to successful communicate their desires with words and sentences, then it becomes your job to teach them how to trade responsibilities for privileges.

Conditioning your kids to complete their responsibilities first is not difficult, but it does require a proactive effort on someone's part. It also requires some parental consistency. My motivation for this conditioning is very simple. I don't want to be constantly nagging my children to do their homework, do dishes, or finish their chores. Moreover, I don't want my kids to be constantly upset with me because I am unwilling to grant their every wish.

Where a parent's involvement becomes critical is in setting the terms of the deal. On the way home from school one day, for example, you might announce, "If you guys can completely finish your homework, I will take you to get an ice cream cone after dinner." It helps to make it something worth working for, but there's no need to go overboard with lavish rewards.

Taking the opposite position works, too. You can just as easily let your child know that, "If you don't have enough time to finish your project, then you surely won't have time to go to the dance this Saturday night."

We are not talking about asking a child to perform farm labor, here. In fact, kids who do the least are often the ones who complain the most to their parents. So, be prepared because you might just get an earful of complaining when you first implement this. In fact, your child might have to miss out on a birthday party or two before they fully understand the true meaning of tit-for-tat. But, I encourage you to invest the time to help them to understand your position.

Call a family meeting if you need to. Give them some perspective by saying, "It's relatively simple. I want you to play with your friends, talk on the telephone, play computer games, and go to the dance! And all of that can happen, if you are willing to uphold your end of the bargain." Your children might as well learn this concept of tit-for-tat negotiation at an early age, because that's how the whole world operates.

Let Your Kids Rise to the Occasion

A few weeks ago when I was in Seattle, I had the opportunity to catch up with one of our long-time clients over dinner. My friend Mike is a family man with an eleven year old son and a nine-year-old daughter. Slowly our conversation circled around to the upcoming release of my fourth book (this one), and we shared war stories about parenting like friends often do when they haven't been together in a while. Then, Mike asked me a question that I suspect a lot of other parents also have.

"Tom, is there a way to teach a child how to become a good negotiator, particularly if they aren't a very aggressive or desirous child by nature?" He explained that his oldest son Justin is a highly motivated and precocious kid who was born with the ability to persuade a sailor on leave to part with his last nickel. "Trust me," Mike said, "Justin is a natural negotiator." His younger daughter Jenna, apparently had the opposite style personality. She was a get-along, go-along type of kid, the kind that is fairly content with whatever is happening around her. My first thought was, count your blessings. There have been many days when I wished my kids were more amiable and accepting.

Although I have two daughters and Mike had one of each, our kids share the same personality mix. My oldest daughter is constantly thinking of ways to improve her situation while our youngest is an easy-going, roll-with-the-flow type of kid. We love them both, and we enjoy them both. Children are all different, and what may be a natural strength for one child may not be apparent in the other. But, since I would like both of our girls to learn how to fend for themselves by the time they leave the nest, I gave Mike the same question-based advice that we had implemented with our daughters a couple years earlier.

First, let me use a simple metaphor to make a point. During my spare time, I love to play golf. And, because I have been a golf nut for many years, I understand that a tremendous amount of time and effort is required to properly maintain a championship golf course.

The most common form of vegetation on a golf course is grass. Different courses use different varieties of grasses, but keeping the grass in excellent condition is one of the primary responsibilities of the golf course superintendent. What do you suppose happens if it doesn't rain for a long period of time and no one waters the grass? The answer, of course, is that grass will die without proper nourishment. Everyone understands this, which is why most golf courses nowadays have very sophisticated sprinkler systems.

Several years ago, I joined a country club in Atlanta just before they lost all of the grass on the greens one summer, making the course virtually unplayable, and the membership was very upset. You couldn't blame the greenskeeper for not watering because the greens were being watered heavily every day. After a brief investigation, it was determined that the greens actually had received too much water. Guess what happens when you put too much water on grass? The root systems don't grow to the desired depth because there's always plenty of water at the surface. As a result, the roots aren't "trained" to grow deep enough to sustain the plant when a summer heat wave strikes. The net result is, making it too easy on the grass to find nourishment can be detrimental to the stability of the plant when conditions are not perfect.

Back to the advice I offered my friend Mike. It's what we started doing with our youngest daughter, Mary Claire, who was always respectful but not very assertive. Whenever she asked for something, like, "Dad, can I go outside and play?", instead of just responding with a simple yes or no answer, I responded with a question of my own.

"That sounds like a good idea," I would say. "Can you give me more information so I know whether or not it makes sense to say yes?"

At first, my daughter just looked at me with a blank stare. She obviously didn't expect to have to think, but silence is definitely golden in these moments. Having to think on their feet and then communicate with you is what causes a child's roots to grow deep. "What information?" she asked.

"Do you have any homework? Have you finished your responsibilities around the house? Where are you going? What time will you be home? Those are the types of things I need to understand in order to say, yes." I would say.

At first, you can expect one word answers, especially from a child who isn't naturally assertive. That's because they don't teach presentation skills in Kindergarten. The key is being patient enough to let them find the words. Note: You may have to hold your tongue and prompt them a bit by saying, "I still don't know enough about your plans to say yes. Can you please tell me more?" Resist the temptation to interrogate them with a barrage of questions. If you do all of the work in the conversation, then they won't learn to think for themselves.

A couple times when Mary Claire was younger, I responded to her request by saying, "I'm sorry, but I still don't have enough information to say yes." You will notice that I didn't necessarily say no. I just didn't have enough information to say yes. This is a learning experience for the child. Their shoulders may slump as they turn and sulk out of the room, but I can guarantee you the wheels are turning at full speed as they wonder what they could have done differently to change the outcome. There is a powerful lesson here for parents as well. If a child knows that you are going to require a more detailed understanding of where things stand before you are able to say yes, they will begin to position their requests differently in order to ensure a positive result.

Today, rarely do our daughters make a single request like, "Can I do this or that?" Instead, they come to us saying things like, "Mom, my homework is finished and I fed the dog. I am planning to take a bath and wash my hair after dinner, and then study a little for my English quiz. But, since we have about forty-five minutes until dinner, would it be okay if I ran down to Hannah's house to play on her swing? She has already asked her parents, and it's okay with them if it's okay with you." You should hear some of the presentations my kids will make. We just smile and nod and let them go. Once in a while, we will ask a question if an important stone has been left unturned. But, it's rare. You will be amazed how quickly a child's confidence can grow as they transition from a passive wall flower just asking permission into someone who can proactively present a case which makes their request good for both parties. That's how negotiation works.

Let me give you a couple extra parental tips on this idea. First, you and your spouse may end up howling after one of these interactions, but you must never laugh or chuckle as your child presents his or her case. They are working very hard to justify their position and earn your respect, and a child who is doing their best deserves your full and undivided attention. Second, even if your child makes a compelling case, raise your eyes and look off in the distance for two or three seconds before granting their request. If a child knows you are going to carefully consider what they say, they will naturally be more thoughtful in their communications with you.

The Take Away Effect

Negotiation isn't always about granting permission. Sometimes, you will have to decline a child's request no matter how well the justification is presented. For kids, part of learning how to negotiate is understanding that they won't always get what they want. And, they also need to realize that if they push too hard, the status quo can actually get worse.

The classic example of this happens in our household around bedtime. "Mom, why do I have to be in bed by 8:30pm?" our youngest might complain. Fortunately, their mother is very smart.

"Because you need lots of sleep to do your best." Laura will say.

"But, mommmm! That's too early." Instantly, the bedtime negotiations are in full swing.

"What time would you like to go to bed?" Laura might ask, already knowing what's coming next.

"Nine-o'clock," my daughter suggests emphatically.

"How about eight-fifteen tonight?" Laura might counter. Like magic, going to bed at eight-thirty suddenly sounds pretty good to a child when they realize that are actually losing ground in the negotiation.

What if your child pitches a fit because they don't like what you prepared for supper? We have made the mistake of giving in and fixing something else that is more appealing to the child. While that may subdue the issue for the moment, I can tell you right now that giving into a child's tantrum will likely create a recurring problem. Instead, why not calmly offer them the option to skip dinner and not have anything until breakfast? Sometimes, even their least favorite meal looks a whole lot better once they realize that the alternative is no food at all.

When it's time to get out of the swimming pool during the summer months, we usually give our kids some advance notice. Giving a five-minute warning only seems fair after a couple hours of independence. But, when they are in the middle of playing a game with their friends, the message to "get out" isn't always well received.

"Whee-hoo," I might whistle to get their attention. "We'll be leaving in five minutes."

"Daaaaaad! Five minutes is not enough time," they sometimes say.

"How about two minutes?" I will counter.

"Five minutes sounds great, Dad." Suddenly, everyone is happy with the original plan. And, my children understand that when five minutes are up, it's time to get out of the pool without any fuss. I talked about this earlier. How did they learn this? Mostly from the school of hard knocks. Through previous experience, my kids have discovered that their ticket back into the pool next time is largely dependent on their willingness to be cooperative when it's time to leave. The same philosophy applies to going to the movies, playing computer games, or riding horses. The best way to get what you want in life is to make sure that other people also get what they want in return.

This is not a power play on my part, as my ego does not yearn to have control over my kids. The thing I yearn for is peace and goodwill toward men (and women) at the Freese house. What I really want is for our children to have control over themselves, and in exercising that control, I want them to be honest, hard-working, and hopefully, use good judgment. Our job then, as parents, is simply to help our kids understand that their actions and decisions often affect people other than themselves, whether it's as simple as getting into bed on time, or something bigger like being disrespectful to another adult.

It is to your advantage to instill this tit-for-tat philosophy early in your child's development. Two years old may be too early, because two-year olds are often just learning to talk. Waiting until a child is five years old, however, is probably too late. Trust me when I say that a lot of expectations in the way you interact with your child are going to be set between the ages of two and five. Use your judgment for your own children, but I encourage you to push yourself to step outside your comfort zone and try it.

It's easy to practice on small issues. "Dad, can I have a snack?"

"Yes, after you wash your hands and put away your game," I'll say. It's amazing how fast a million-piece game can be put away by a motivated toddler.

"Hey, Dad, want to play catch in the front yard?" a child might ask.

"Sure, can you get the ball out of the garage and meet

me outside?" I might respond.

For a younger child especially, asking for their involvement is actually an affirmation of their capability, perhaps even a sign of trust. The underlying message that gets communicated is, "Because I have confidence in your abilities, I will grant your request, if you are willing to do something that helps me, too." These are the emotional building blocks that will help your child form and maintain successful partnerships for the rest of their life.

It's also worth noting that in the world of negotiation between kids and their parents, we parents are not always correct. In some cases we change our minds. Other times we are just plain wrong. And, while we may ultimately have the authority to force an issue if we choose, sometimes it's better just to say, "I'm sorry," than to indignantly defend an invalid position. Good news. If you do have to back down, you demonstrate one of the most valuable lessons a parent can teach a child about humility and grace. Another powerful phrase that you can try is, "Son, I was mistaken. Will you forgive me?" Being willing to openly admit that you aren't perfect is a humble, but very strong negotiating position.

Teaching Children to Manage Money

While we deal with the issue of negotiation, we might as well talk about money, since it's the primary currency of the world. Someone has to start teaching our young people how to manage their money. Just look around. Credit card debt has sky rocketed in this country, college graduates are moving back home in record numbers, and a large percentage of the general population has slipped into a lifestyle where people are living far beyond their means.

I'm a big fan of looking for opportunities to have kids share in the cost of doing business. Life is certainly not free, so they might as well learn something about the real world at an early age. Don't get too excited. I am not suggesting that you should hand your children a monthly invoice for room and board. That's probably a little over the top. But if your kids get a weekly allowance, they can certainly afford to pay for their own Skittles. Once they start driving, they can also help pay for their own gasoline.

Fortunately, when I was young, I had the best teacher when it comes to managing money and learning the true value of a mere fifty cents. Her name was Aunt Doris. I was twelve years old.

My aunt, Doris, used to visit us in upstate New York every summer. Somehow, a trend got started where whenever one of her nieces or nephews reached the age of twelve, it was prearranged that the "almost teen" would drive back to Chicago with Aunt Doris and spend a week in her home. Better yet, we got to fly home. In fact, the trip back to Rochester was my first time to fly in an airplane. The Chicago trip, in many ways, was a rite of passage into young adulthood.

My older brother Larry had gone to Chicago the previous summer, so I had heard many stories about things he had seen and done. After visiting Niagara Falls, they stopped to pick fresh blueberries, and took lots of pictures. One of the highlights from Larry's trip was eating straw-berry pie at the Big Boy Restaurant. I was a nut for strawber-ries, and when I heard that a giant slice of strawberry pie was waiting for me in Chicago, I got very excited.

When Aunt Doris and I left our house in New York, I had twelve dollars in my pocket that was supposed to last the entire week. Sounds like a pittance now, but it seemed like a ton of money at the time. Aunt Doris knew about my enthu-siasm for strawberries, so she advised me to put fifty cents aside for a piece of pie. Early in the trip, I had so much money, her suggestion seemed like unnecessary advice at the time.

Along the drive, I bought some candy in Ontario and purchased a few picture postcards in Detroit. Once we arrived in Chicago, Aunt Doris pretty much provided every-thing I needed, so money was no object. Therefore, I put money into every candy machine I came across.

On the last night of the visit, Doris had planned to take me to the Big Boy after dinner for that coveted slice of straw-berry pie. "Grab your fifty cents and let's go," she said. As soon as the words came out of her mouth, I realized that I was completely out of funds. I had unwittingly dropped my last few coins into a Coke machine at the youth center earlier in the day.

"I forgot to save fifty cents," I reluctantly admitted to Aunt Doris.

"That's a shame," she said, shaking her head. "You would have really enjoyed their strawberry pie."

I still remember bursting into quiet tears. Aunt Doris had offered to take me to the Big Boy, but it had been clearly understood that I would need to pay for my own piece of strawberry pie—and no money meant no dessert. I sat by myself in her guestroom feeling ashamed that I could be so stupid.

Aunt Doris let me *stew in my own juices* for about twenty minutes before she appeared in the doorway. "I found two extra quarters in the kitchen," she offered. "Would you still like to have some pie?"

The strawberry pie at the Shoney's was better than advertised. I had never put something so good in my mouth. While I was not aware of it then, my Aunt Doris was a very smart lady who knew exactly what she was doing. She didn't lecture me at the Big Boy—she didn't have to. For the small cost of fifty cents, Aunt Doris taught me a priceless lesson about managing money, which has been one of the most unforgettable lessons of my life.

I encourage you to apply this logic with your own children. The single best way to teach kids the value of money is to let them run out a few times. If Mommy or Daddy is always there with a handful of fresh bills, let's not be surprised if the child doesn't learn to appreciate the value of a dollar. For most of us, money is a limited resource. Therefore, it should be handled with responsibility and respect. In our family, Laura and I actually look for opportunities to have our kids operate within a fixed budget. During a trip to the movies, for example, I would much rather give my child a specific amount to cover the cost of a ticket and a light snack, as opposed to handing them a large bill and letting them choose to spend as much as they want.

Since entering the credit card era, some parents are even giving their teenagers no-limit credit cards, which the parent then pays off every month. What lesson does that teach? I can see the logic behind providing a credit card for use in case of emergencies, or issuing a debit card to cover monthly expenses when your child leaves for college. But, if you are going to bail your children out every time they run short on cash, you are setting yourself up to be bailing them out for a very long time.

Using Humor to Make a Point

My aunt taught me a valuable lesson about managing my personal finances that still impacts my choices and decision making today. However, all of life's lessons don't have to be learned the hard way. Sometimes injecting a little levity into the situation can actually be an effective way to make a point.

A few years ago, for example, my daughters were both upstairs after finishing their assigned chores on a Saturday morning. Again, we are not running a sweatshop for child labor, but I do believe that as part of the family, children should be expected to help around the house.

I happened to pass by the upstairs playroom, which was in various stages of disarray. So, I summoned the girls from down the hall to ask if they would please pick up their things. By their reaction, you would have thought I had asked them to repaint the house! "If you put your mind to it, cleaning up should only take a few minutes," I said.

"But, Daaaad, that's not fairrrrrr!" they both complained.

Without hesitation, I walked over and sat down on the rug in the corner of the playroom. Patting the carpet next to me, I said, "Sarah, can you please come sit right here?" Patting the carpet on the other side, I continued, "Mary Claire, would you please sit right here?" And, there we sat on the carpet facing the center of the room.

After a few seconds passed, Sarah broke the silence by asking, "Why are we sitting here?"

"We're watching," I said.

"What are we watching for?" Sarah asked.

"We're watching to see if the playroom picks itself up," I answered.

It was difficult to keep from chuckling once I noticed Mary Claire on my left (five years old at the time) straining her neck to see how this miracle was going to occur. Sarah had already figured out what dad was doing.

As if on queue, my wife Laura peeked into the room and saw the three of us quietly sitting on the floor in the corner on the room. She studied us for a couple seconds and then asked, "What are you guys doing?"

"Sarah, tell mom what we're doing." I said.

"We're watching to see if the playroom straightens itself," she said.

Being the question-based parent that she is, Laura asked. "How's that working out?" and then she left as quickly as she had come. The three of us just sat there, watching. The entire episode probably didn't last sixty seconds, but nothing in the room moved an inch during that whole time. To the girls, I bet it seemed like we sat there for an eternity.

"How long are we going to have to sit here?" Sarah finally asked, and I knew she could tell that her question was a loaded one.

"That's what I was just about to ask you," I replied.

"Okay, okay, c'mon Mary Claire, let's clean up the playroom," Sarah said in a resigned tone.

Rumor has it that after I left the room, both girls agreed it was good that Sarah had broken the silence because they were pretty sure Dad was ready to sit there for a very long time. Frankly, I don't mind if my kids think their father is a little off-center sometimes. It keeps them guessing, and it also keeps me somewhat entertained.

Logic Works Just as Well as Humor

Child safety is a concern for all parents. As a result, some things are simply non-negotiable. Jumping up and down on the bed, for example, is one of those things for me.

It creates a vision where a child is just one misstep away from having a potentially dangerous accident. I happened upon an episode of bed jumping one day when I walked into my oldest daughter's bedroom. Apparently, she had just discovered that a bed and a trampoline have a great deal in common, and she was having a world of fun bouncing up and down. She didn't notice me at first. But as I stood there, I grew especially concerned because she bounced very close to the edge of the bed several times, which could have spelled disaster. At the age of four, she was clearly oblivious to any potential risk. She was having the time of her life.

Commanding a child to, "Get down from there this instant!", is a tendency that many parents share. I understand the rush of emotion that can occur when you see a child at risk. Delivering an order like this one with an unmistakable harshness in your voice would probably succeed in achieving the short-term objective of getting them to stop a dangerous activity. Most kids would immediately stop jumping and get off the bed. But does this type of intervention, by itself, accomplish the larger objective of teaching the child to recognize dangerous situations on their own? Someday your kids will climb in behind the wheel of a two-thousand pound automobile and their mommies and daddies won't always be there to alert them to every danger. From my perspective, helping children learn how to recognize risk requires some thoughtful seeds to be planted well in advance of when they might actually be needed.

My first instinct as a question-based parent was to ask my daughter to stop jumping on the bed. I modified the question slightly in order to ask, "Sarah, could you please come down here for a minute?" Ironically, she hopped down just as fast as if I had issued a command. But since I wasn't yelling at her with a harsh tone, she didn't feel the need to put up her natural defenses to start the conversation.

"Why are you jumping on the bed?" I inquired. I was really interested in hearing what the answer was.

"Uhhhh, because it's fun?" she answered sheepishly. Kids are smart. I was pretty sure that she knew jumping up and down on the bed was probably not a good idea.

"It looks like a lot of fun," I said. Now she was confused. Was jumping on the bed okay with Dad, she wondered?

"Have you thought about what might happen if you fell?" I asked, like I was wondering out loud. That was a good question! She didn't say anything, but I could tell she was thinking about it, which was okay because I hadn't yet made my point. "If you slipped and fell," motioning toward the nightstand with my finger, "what would have happened if you bumped your head right here on the corner of the table?"

She give me a concerned look, but no verbal response. Most kids don't like to think about what might happen if they split their head open as a result of hitting the corner of a bedside table. Most parents don't like to think about those things either, it turns out.

But, if you are going to ask a legitimate question, then it's important to wait for an answer. A few moments passed, and she said, "I wasn't going to fall." Touché, the kid is a tough negotiator.

"Yes, but if you did fall you could have really hurt yourself," I said. I went for the close by asking, "Can you see that?"

Sarah is almost fifteen now, and to her credit, she has become a very safety conscious person with regard to herself and others. We are particularly hopeful that this will pay dividends in the coming months as she continues working toward getting her driver's license.

I don't attribute the high levels of awareness that she

now demonstrates to any one incident. Lord knows that we have experienced our fair share of close calls over the years. Consistency, however, tends to have a cumulative effect, and she would be the first to tell you that rational logic and a calm explanation is preferred to being on the receiving end of a parental barrage of harshness every time something happens, or almost happens.

The downside to being question-based lies in the fact that a larger time investment is often required when dealing calmly and rationally with a child. That's okay because question-based parenting is not intended to be a quick fix. Rather, what I am talking about is more of a longer-term development program to maximize your ability to communicate with and educate your children as they grow and mature. The question is, when something unexpected happens, can you hold off the natural rush of emotions long enough to have a productive exchange of information and ideas with your child? How else will your kids learn how to recognize and avoid unnecessary risks, and begin to think ahead about how their actions right now might pose an otherwise unanticipated risk at some point in the future?

Schoolwork and Grades

A significant portion of the negotiations that occur between children and their parents revolves around the issue of homework and grades. From a parent's perspective, school is very important. We know from experience that having a good education is one of the things that will create an abundance of opportunities later in life. But I must tell you, the idea of pressuring young people to achieve stellar grades is overrated. I am not giving away a parental secret here, as both my daughters know exactly where I stand on this topic.

Bringing home a report card filled with excellent grades is fantastic, and I am more than ready to give out high-fives and pats on the back. Too often, the opposite scene is played out, where parents are distraught when the report card comes home and does not reflect good news. In our house, we have made a commitment to our kids to focus on the effort that was invested, and not just the results. While grades give you some indication of whether your kids are on the right track, if my child has done her very best and put forth a sincere effort in terms of time and preparation, then I don't care that much about the grade.

Not every child is going to come home with straight A's. The truth is, your child might be a gifted artist or musician who will always struggle with analytical subjects like science and math. Someone else's child might be a struggling reader, which could challenge them in other subjects like English or History. Which subjects did you struggle with when you were a kid? To me, it is important to recognize that kids are going to have different strengths and weaknesses. That said, every child does have the ability to *try their best* in school. The only remaining issue, then, is whether or not your child has the desire and motivation to put forth the effort.

Desire is one of my top two issues regarding schoolwork. I understand that times have changed, and in our hustle and bustle world, kids are pulled in many different directions. Even so, I believe that extra-curricular activities like after-school sports, playing with friends, and weekend outings are privileges that come secondary to completing your schoolwork on time and with reasonable quality.

In the Freese house, we hit the wall on this a couple

years ago. All of a sudden, a few zeros started appearing on homework papers, test grades dipped significantly, and self-confidence was noticeably absent. From personal experience I can tell you that it's easy to get frustrated at a child for underperforming when you know they can do better. But collectively, let's take a deep breath. A child's grade point average isn't likely to suddenly skyrocket because a parent displays an outburst of anger. As an alternative, the next time you sense that the train is off the tracks relative to the child's schoolwork, make it your objective as a question-based parent to first understand the root cause of the problem. And, since your child is closest to ground zero on almost everything that is happening in their world, you might as well start by asking them a few honest questions.

"Is something happening that's causing your grades to suffer?" I might inquire. Our culture is based on the presumption of innocence, so it's important not to be angry when you are gathering information. Frankly, I really want to know if something is adversely affecting my child's performance. Once a line of communication is opened, you might discover your child simply has a puppy crush on the redhead in the second row. Or, for whatever reason, they may be in conflict with a certain teacher. Things like this happen. By the way, I am not looking for a list of excuses. I just want to know if something beyond our awareness is contributing to the recent change in results at school.

When it comes to actually dealing with the situation, it's important not to use your parental authority as a sword to dictate corrective action. If your child doesn't buy into your plan of attack, they probably won't follow your advice anyway. So once again, a negotiated settlement is preferred.

After exploring the root cause of the problem, I would probably ask, "What can we do differently, either to increase the amount of effort you are putting into your school work, or get better results from the time you're already investing?"

It's a fair question. If you can button up long enough to listen to the answer, you might end up solving the problem right there and boosting your child's confidence in the process. After all, there's a big difference between working *with* the child toward resolution, as opposed to just making them the recipient of a frustrated parent's wrath.

Here's my deal with our kids. Put in enough time and effort to demonstrate that you are indeed doing your best, and I won't complain about grades. How much time and effort is enough? That's a negotiation where both parent and child discuss what is reasonable and then come to an agreement. If you need help quantifying what constitutes reasonable time and effort, ask for a teacher conference with yourself and your child. Ask the teacher, "On average, how much time should Bobby be spending on schoolwork on the typical day?" The amount of homework that we have been advised to expect is twenty minutes per day per subject (on average).

It's worth noting that reasonable effort with regard to schoolwork includes more than just those things that Bobby has to turn in tomorrow. Homework should include preparation, organization, study, and review, in addition to daily assignments and longer-term projects. While that might sound like a lot, school is much more manageable if your child has a plan and you are consistent with regard to helping them stick with it.

The one other requirement I have regarding school is that Laura and I want to hear about grades directly from our children. I don't want to find out two weeks from now that there is a problem when the teacher sends home a note. Frankly, I don't want to miss hearing about perfect scores, either. Good or bad, whether it's a quiz, test, homework, or project grade, the message has been clearly communicated to our kids that we don't want any surprises when the report card comes home. All we ask is that you do your best, and let us know what's happening, when it's happening. And they do.

By the way, since our communication improved, my children *are* doing their best, and they are independently putting forth the appropriate time and effort. As a result, their grades are better than mine when I was their age, and their level of self-confidence and self-reliance has skyrocketed. Of course, this makes everyone in the house happy!

Teach Your Kids How to Talk with Adults

When it comes to dealing with other people, I would encourage you to please not answer for your kids. Learning to speak with confidence to adults other than parents is a very important skill for children to acquire if you want them to be able to fend for themselves. But it can only be learned through practice. If you think about it, people are always impressed when a child can stand up straight, look you in the eye, and confidently say whatever happens to be on their mind. Parents, however, have a funny way of jumping in and speaking for their children.

When I taught the first grade Sunday school at our church, parents would often drop their kids off at the classroom door. Particularly early in the year when we were just getting to know the children, we always tried to greet each child, saying, "Good morning, Elizabeth. How are you this morning?" Or, "Hello, Adam. Did you have a good week?"

I was shocked at how many parents would butt in to answer these simple questions for their kids. It was amazing.

"Ethan, are you having a good morning?"

"Ethan is a little shy," the parent would say, while Ethan just looked down at his shoes.

"What school do you go to, Ethan?" I sometimes asked.

"Ethan goes to Smithfield Elementary," the parent would answer.

"Who's your teacher?" I might continue, trying to engage the child.

"He has Mrs. Granger this year," the parent would respond. At this point, whatever level of interaction is really with the parent, with the child just standing to the side like a ventriloquist's dummy.

Mothers and fathers are so quick to jump in and answer for their children. In addition to discounting the child's capabilities, this behavior on the part of a parent is just plain crazy. What motivation does a parent have to answer instead of their child? Will the Earth stop rotating on its axis if a question intended as a pleasantry is not responded to promptly enough by a first or second grader? If you want your children to learn how to become independent and self-reliant, you might as well let them have a shot at fielding some of life's most basic questions. The question-based parent understands that children learn to communicate by doing. In fact, it's the only way they will learn.

An easy place to start is in restaurants, where it's a great idea to allow children to order their own meals. Both our daughters starting ordering for themselves when they were old enough to speak clearly. It's just not that hard to speak up and tell a waiter what you would like. With younger children, you might have to ask them to speak up or repeat difficult words. If some interpretation is needed, do it covertly so as not to take away from a child's pride for having accomplished the objective. Then, if your child needs something during the meal, like ketchup or an extra napkin, flag down the server, but then defer to the child to communicate their request.

What if your youngster happens to be shy or just doesn't want to order for themselves? If a child is having a bad day or they feel totally intimidated for some reason, it's okay to help them out. But, I generally draw a pretty hard line on this. If a child wants to eat, they will very quickly learn to speak up.

Children who are uncomfortable talking with adults actually feel most intimidated when they feel judged by their doting parent's watchful eye. In the earlier stages of social development, your kids simply can't think as quickly as you can. It's intimidating for a child who knows that if they don't answer quickly enough, their parents will jump in and speak for them. Equally bad is the parent who continuously prompts their child by telling them what to say, or edits the child's sentences as they come out.

"Hi, Chandler, how was your week?" I might ask.

"Tell Mr. Freese that you're doing fine," the parent responds.

It's hard enough for children to decide how to respond to adults without also having to respond to their parent's commands at the same time. Plus, what message are you sending if you don't trust your child to answer simple questions about how they are doing today, what school they attend, or who their teacher is? Go ahead and tell your kids *not* to talk to strangers. That's fine. But, you must also teach your children how to talk with adults when appropriate, and then give them an opportunity to practice. That includes encouraging them to look other people in the eye and use full sentences. (The full sentences comment is for parents with teenagers.) Just saying, "Nuh-uh," is not enough to qualify as sufficient communication.

Please note that teaching social skills may require a little extra patience on your part. Remember, you have been practicing your social skills for many years and your children are just cutting their teeth. So, don't jump in and answer questions posed to your kids. I also recommend against constantly correcting a child's syntax in front of other people, like making them say it again (the proper way!). If you are one of those parents who needs validation that you are indeed smarter than your child, call me and I will tell you, "You are indeed smarter than your kids." Otherwise, constantly demonstrating that you are more capable than your children doesn't do much to boost their self-concept. Ultimately, you want your kids to learn how to think for themselves without being prompted. If you can bite your tongue long enough to give them a chance, your kids might just surprise you with how capably they can handle themselves.

Chapter 4

Delivering Bad News Gracefully

"You can't always get what you want."
—Mick Jagger, The Rolling Stones

We can talk about the intricacies of parent-child negotiation, but at the end of the day, I sometimes get tired of saying "No" to my kids. I'm sure my children would tell you they get tired of hearing it, too. Nonetheless, part of the human condition is that children are going to test their boundaries, challenge the status quo, and push the limits of every parent's patience. They push and push until the answer we must give is simply, "No." "Why not?" they ask. "Because I said so, that's why!"

At some point, the answer *is* going to be, "No." That's because life is filled with schedules that need to be kept, responsibilities that must be fulfilled, and some degree of reasonability that unfortunately counterbalances the wishes and whims of an otherwise happy-go-lucky child.

"Can we play a game?" is a wonderful request to hear from an enthusiastic young person. But it's not a reasonable request if the school bus is chugging down the street toward your house in the morning. "Can I have another dinner roll?", seems like an innocent desire, but it's not a reasonable request if the child has already devoured three rolls without touching their vegetables. In these and many other cases, the answer just has to be, "No."

One of the main reasons parents need to be in charge is that you have a broader perspective with regard to what is reasonable and acceptable that your children do not yet have. How could they? They have very little "been there, done that" experience to draw upon. You and I didn't have a mature perspective when we were young. It's something we acquired as we matured. And someday, when your kids grow up to become well-rounded adults with kids of their own, their perspective will broaden just like ours, where they will begin to think differently about the health, emotional well-being, and overall welfare of the family, as opposed to acting on whatever craving pops into a young person's head at the time.

Part of our job as parents is to recognize the bigger picture when determining what's best for our children. As such, we have a certain responsibility to field requests from our kids with an objective point of view and a certain evenhandedness with regard to what's fair. In essence, you are the judge and jury, the one who will ultimately determine whether the answer is, *"Yes"* or *"No."* You are also the one who will either receive positive gratitude, *"Thank you. You are the best daddy in the world..."* or have to deal with the child's resulting contempt, *"You are so mean,"* ...*stomp, stomp,* ... *"I hate you, I hate you."*

You mustn't be dissuaded by tantrums. We have all ridden the emotional rollercoaster of both loving and hating our parents at times when we were young. Much of this you can chalk up to the circle of life. As parents, we don't want to be seen as a mean father or an uncaring mom, and we have all had to wrestle with the desire to please (a child) versus the need to stand firm. No matter how much you tell yourself that it doesn't hurt, it is very difficult to be the one who is constantly disappointing your children with the word, "No!"

For a while, you toe the line because you understand the magnitude of a parent's responsibility, and you, too, want to raise impressive children. At some point, however, the nature of the ongoing conflict between children and their parents beats you down until you no longer have the energy to continue battling your kids, so you just give in. "Do whatever you want," you think to yourself. "I just don't want to argue anymore!"

Have you ever experienced a weak moment where you felt like this? It's okay; every parent has. And now that we have a tough negotiating teen in our house, we seem to be experiencing these moments more frequently. But, what if parenting didn't have to be so conflict-oriented? What if it were possible to enforce the rules of the house, and at the same time, sidestep much of the contention you get back from your children? What if it were even possible to deliver bad news or say "No" in a way that would diffuse the otherwise hurt feelings between parent and child?

I have good news for parents. If you want to change the tone of your communications at home, there is something you can do that will considerably change the way you interact with your kids. It will also change the way your kids interact with you. You can achieve phenomenal results by simply implementing a very specific question-based technique that we call "delivering bad news gracefully."

Can I Have a Treat?

Some of the best material I have ever written has come to me purely by accident. Particularly at home, when something I am doing is not working, out of sheer exasperation, I sometimes try a different approach—even doing it the total opposite way as before. Lo and behold, it works! Suddenly, I have a new strategy for dealing with a certain issue.

My wife (Laura) and I had such an experience at the dinner table one mid-January evening in 1998. Our oldest daughter (Sarah) was in Kindergarten at the time, and Laura was pregnant with our second daughter who wasn't due for another month.

We try very hard at the Freese house to have some semblance of order at the dinner table, and thus, there are a few simple etiquette rules we all try to follow. For example, it's impolite to talk with food in your mouth. We can wait until you stop chewing. Similarly, let's not have everyone talk at the same time. There's no need to interrupt someone in the middle of a story. Lastly, if you eat a good supper, you can have dessert. These rules apply to everyone at the table, parents and children alike. I would guess that most of you have similar statutes in place at your dinner table. To me, expecting a child to finish their dinner before satisfying their sweet tooth with dessert is a fair trade. But, logic doesn't always stop children from testing their boundaries or your resolve.

On that particular evening, about half way through dinner, Sarah, who was five years-old at the time, turned to her mother and asked, "Can I have a treat?" That's her word for dessert.

Sarah had always been a good eater, so this request was somewhat of a surprise to both Laura and me. Upon noticing that Sarah hadn't yet eaten much of the food on her plate, Laura took the helm and said, "No, you may not have dessert until you finish your dinner."

Whenever Sarah isn't pleased with the answer she receives, she sticks out her bottom lip and pouts. I call it the *grumpies*. Even though my wife was doing the right thing to enforce our rule about eating a good supper before having dessert, Laura had suddenly become the bad guy—the one standing in the way of Sarah's desire for a treat. *Grump, grump, grump!*

This same scenario played out the next night, and then the next. Night after night, Sarah would eat some fraction of her meal and then defiantly turn to her mother asking, "Can I have a treat?" Night after night, Laura stuck to her guns and would not allow Sarah to have dessert until she finished her supper. Have you ever noticed that "the grumpies" can escalate from a pouting lip into an all out "I'm going to show you" type of fussiness?

After an almost week-long war of wills at the dinner table, this relatively small issue had somehow escalated into an international incident. Finally, I conferred with Laura in a quiet part of the house before dinner. We simply could not continue down this path of rapidly spiraling emotional hostility between my wife and a five-year-old.

"Honey, if Sarah asks for dessert again before finishing her dinner, can I have a turn at answering?" I asked. My wife likes to fight her own battles within the household, so I didn't want to usurp her authority. "This may not happen again tonight, but if she does ask for a treat before finishing her dinner could you route that request down to my end of the table?" Since Laura had reached the end of her patience with this one, she was more than agreeable. "You got it," she said.

That evening at dinner, I was watching Sarah's plate out of the corner of my eye, and I knew that Laura was on full alert as well. Sure enough, after finishing about half her meal, Sarah turned to her mother and delivered those fateful words, "Mom, can I have a treat?"

On queue, Laura said, "Tonight, why don't you ask your father?"

Caught off guard slightly, Sarah cautiously panned down to my end of the table and sheepishly asked, "Dad, can I have a treat?"

"Yes, Sarah," I said with an enthusiastic tone, "You may absolutely have a treat."

Both my daughter's and my wife's eyes popped wide open with surprise. "What did he just say?" they were both thinking to themselves. My wife could have been thinking some other things as well, but we'll probably never know about that.

"You may absolutely have a treat," I continued, "...as soon as you finish your supper."

Sarah glanced at me, and then at her plate of food. Her parent's authority was no longer the obstacle standing between her and her desires. She could absolutely have dessert as soon as she finished. Suddenly, Sarah's destiny was completely within her own control. Just as a coach would have drawn it on a chalkboard, the play worked to perfection. Sarah eagerly finished up her dinner, enjoyed her dessert, and to this day, the issue of asking for a treat before finishing dinner has never resurfaced at the Freese house.

It's worth pointing out that Laura and I were totally on the same page with regard to expecting the child to finish her dinner before having dessert. The only difference was how we actually enforced the rule. Laura said, "No, you may not have dessert until you finish your supper." I would guess that this is a typical parent's position, and probably what I would have said, too, if Sarah had asked me first. But, once it was clear that the typical approach was not working, a different tactic was needed.

By adjusting my position slightly, not only did I avoid the harshness that comes with the word, "No," my actual response to her was, "Yes, you can absolutely have a treat." *Sure! Go for it!* As soon as you meet these conditions that we (as your parents) feel are reasonable.

The lesson in this story is simply this: Kids are going to push the envelope with regard to what is reasonable, and in many cases, the answer should be a resounding "no." But there is more than one way to skin a cat when it comes to delivering bad news to your children. Therefore, the next time one of your kids, friends, neighbors, extended family or even one of your customers at work asks for something beyond what is reasonable, rather than just saying, "no," try repositioning your response such that you can say "yes,"— if certain conditions can be met in a way that makes the request mutually beneficial.

Softening the Blow of Rejection

One of the neighbors on our street has a beautiful redwood outdoor play set in their backyard. It came with dual swings, a built-in climbing fort, a rope ladder, and a large plastic slide. Of course, the thing attracts the neighbor kids like flies.

Being popular in the neighborhood is great, except when you want to have some privacy. Dedicated family fun is important, especially during those special times like when you are wrestling in the grass with your oldest boy, or you want to push your daughter on the toddler swing. During these unique moments, nothing else in the world matters—that is, until the neighbor kid hears someone on the play set and comes running over wanting to join in.

Have you ever noticed that kids don't always know how to take a hint? Even if you say something like, "Andrew, tomorrow might be a better time to come over," they respond by saying, "Don't worry, my mom said it was okay for me to play."

Somehow they missed your point. Consequently, you either have to acquiesce and let them join in or be more direct in order to successfully communicate your actual message. Being too direct can be problematic, however, because it's so easy to damage a young person's fragile ego. Personally, I would not feel comfortable telling a neighbor's child to go away because we don't want them in our yard. But, you can use this same question-based technique of delivering bad news gracefully to soften the blow of rejection.

As a side note, if you need to communicate a message that yours or any other child may not want to hear, it's important that you talk with them one-on-one, as opposed to yelling across the yard.

"Billy, can you come over here for a second?" is a great question-based opener. Once he does come over, you simply say, "I wanted to ask a favor." Of course, Billy nods. "Would it be okay for us to have a little family time this morning, and then you can come back and play on the swing set after lunch?" That's a much softer way of asking for privacy, while at the same time, letting the child know they are welcome to come back later in the day.

That's not for (Child's Name)

When I was a brand new father, I couldn't wait for our baby girl to learn to walk. I coached her on standing, and even held toys at arm's length to encourage her to step out. When she took those first few steps, I was tremendously excited to be there as a witness. Within a few days, however, our easy little bundle of joy had mobilized, and she was suddenly motoring all over the house—and getting into things she shouldn't. My momma always told me to 'be careful what you wish for.'

As is often the case, our new walker was also learning to talk. Her vocabulary was limited to a few starter words like "ball", "dog", and, of course, "Dada." She also understood the word, "no."

As the days and weeks of her newfound mobilization rolled by, it turned out that she was being exposed to the word "no" more than any other word in the universe. That's because her mother and I dutifully followed her all over the house saying things like, "No, don't touch," "No, leave that alone," or just simply, "No," when she was doing something that could create a problem. Even after child proofing our home, we still found ourselves following the little explorer around the house getting ready for the next opportunity to say, "No."

One day it occurred to us how difficult it must be for a toddler to interpret the word "no." Does it mean, "Stop immediately because you are in danger" or perhaps something less urgent, like: "Honey, it probably isn't a good idea to give your pacifier to the dog?" We also wondered how many times a day a toddler hears the word "no." And, after being rebuffed a hundred times since breakfast, does hearing it so often takes away its credence?

"No, no, no, no, no, no, no, no, no, no!" How does that make you feel?

Fortunately, a friend gave us a parenting tip that was instantly applicable with our toddler, and the same advice worked for many years afterward. Instead of using the same two letters for every correction, you would be better served to reserve the word "no" for specific "stop the child in their tracks" emergencies. For example, if your child reaches toward a pot of boiling hot water, you should absolutely exclaim, "No. Don't touch that!"

To avoid diluting the impact of the word "no," however, Laura and I made a conscious decision to adjust our phraseology, so that when our curious eight month old (at the time) reached her hand out to test the stability of the Christmas tree, we would just say, "That's not for Sarah." If she wandered over toward the dog's food dish, with the intention of doing a taste test between Gerber and Purina, it was easy to say, "That's not for Sarah." Not only did we feel better about not blurting the word "no" every twenty seconds, but she also responded much better to the built-in softness of our new phrase.

Saying, "That's not for Patrick," is a much softer way to communicate boundaries to your child. In addition to being easier to hear, the underlying message that something is "Not for Emily" will help them to understand that they should steer clear of said item in the future. The next time your little boy cruises past the dog's bowl, for example, you want him to be thinking, "That's not for me."

A discerning reader might recognize and point out that I am using statements here as opposed to asking a question. That's a keen observation. Keep in mind, though, that being question-based is not the same as being limited to question-only conversation. In fact, the beauty of this technique is that it provides parents with a wonderful education mechanism. It conditions the curious child to always be thinking to themselves, "Is this for me?" For a child who is rapidly becoming cognizant of their newfound abilities and boundaries, causing that child to ask themselves a few questions about how best to behave is a very different thought process than just having the child aimlessly motor around the house until someone blurts out the word, "No."

Being Influenced by Peer Pressure

Speaking of boundaries, as your children grow up, their boundaries will naturally expand. When that happens, they will begin to experience the effects of peer pressure, as will you, especially when your child's primary motivation for wanting something is based on the impulsive rationale that, "Everybody else is doing it!"

A couple years ago, our oldest daughter was the only one in her grade who didn't own a cell phone, or at least, that's what she said. "Everyone else has one," she asserted. I should point out that I am not against kids having cell phones. I'm just not willing to purchase an expensive item for a pre-teen just because everyone else has one.

One of the burdensome characteristics that comes with being part of the male species is that I naturally gravitate to using logic. "Are you sure everyone else in your grade has a cell phone?" I asked.

"Yes," she confirmed.

"Does your friend Elizabeth have a cell phone?" I asked. Because we knew Elizabeth's parents fairly well, I knew that they too were holding out, not wanting to purchase a cell phone just to be used as a toy.

"No." Sarah remembered.

"Does Lydia have a cell phone?" I asked, once again knowing that I had successfully poked another hole in the "everybody else" defense. I walked away feeling like I had won that battle, but in a house full of girls, I have learned that sometimes winning the argument can be a losing proposition.

Laura has the best approach for dealing with peer pressure. First, she simply asks our girls, "How do you feel about that?" Oftentimes, there's a level of indifference lying just beneath the surface of many spontaneous requests, to the point where the child doesn't really want the item as much as they want to test to see if you would allow it if they did. When it becomes clear to the child that something is really not a "have to have" item, the sense of urgency to acquire it often dissipates like fog in the morning. Kudos to Laura for having the insight and patience to find out what is actually driving the need.

With those requests that retain life or death status because "everyone else" is doing something, Laura still has the best response.

"But, mom," my daughter might say, "everyone else at the party will be staying way past midnight!"

Laura usually responds by saying something like, "I'm not everyone else's mother." Sometimes she uses a variation of this same idea, by saying, "Everyone else doesn't live in this house." This response is along the lines of "because I said so," but it's softer by design. My wife's softness is no less authoritative, however. As far as I know, there is no clause in the Freese Family Rules dictating that we must change our perspective on what is reasonable just because some other parent approaches things differently.

If you want to be a question-based parent, then it's

incumbent on you to be an excellent listener, because your child might actually have a point. As I said, Sarah is a good negotiator and we did end up purchasing a cellular telephone for her to use, but not because everyone else had one. Instead, once she thought about what might make the idea more appealing to us, she started communicating the advantages of having a mobile phone that included things like personal safety, and making her more available when she is babysitting at someone else's house. In fact, she made several valid points to support her request. Sarah will definitely make a great salesperson one day.

One of my company's certified trainers in the Southwest, Alan Rohrer, tells the story of his teenage daughter who wanted badly to go out one evening to see a band play at a local club in Phoenix. "C'mon dad, so-and-so's mother is going to take us, and everybody's going to be there," his daughter pleaded.

"Where exactly is this club?" Alan inquired.

Alan discovered that the band she wanted to see was playing at a bar in a seedy part of town known as the Warehouse District. Sending a fourteen-year-old girl to a bar on the south side of town on a Friday night didn't seem like the right thing, no matter how many of her friends would be there. In fact, Alan even took the extra step to call the owner of the club. Apparently, the bar had a separate room that was blocked off, so kids could be separated from the adults in an attempt to minimize underage drinking.

"Do you have kids of your own?" Alan asked the club owner.

"Yes. Two teenagers," the bar owner replied.

"If you were me," Alan continued, "would you let your own kids go to this type of event on a Friday night?"

"No way!" the bar owner quickly replied.

Have you ever noticed that a parent's first intuition about a questionable situation is generally correct? As it turned out, even though his daughter was convinced that "everyone else" was going to be there, none of her friends ended up going to the concert on the south side of Phoenix that Friday.

If what everyone else is doing, or the possessions that everyone else has, is going to be the standard for decision-making within your family, let me suggest that you encourage your children to consider all the other kids in third world countries who are significantly less fortunate that most of us. The truth is, everyone else doesn't already have a cellular phone, an MP3 player, laptop computer, designer jeans, Nike shoes, or a new outfit for the school dance on Saturday night. As I'm writing these very words, my mind is flashing back to the days when my grandfather used to say at the dinner table, "You better eat everything on your plate because there are kids starving in India."

Talk with Your Child About Implications

It is perfectly acceptable to have rules. You should have rules, and you should also have the fortitude to stand behind them if they are breached. We certainly do at the Freese house. But, we don't have many rules that are based on the sole justification, 'because we said so." What I really strive for is to have my children understand why certain rules are in place, and the implications of crossing the line.

For example, like many families, we require our kids to wear a helmet when they ride their bikes. This isn't some whimsical regulation Laura and I dreamed up one day just to agitate our children, and it didn't get implemented because we own stock in a helmet company. Somewhere along the line we realized that it doesn't take much to cause an accident, and if your child falls off a bike, the concrete always wins. The cost of a bike helmet is also significantly less expensive than a trip to the emergency room.

But most kids, before they have a serious accident, never ponder what a trip to the emergency room might be like. How many novocaine shots does it take, for example, to numb the skin before the doctor sews up an open gash with fifteen stitches? Just the thought of that scenario makes me cringe.

We have also taught our kids not to talk to strangers. When our girls were younger, we sat down and talked with them about what they should do if someone unfamiliar approached them. Most kids haven't ever thought about what could happen after they accept a handful of free candy from a perfect stranger. I am not advocating that you should try and scare your children, but there is definitely an opportunity for parents to be proactive on an important issue like child safety.

One of the most common ways parents try to get their point across is by threatening their children with consequences. "You better wear a bike helmet, or else...!" The point is here not to threaten a child into compliance. Instead, you simply want them to have a healthy respect for your underlying concerns, which is what ultimately drives most of your rules.

It might be something as simple as educating children about the possible implications of failing to use good judgment. The reason kids need to go to bed on time on school nights, for example, is not because something terrible will happen if they don't. Rather, it's because you want them to be healthy and happy and ready to learn in the morning, and consistently getting a reasonable amount of sleep each night contributes to attaining that result. Likewise, we want kids to wash their hands before supper, because it's the right thing to do with regard to person hygiene. Will something terrible happen if they forget to wash their hands before one meal? Probably not. But, I can tell you that it's much easier to get a child to wash their hands (or bathe) if they understand *why* it makes sense.

How can you help children understand the implications of their behavior? The question-based parent starts by asking questions to gauge the child's current perspective, in order to then fill in any gaps. With a younger child, start with easy questions like, "Susie, do you understand why it's important to wear a helmet when riding your bike?" Young kids love to answer questions correctly. Make a big deal about thoughtful responses, as it will bolster their confidence. If they truly don't know why, that creates a perfect opportunity for you to communicate some very important information to your child.

Questions are valuable conversational tools because they involve the child and show that you are truly interested in their opinion. I use the same technique with older kids, although I generally notch-up the sophistication level of the conversation. Don't be afraid to cover the basics, though. When a teenager is first learning to drive, a parent should ask some rudimentary questions like, "Do you understand the difference between solid lines and double lines on the road?" Funny thing, teenagers love to answer questions correctly, too. They will also give you feedback on the validity of your question, letting you know with an eye roll or a grunt if a question you ask is redundant or just plain foolish-sounding.

We're talking about understanding what if—the "what if" implications of a child's daily choices. I think the key to creating a good prevention strategy is to paint verbal pictures that will resonate with the child. My earlier reference of sewing up an open gash in the emergency room, for example, is probably too graphic for toddlers. They would completely miss the point. Getting a boo-boo on your knee might be closer to what a young child understands. On the other hand, painting a vivid picture of what could happen if a student driver was talking on his cell phone while turning left in front of a speeding truck, might be exactly what is needed to create the appropriate level of respect for the road. Understanding the implications of our actions reinforces the reasoning behind the rules we put in place for our families. It just might be the best bad news you can deliver.

Dealing with the Child Who Repeatedly Gets Out of Bed

Just after our youngest daughter (Mary Claire) turned four, she went through a period of waking up in the middle of the night. The waking up part wasn't so bad, except that each time she would then make her way downstairs to the master bedroom and wake us up. She wasn't afraid or upset, just awake and wanting to share it with someone. Coming downstairs wasn't even a big deal, except that when she was ready to go back to bed, she wanted someone to escort her back upstairs to her room.

A few times of waking up in the middle of the night soon turned into a trend, and we were suddenly faced with a taxing nightly routine. Lucky for me, little girls tend to love their mommies much more than their daddies at three o'clock in the morning. So, for several days in a row, Laura was making the weary trek upstairs to put Mary Claire back to bed, sometimes multiple times per night.

Yelling at a four-year-old in the middle of the night or administering some sort of parental punishment to deter the behavior would not have worked because Mary Claire was only half-awake during most of her late night visits. And, talking about it during the daylight hours wasn't helping either because she wasn't consciously misbehaving. But, I can tell you that something had to be done. Continually waking mommy up in the middle of the night is a bad formula for spousal bliss.

Fortunately for us, question-based communication techniques work around the clock. "What if we changed the batting order?" I suggested to my wife. "Let's see what happens if she has to deal with daddy." Later that night, at o-dark-thirty, we heard the familiar creak of the bedroom door opening. The pitter-patter of a four-year old's little feet is unmistakable. Mary Claire was right on schedule, and as usual, she headed toward Laura's side of the bed.

"MC, would you please come around to my side?" I whispered. Laura pretended to be asleep, as was our plan. Reluctantly, Mary Claire came around the end of the bed towards me.

"What's the matter?" I asked. I didn't even raise up, because when I was lying down and she was standing, we were exactly eye level.

"Umm, I had a bad dream," she replied. She had discovered that having a bad dream generated the most loving response from her mama.

"What would you like me to do?" I continued softly.

"I don't know," Mary Claire responded. If nothing else, it was obvious that I had knocked her off her game plan.

"Would you like a drink of water?" I asked.

"Yes," she answered.

Knowing that most four-year-olds know how to hold a cup and turn on a faucet, I suggested that she go into the bathroom, get a quick drink, and then come right back.

"Do you need anything else?" I calmly whispered, as she once again stood directly across from me, nose-to-nose.

"No," she said softly.

"Would you like me to take you back upstairs?" I asked. She nodded, still a little unsure of where this was headed.

I took her back to bed. I wasn't harsh, but I also didn't coddle her, and there was minimal conversation. Making it fun and exciting to come down to a parent's room in the middle of the night creates an incentive to repeat the behavior. I even attempted to prevent a recurrence.

"If you need something," I whispered, "you can always come find me. But, if you don't need anything, I would ask you to stay right here, okay?"

"Okay, daddy," she said.

I came back downstairs feeling like I had conquered the world. Laura was miffed. "I bet it doesn't last, Mr. Big Shot," she mumbled.

And, she was right (again). Shortly after drifting back into my happy place of deep sleep, once again came the pitter-patter of little feet as the bedroom door opened.

"Over here, Mary Claire," I said, cutting short her otherwise deliberate beeline to her mother's side of the bed. It would have been so easy to hoist her up into our bed, and we could cuddle like three bugs in a rug. But, that just might be what created this problem. It had obviously become more desirable for Mary Claire to come downstairs than to stay in her own room.

"Why are you here?" I asked, and then patiently waited for an answer.

The effectiveness of this technique is buried in the

subtlety of my question. You see, there was no good reason for her to wake up and come downstairs every few hours. Laura and I knew it, but Mary Claire hadn't yet figured it out. So, I patiently waited for her to respond. There was nothing but silence.

"You don't really want to be here, do you Mary Claire?" slowly she shook her head. Even little kids are smart. When they recognize that there is no logical explanation for their behavior, their perspective changes. To seal the deal, I asked, "If I take you back upstairs, will you promise to stay in bed?"

Now, we would definitely want our children to come to us if they felt sick or truly needed something in the night. But since getting up in the middle of the night is not fun for adults, it was important to make sure it wasn't enjoyable for our daughter, either. MC (as we sometimes call her) is now nine years old, and her days of getting out of bed for no reason ended pretty much that night. I'm sure she had times when part of her still wanted to come downstairs and garner some extra attention. But, a bigger part of her didn't want to be standing nose-to-nose with a dad who was certain to ask some legitimate questions.

Staying Home Sick from School

An effective parent has to fulfill many different roles, including being a nurse when the kids are home sick from school. Especially during the cold and flu season, the all-too-familiar symptoms of runny nose, sore throat, fever and cough tend to circulate around the entire family.

Being sick is the pits. I know from personal experience that few things are more heartbreaking than seeing a pitiful child wrapped in a blanket and lying on the sofa when they aren't feeling well. A couple doctor visits later, often with the help of some mild antibiotics, your child is back turning cartwheels around the house as usual. Time, patience, and a little extra loving from a caring parent continue to be some of the best medicines in the world.

However, sickness aside, it's possible that your child doesn't feel well for some reason other than the flu. Have you ever had one of those days where the alarm clock buzzes a couple hours short of a full night's sleep, and you really have to drag yourself out of bed in the morning? Kids feel this way sometimes just like we do. And, if you're a middle-schooler who hasn't studied for a big science test that day, you might start feeling even worse.

My physical education teacher in the fifth grade liked square dancing. Every spring, he dedicated two classes to teaching the entire grade how to square dance. I didn't attend either one of those classes. Do you know why? I was "sick" both days. It wasn't hard to convince my mother that my throat was scratchy and my head felt hot. Instead of being at school and being forced to dance with a *girl*, I stayed home and watched TV. Nothing to it!

Sorry, but that experience translates into some bad news for someone in our family who stays home from school. My philosophy is: If you are too sick to attend school, then you aren't well enough to play computer games, surf the Internet, or watch television at home. I am not against caring for a sick child. I just want to make sure we are not creating an incentive system that actually rewards someone for not feeling well.

My friend Candice has an even better solution. In her house, if you have to stay home from school because you are sick, then you must stay in bed the whole day. "The whole day?" her children complain. The rule is that you must remain in bed until the usual time you would have come home from school. If a child really is under the weather, they will benefit immensely from the extra rest. If their illness was more psychological than physical, they'll be bored to tears and more than ready to bounce out of bed when the bus rolls by at three o'clock.

The point is not to punish a child for being sick. Nurturing them back to full strength is the primary goal. But defining the boundaries for sick days accomplishes a longer term objective, which is that you want your children to "want to" be healthy. I am not suggesting that every child who stays home sick from school is faking an illness. I'm merely saying that no matter how healthy your kids are, they won't always feel like going to school (or to work later in life). And, when the time comes where they have to choose, I want my kids to realize that staying home and being B-O-R-E-D for seven hours, and then still having to make up the school work, is not the easy way out.

If one of your children seems to be dragging more than usual, the question-based parent might seize the opportunity to first diagnose the situation *before* jumping to a conclusion or making a decision. Frankly, I don't want to be in the awkward position of accusing one of my kids of faking an illness. What if you are wrong and they really are sick? Good luck rebuilding that child's trust in you. Instead, I want to ascertain if they are experiencing real symptoms or are feeling sluggish for some other reason. And, if it's the latter, with a little curiosity and persistence, you might just find out what's wrong. Maybe your child is struggling in a certain subject. Or, maybe they have recently found their way into the crosshairs of a schoolyard bully. Who knows? Maybe they just don't like square dancing.

Taking good care of a sick child is prudent parenting. Dealing with any of those other problems, by just letting your child stay home from school and watch television or play video games is *not*. The consistent theme throughout this book is: ask the right questions, and listen for the answer, before trying to dictate a solution without first knowing the facts.

Use Humbling Disclaimers

In business, salespeople are taught to ask the "hard" business questions—about things like budget, the timeframe for making a decision, and who are the decision makers. But, when a salesperson poses these types of questions to customers, they have to be careful because asking probing questions can sometimes be seen as pushy, or manipulative. That's why we call them the *hard* questions.

When I first created Question Based Selling, my advice to salespeople was to refrain from asking any more "hard" questions. You see, I had discovered over time that most customers don't want to be pushed or manipulated. I am not suggesting that salespeople should avoid asking business questions about the customer's budget or decision timeframe, because it is appropriate at some point to qualify whether a pending sale is indeed going to happen. I just make the point that sellers should stop asking non-fruitful questions.

Do you know what makes a question "hard?" The answer is risk. If a probative question has a high probability of making the other person feel pressured or uncomfortable, then you risk turning the other person off, to the point where you might actually get less information than if you hadn't asked. You can greatly reduce the risk of making people feel uncomfortable by using a simple questioning technique we call humbling disclaimers.

The concept of *humbling disclaimers* was originally developed to lower a salesperson's risk when asking business questions. For example, if a salesperson wants to ask about a customer's budget, they could easily say, "Mr. Customer, I appreciate your sharing the goals and objectives for your new employee benefits package, and *I don't want to be too forward,* but do you mind if I ask about the budget?"

Did you recognize the humbling disclaimer (in italics)? Technically, the answer to this question is either, "Yes, I do mind if you ask about the budget," or, "No, I don't mind," although you will rarely receive such a literal response. Instead, you might be surprised how quick customers are to open up and say something like, "Let me tell you about our financial projections."

The reality is simply this: If someone doesn't want to share with you, then it doesn't really matter what type of question you ask. On the other hand, if someone does want to share, using a humbling disclaimer will often enable you to have a more in-depth and more valuable conversation. What is it about this technique that causes people to want to open up and share information? It's the respect your question displays toward the person you are asking. The logic is simple: If you are respectful of another person's right *not* to share with you, it's amazing how much information you can get.

Here are more examples of humbling disclaimers:

"I'm not sure the best way to ask, but would you mind..."
"Without stepping on anyone's toes, could I ask about..."
"At the risk of sounding too forward, would it be okay ..."
"I don't want to say the wrong thing, but..."

At some point between the time when I first wrote about humbling disclaimers in the mid-1990's and today, it has become clear that the application of this technique extends far beyond traditional business conversations. In fact, it turns out that a child doesn't want to be pressured by a parent asking "hard" questions any more than a customer wants to be probed by a salesperson. Maybe you've noticed that asking probative questions turns out to be one of the quickest ways to cause a teenager to clam up.

It's important to always be sincere with your humbling disclaimers, as opposed to sounding sarcastic. Fortunately, this technique makes it easy for parents to sound sincere, because humbling disclaimers expose your vulnerability as part of the question itself, and this humility helps to facilitate better conversations. Any family counselor will tell you that kids are more reticent to share information with a parent who comes across as pompous or all-knowing. I think you'll find that injecting small amounts of humility into your questions will dramatically enhance the quality and quantity of the responses you receive from your children.

Suppose for example, I wanted to ask one of my daughters about something personal. It would be very easy to initiate the question by saying something like:

> *"I don't want to say the wrong thing, but I would like to ask you about…"*
> *"I'm sorry to interrupt you, but would you mind if…"*
> *"I am not trying to be critical, but could you help me understand…"*

Humility is a very attractive human quality, whether you are dealing with grown ups or children. It also tends to reverse the effect that makes someone feel pressured when responding to probative questions. That's because humbling disclaimers soften your questions with small doses of humility, which ultimately causes people (especially children) to feel more comfortable and share more information. Once someone feels comfortable enough to share, the task of asking the right questions gets much easier.

Time for a Softer Touch

Parents are often put in the awkward predicament of having to say, "No," to the very people we love more than anything else in the world. But if you look at a parent's motivations, one of the main reasons to stop your child from doing certain things is because you love them. If a toddler, for example, reaches across the counter toward a sharp knife, you say "no" to stop their progress. Because you love them, you want to prevent them from hurting themselves. An older child who misses a high school dance because they are grounded for the weekend, might not understand at the time that we ultimately make those decisions, too, because we love our children. Giving into a child's every desire is a formula for problems, because you will never be able to fully satisfy a child's expectations by always saying "yes."

One of the main differences between questions and statements is the respect you demonstrate to those people we so dearly love. The question-based parent can still decline a child's request by answering, "No," but that message is much easier for that child to hear if it gets delivered with a softer touch.

My wife Laura always says, "It's not *what* you say, it's *how* you say it." The tone of voice, your choice of words, and your facial expression are all important factors that contribute to the overall message you are sending to your children. While some people are naturally good at saying things the right way, the rest of us have to really think about what we say and the message that gets conveyed as a result. Here's the good news. Take the good intentions you already have and mix that together with some sound question-based communication techniques, and you will end up with a very potent formula for dealing with children in a way that shows your love for them and continues to foster their respect for you as their parent.

What happens if you use every trick in the book to communicate with your child, and their behavior is still unacceptable? At that point, it's time to deal with the issue of parental discipline, which is the topic we will discuss next in Chapter 5. My disciplinary philosophy might surprise you, however, because it's less about handing out consequences to punish a child, and more about teaching parents how to be better stewards of our authority.

Chapter 5

The Balancing Act of Discipline

The old adage, "Rules were meant to be broken," was obviously not created by a parent. This saying was more likely concocted at a fraternity party. The truth is, rules were meant to be followed, and maintaining some semblance of order within the household is a role that only a parent or guardian can fulfill. Otherwise, you will have chaos.

—Anonymous

My philosophy on discipline has changed dramatically over the years, particularly since we started having kids of our own. I used to think punishments were administered by parents for the sole purpose of "penalizing" a child for their poor judgment or bad behavior. I also assumed that the severity of the consequence should be dictated by the magnitude of the offense. I could *not* have been more wrong.

Rest assured that I derive no pleasure from punishing a child. If it were up to me, everyone in the Freese house would *always* make good decisions and our home would be known around the world as the most peaceful place on earth. Unfortunately, the realities of life usually awaken me from this fantasy just in time for Laura, myself, or a specially-equipped team of UN negotiators to come in and restore the peace.

Maintaining an appropriate level of discipline has always been a balancing act. Having no rules within your household is a formula for disaster, where lawlessness and mayhem will soon take over. Conversely, having too many regulations that are unnecessarily harsh can lead to anarchy and rebellion. If you want your children to develop any sense of responsibility and respect for others, then they must learn how to abide by certain guidelines. The parent's role is not just about enforcing this set of rules and regulations, however. Rather, it's about teaching our kids the necessary social skills that will enable them to live in harmony with their friends, family, neighbors, teachers, clergy, and the rest of society.

Interestingly, my roots as a sales professional have served me well in my quest to become a more effective parent. The goal of a salesperson is ultimately to motivate prospective customers to want to work toward a mutually desirable result. By mutually desirable, I mean working toward a transaction that is good for both parties—the paying customer gets a valuable product or service, and the selling company recognizes revenue in exchange. As it turns out, the role of a parent has strong parallels, where the primary goal of most parents is to motivate their kids to behave in ways that will produce a mutually beneficial result. The trick is fostering an environment where children "want to" act responsibly and be respectful toward others. This is ultimately accomplished through training, and good training requires discipline on the part of both parent and child. Motivating your children to want to abide by your rules is one of the most important ingredients in the formula for raising impressive kids.

What is Good Discipline?

We should start by defining the concept of parental discipline. One of the greatest responsibilities we parents share is to help our children understand the difference between right and wrong—plain and simple. We accomplish this using a mixture of positive reinforcement and negative consequences, hoping that our children will gravitate toward those things that reinforce positive behavior and away from other things that lead to disciplinary action.

Are your kids going to step out-of-bounds at some point along the way and partake in some incredibly brainless acts? The answer is yes, probably. Unfortunately, there are no magic potions that will eliminate bad behavior or poor judgment in young people. Your children are going to make mistakes, just like you and I did. It's all part of growing up. I just want to make sure that when one of my children steps out of bounds, they are in a position to learn from their experiences, so the likelihood of repeating the same offense in the future is greatly diminished.

The literal definition of the word discipline means: *training one to act in accordance with rules.* Notice that I am not just talking about children here. We live in a society where people are responsible for their own actions. If a man robs a bank, he should expect to suffer the consequences associated with his blatant disregard for the law. On a smaller scale, if you hurt someone's feelings, you should apologize, whether you meant to hurt their feelings or not. Passing on this sense of personal responsibility and self-reliance to our children is very important, I believe. At the end of the day, this is accomplished by having the fortitude to uphold a reasonable and consistent set of personal values.

Providing consistent discipline requires a proactive strategy on the part of every parent. This includes a willingness and resolve to educate children on what is considered to be acceptable behavior, and what isn't. Understand that discipline is not just about handing out an assortment of punishments, however. You can punish a child until you are blue in the face, but if the punishment doesn't have a positive impact on their decision-making, judgement, or future behavior, then you have accomplished nothing.

Therefore, rather than just looking in the rear-view mirror and punishing a child for what they may have done wrong, the question-based parent is really looking ahead and thinking, "What needs to happen in order to prevent similar incidents from happening again?

Don't get me wrong. Laura and I are both fairly tough disciplinarians, and believe me when I say that there are plenty of potential consequences available to deal with whatever issues may arise in the Freese house. Our intention when handing down a consequence, however, is not just to penalize the child for a lapse in judgment. Certainly, we would want them to recognize their error regarding whatever infraction has been committed. But the real objective of sound discipline is to deter the young person from making the same mistake in the future. Helping your kids understand the downside of unacceptable behavior or bad decisions, therefore, becomes a legitimate part of a parent's responsibility, and the child's maturation process.

I am not introducing new social policy here. The entire criminal justice system in the Western world is predicated on this concept of prevention. Think about it. It's in no one's best interest to fill the country's jail cells up with bad people. What we really want is for our elected officials to create laws and legislate consequences that are penal enough to serve as a deterrent for undesirable behavior, thus reducing the probability and number of criminal acts.

Capital punishment is a good example. Wherever you stand on the issue of the death penalty, the only reasonable argument in favor of capital punishment is its value in helping to deter would-be assailants from committing heinous crimes in the future. The Internal Revenue Service is another example. Your friends at the IRS want you to understand that the penalties for tax evasion or fraud are quite severe. The objective of these punishments, however, is not so much to penalize tax evaders as it is to create significant disincentives that will deter the masses from trying to cheat the system.

With children, the penalty doesn't have to be harsh to deter undesirable behavior. Small infractions can easily be dealt with verbally. Asking one sibling to look another in the eye and apologize can do wonders to prevent similar squabbles down the road. Or, spending a specified number of minutes sitting quietly in a time-out chair provides an excellent opportunity for a child to reflect on what happened and think about what they might do differently next time. The fact that most kids don't really want to apologize or sit in time-out creates an effective deterrent that can prevent similar undesirable behaviors in the future.

Of course, the severity of the consequence should escalate if you are dealing with a more egregious offense, like being disrespectful to an adult or not telling the truth. No matter how harshly you punish a child, however, the severity of your backlash won't undo whatever they have done wrong. Whatever happened has happened, and it's over. While you may still be upset by your child's judgment or their actions, the goal of any punishment you deem appropriate must be forward-looking. It should also be delivered in a way that will help the child understand the difference between right and wrong, and also create enough of a deterrent to cause them to avoid making the same mistake down the road.

Remembering to be proactive can be difficult for parents, particularly in the heat of the moment. Our emotions often run high when one of our children is out of line, especially if we (as parents) have already lost our patience. That's why it's so important to have a consistent strategy for discipline within the household, rather than just reacting with punishments that don't accomplish the longer-term objective of serving as a future deterrent.

Ultimately, you want your children to learn to govern themselves. The very best kind of discipline is always going to be self-discipline. As your kids mature into young adult-hood, mommy and daddy aren't always going to be around to lay down the law. And, when the time comes for them to choose between what they know is right, and whatever else they may be tempted to do, you want your children to "want to" make wise choices.

I made the point earlier that being a question-based parent is not just about asking a bunch of questions. Sometimes, your most powerful ally is the ability to tap into a child's conscience so they will begin to question their own behavior. Don't worry; there will be plenty of times when the devilish little voice inside your child's head will be tempting them to do something stupid. During those times, it's easy for kids to rationalize poor judgment by thinking; "It'll be okay. There's no one around to punish me." And, if there are no consequences to worry about, what's the deterrent for bad behavior?

The long-term goal of the question-based parent revolves around the idea of creating an even more powerful voice inside your child's head that asks them questions like, "Would my parents want me to do this?" Or, "What would be the right thing in the current situation?" Perhaps you have seen the WWJD bracelets that some kids wear, that poses the ultimate question, "What would Jesus do?" If you cause your children to pause long enough to consider the consequences of their actions before giving into whatever temptations they may face, you are way ahead of the game as a parent.

There Needs to be a Downside for Bad Behavior

You begin setting a child's expectations about discipline at an early age. Exactly how early depends on your child, but I can pretty much guarantee that most kids have fully tested their parent's patience and they have also calculated your resolve by the child's third birthday.

The initial data children collect from their parents is primitive but telling. In their eyes, you are either a pushover, or you aren't. From a disciplinary standpoint, you either have enough conviction to say what you mean and mean what you say, or you don't. They've got you pegged. Don't expect your toddler to share their findings with you, as they are generally very reluctant to give up the manipulative advantage that comes from having such emotional leverage over their otherwise out-of-control parents.

Earlier in Chapter 2, I made the point that babies cry to get what they want, because crying is the only mechanism they have to communicate their needs and desires. Of course, the more they want something, the louder they cry—and they quickly learn that working themselves into a red-faced tantrum tends to speed up delivery. That's how the relationship with your child began—they cried, whined, and fussed, and you, the enthusiastic new parent, jumped through hoops to try and provide rapid comfort to your little 'chip off the old block.'

Even as they start to develop communication abilities, young children still gravitate to fussing at their parents or throwing a fit when they aren't getting what they want. How do you handle these manipulative meltdowns? Sometimes, our initial instinct as parents is to fuss right back at them. Am I right? We raise our voices to a harsher level and say a lot of words, and maybe even wag our fingers in their general direction. And, if our frustration level reaches a certain boiling point, we stare at them with a blotchy red-faced look of our own.

If a parent angrily responds to a child's tantrum by fussing back at the child, what is that child learning? Is he learning that the best way to communicate with people we love is to escalate the argument? Probably, and the bad news is, your child will be cataloguing this behavior for later use during their teenage years. Parents of teenagers know what I'm talking about here.

"But when I remain calm, my child just ignores me and continues the same undesirable behavior," frustrated parents complain.

This brings us to the single most important point with regard to maintaining good discipline within your household. *There has to be a downside for bad behavior.* Trying to pacify a poorly behaving child by giving in to their demands is a formula for creating even poorer behavior in the future. At some point, every child needs to learn that demonstrating desirable conduct will lead to good things, while unacceptable behavior will lead to certain consequences that the child definitely does not want.

There absolutely has to be a downside for poor behavior, but let's not be too quick to start dishing out punishments. In fact, you might be surprised to hear me say that most parental punishments are overrated. It's almost too easy to put a cranky child in time-out for a few minutes, or "ground" a teenager for an entire week if they commit a more egregious offense. We will talk more specifically about suggested disciplinary consequences later in the chapter. For now, I am merely suggesting that if your child does not incur a meaningful downside for bad behavior, then you will have missed the whole point of discipline, because there is no disincentive to deter poor behavior in the future.

For example, show me a child who can smart-mouth a parent without any repercussions, and I will show you a child who is going to be consistently disrespectful to one or both parents, and probably to their own children twenty years from now.

Being respectful to other people, especially your parents, is a learned behavior. Some kids are wise beyond their years and having a pleasant disposition just comes naturally. Most children, however, won't understand the importance of respecting authority until they learn that there are consequences for crossing the line. If one of our parental responsibilities is to teach our kids the difference between right and wrong, then we must create separation between those behaviors that are appropriately respectful and those that are not. Again, this education may require some effort on your part, but it is an investment that will ultimately pay big dividends over time.

What's the downside of poor behavior in your house?

Ironically, that question is not just for parents to ask their children. Rather, it's a question that you want to teach a self-reliant child to ask themselves.

In the Freese house, we have used a variety of different vehicles over the years to serve as punishments for poor judgment or unacceptable behavior. We also have a laundry list of consequences that aren't necessarily punishments, but also serve the purpose of creating a significant downside to further deter future occurrences.

Asking a child to apologize to someone for their thoughtless behavior, for example, is not a "punishment" in the traditional sense. But, I can tell you that being in this situation once or twice definitely creates a substantial downside that most kids will do almost anything avoid. Being called into Dad's home office to discuss an incident that occurred earlier in the day is not a punishment either, but again, my kids would rather avoid that scene if they can.

One note: I would strongly encourage you to do everything in your power *not* to unleash your anger from across the room. There is nothing to be gained from embarrassing your child in front of their siblings, peers, or other adults. While wielding our parental sword by raising one's voice may make us feel powerful for the moment, correcting your child in front of other people will end up hurting you both in the long run. Instead, try this. The next time your child pitches a fit, calmly put out your hand out (palm up), and motion with your index finger for them to come over to you. No words. The less said, the better. The first time you may need to prompt the child, "Peter, could you please come here for a minute?" Be serious, but not angry or tough. If you are with a group of people, move away from the crowd so it's just you and the child (mano e mano).

Be patient, because a chagrined child who is exhibiting

poor behavior tends to move slowly across the floor. That delay actually works to your advantage, because it gives them time to reflect on the situation before you even say anything. Their little minds will start racing. "Oh no, I'm in big trouble," they think to themselves. Trust me when I tell you that kids who are behaving poorly don't want to be on the receiving end of the "come over here" signal from one of their parents.

Notice that this technique is not about the punishment, at least not yet. It's about you establishing your authority as a parent, and causing your child to recognize they may have stepped outside the boundaries of what's acceptable. When they finally arrive, the first thing the question-based parent does is gather information. Like a doctor, you shouldn't prescribe a solution without fully understanding the problem. "Do you know why I called you over?" you ask in a measured voice. Then, calmly listen for their response.

If your child is not willing to come over, then you go to them. Remain calm and say as little as possible. It's easy to get frustrated with an obstinate child and unleash your anger, but you must refrain from getting upset—the bigger picture is much more important. Instead, you gently but firmly remove them from the situation so you two can communicate. Assuming your child is old enough to walk, simply wrap your hand around their little forearm (not their hand) and lead them to a neutral spot. The reason I suggest you hold their forearm is because holding hands is reserved for more tender moments, and there is no need to confuse this disciplinary action with a tender moment. I am not suggesting physical force. You just want their full attention.

Here's another important point. There is no need to raise your voice when talking with a child one-on-one. If you listen carefully, they might share a piece of information that changes your perspective on the event. For example, their actions may have been in response to a sibling hitting them or grabbing something away. Maybe their tummy hurts, or they are just tired. Before punishing a child for an inappropriate offense, I first want to understand the nature of the incident. Why, you ask? It's because there is a big difference between something that happened accidentally and disrespectful behavior. Accidents can't always be helped, but malicious intent on the part of a child needs to be dealt with as a disciplinary issue.

Our kids learned at a very early age that I am happy to discuss whatever is making them unhappy. I remain calm and talk with them in a low voice. In fact, these little one-on-one parental meetings aren't always called to correct an inappropriate behavior. I might signal one of my kids to come over and whisper, "Would you like to go play in the yard?" But, both of our kids have learned in no uncertain terms that pitching a fit in our house doesn't accomplish anything. I will say again, I do not want to be constantly fussing at my kids, and I sure don't want them fussing at me.

Do emotions sometimes get the best of me, to the point where I react harshly without really thinking? The answer is, yes, most parents including myself are guilty. But, if my child's initial reaction is a tantrum, I call them over and say, "Why don't you sit in this chair until you calm down. After that, we're going to talk."

At some point the child does calm down, and we have a serious talk. I ask questions and then listen carefully to the responses. If punishment is appropriate, I explain why I am issuing a consequence—I tell them, it's to deter future instances like this from occurring. In many cases, I ask the child, "Will this punishment be enough to prevent this situation from happening again in the future?" If they agree, then

I expect not to be dealing with the same issue later in the day, week, or month. If my child cannot agree that a certain punishment will prevent the undesirable behavior from recurring in the future, then I ask them to help me think of something that will. Can you imagine—a parent asking a child to help think of the appropriate punishment?

I'm telling you, this technique of involving a child in crafting their own punishment works great! That's because it's not the actual punishment that prevents the problem from recurring in the future. It's the recognition from the child that their behavior was not acceptable, and you are serious about dealing with it until changes are made.

When I think of the ultimate story about creating a downside for bad behavior, I remember a former neighbor once telling me about how he handled a rapidly escalating spat with their oldest son when he was a budding teenager. After a sharp exchange between the child and the parent in the kitchen, the child stormed up to his bedroom. The father smartly waited a few minutes to give everyone a chance to cool down, and then headed upstairs to talk with the boy.

Knock, knock.

"Go away," the teenager replied.

"I would like to talk with you," said the father, testing the doorknob with his hand. It was locked. "Please unlock the door," the father insisted. The boy refused, and after several attempts, the father retreated downstairs.

A couple hours later, the son came down for dinner. At the supper table, the conversation was strained from the after-affects of the earlier argument. Everyone finished dinner and then went back to their respective areas of the house.

Upon arriving back upstairs, the teenage boy was surprised to find that the door to his room had been completely removed at the hinges. "Dad, what happened to the door to my room?" he awkwardly asked.

Calmly, the father calmly replied, "If you can't control your emotions enough to unlock the door when asked, then there's no reason for you to have a door on your room." The door stayed off his room the rest of the month.

I love it! Without any harsh words or confrontation, the father just created a significant downside in response to his son's unacceptable behavior. Personally, I liked the father's perspective that if a child wants to have a door on their bedroom, then they have some responsibility to deal with people, especially parents, in a respectful way. This includes opening the door when the father knocks. While we're on the subject, if you (the parent) are responsible for the mortgage on your house, then it's not really *their* door. It's not even their bedroom, for that matter.

With Rules, Less is Better

Some people think that good discipline is about having lots of rules and regulations. They think, if you want to prevent a child from engaging in a certain undesirable behavior, just make a rule against doing it. Then, when someone breaks the rule, they get punished. Sorry, but I am going to jump up and down and pound the table on this point. Having an over-abundance of rules is actually a formula for disaster. In addition to increasing the number of arguments with your children, creating too many rules will undermine your parental authority within the household.

When your children were small, I bet you wanted them to develop good table manners, so you made a few rules about that. Over time, a couple more rules were added to govern bathtub activities and some additional rules were created for playing with friends outside. Even more rules were then implemented for riding in the car, and a few specialty rules applied when visiting Grandma. The start of school spawned a whole new set of rules about getting ready on time, how to behave in carpool, and what was expected of the child in terms of bringing home good grades.

It's okay to have high expectations for your children. We are trying to teach our girls to manage themselves with a level of maturity and independence that is appropriate for their age. The problem is, trying to create specific rules for every possible situation that could arise opens a cacophony of loopholes.

I bet you don't have a specific rule against kids sneaking downstairs to eat an Oreo cookie at three o'clock in the morning. Does that means it's okay to do that in your house? Do you have a rule that kids are not allowed to trample the neighbor's flower beds during the month of April? Have you outlawed hitchhiking home from school? Is there a specific rule in your house that forbids kids from taking a few dollars out of mom's purse when she's not looking? Do you have a rule against your children selling their homework to other kids in the neighborhood? The list of possible loopholes goes on and on, especially as kids get older and wiser, to the point where a rule-loving parent would have to keep a copy of Black's Law Dictionary in the kitchen just to keep up.

Arguing with a child who wants to rationalize poor judgment because a certain act or behavior wasn't specifically forbidden by the parent is a trap I never want to fall into. That's why we actually have relatively few rules in the Freese house. Six, to be exact. I introduced them to you back in Chapter 2 and we still have the document hanging on the bulletin board for everyone to see. For your reference, here is a summarized version of The Freese House Rules.

Freese House Rules!

1.) *People in this house will respect each other at all times.*

2.) *If you lose control of your emotions, you lose your vote.*

3.) *Privileges are not something one is automatically entitled to.*

4.) *Everyone in the family is expected to fulfill certain responsibilities.*

5.) *Disrespectful behavior is unacceptable.*

6.) *Listen to your parents.*

When my children were ten and four, we sat down as a family and discussed each of these points at length. Then, we all signed a document agreeing that these principles would serve as a foundation for what would be considered acceptable behavior in the Freese house. Our house rules document serves the same purpose that our fore-fathers intended when they wrote the U.S. Constitution—a set of overriding principles that can be applied to most situations. Do our children sometimes overstep their boundaries? The answer is yes, just like most kids. But, we don't find ourselves having to invent a new set of rules with every new incident because we are generally covered by these six. We also don't spend a lot of time arguing about loopholes and exceptions that for some reason fall outside the letter of the law.

By having fewer rules, I am not suggesting that parents should lower their expectations. Instead, the key is to think in terms of creating more general guidelines that encourage your children to respect each other at all times, control their emotions, not take privileges for granted, fulfill certain responsibilities, and listen to their parents. At that point, you will be way ahead of the game.

Consequences Don't Have to be Severe to be Effective

What happens when one of your children steps out of bounds? Our two kids are keenly aware that there is a downside for exhibiting poor judgment or unacceptable behavior. They know this from experience. Of course, the actual consequence of their actions is going to depend on the circumstances of the incident and my child's intentions at the time. As any true question-based parent would do, I always want to know the facts before rushing to judgement or making a decision about how best to respond.

But, I need to tell you that we don't threaten our kids with hypothetical consequences in advance of a crime. You will never hear Laura or me say something like, "If you do such and such, there will be no television for the rest of the week!" Or, "If you don't straighten up, you can go to your room and not come down for the rest of the night!"

There's a reason we don't threaten specific consequences in the heat of the moment. It's too difficult. Honestly, I can't think fast enough to assess an inappropriate behavior against my child's intentions, and then issue a consequence that is both fair and will deter the undesirable behavior in the future. Parents who use threats like these usually end up making lots of declarations, and then compromising on their threats later on. Meanwhile, your kids are listening carefully, and once they determine that you aren't likely to follow through on what you say, your haste to enact an immediate punishment will end up eroding your own credibility in the future.

Try this instead. The next time one of your kids gets in trouble, let them know that their behavior was unacceptable and there will be a consequence for their poor judgment. But, rather than selecting a punishment during the heat of battle, ask them to go and sit quietly in the next room. Let them know that you will be there in five minutes, at which time, you will issue a consequence.

Having to wait in another room while a parent decides on an appropriate punishment is gut-wrenching for kids. We all share a fear of the unknown. For children, the anticipation of not knowing exactly what their parent will do creates the same nervous feeling they experience when you take them to a doctor to be immunized. Major tears and whining. Of course, the actual stick of the needle is nothing compared to the emotional trauma children put themselves through on the way to the appointment. So, your misbehaving child is in the other room quietly freaking out because their fate is now in your hands. You can then use those five minutes to take a deep breath and decide what consequence makes the most sense, given the situation.

My disciplinary philosophy works much the same way. Instead of threatening our two daughters with an intimidating list of possible consequences in the hopes of deterring undesirable behavior, we simply let them know in advance what's expected, and they are well aware that there are consequences for stepping out of bounds. What will those consequences be? I don't know exactly. Honestly, we don't like to make empty threats. But, I wouldn't have any problem saying to my child, "I'm not sure what will happen, but I'm pretty sure you wouldn't want to find out." And you know what? They pretty much don't.

Do You Spank Your Kids?

There has been a long standing debate among psychological experts as to whether spanking a child is helpful or harmful to their long-term emotional development. I don't pretend to participate in the psychological arguments in favor or against, but I can tell you that I am very much opposed to physically harming a child in order to control their behavior. What happens if your version of physical punishment doesn't work? Does that mean your anger then escalates to the point where the next level of retribution in your house is abuse?

I don't beat my children, and it's easy for me to say without hesitation that you shouldn't either. But, I can tell you that spanking a child's bottom is definitely on the list of possible consequences in the Freese house. I am neither proud of this fact, nor embarrassed by saying it. We never spanked our children very hard, and we didn't spank them often. But, there were times when one of our kids just wasn't getting the message, and words alone were no longer cutting it.

To me, the days of whipping a child with a belt or switch have long since passed. In fact, I remember making the decision when I was a brand new father that I would never strike one of my children out of anger or frustration. And, I never have. But, I do believe that God formed my open palm to curve in exactly the same shape of my daughters' buttocks for a reason.

Ironically, the worst part of a spanking does not occur when your hand comes into contact with your child's little bottom. Inflicting physical pain is not the goal anyway. The objective of a spanking is the same as any other conse-quence—to create a deterrent that is undesirable enough to prevent the behavior from happening again in the future.

For the question-based parent, a spanking is not just a quick pop on the backside. Rather, it's an entire event. With my girls, whenever a spanking was warranted, I simply said, "Young lady, your behavior is unacceptable and you are going to receive a consequence. Let's go to my office."

Usually, their little hands were glued to their backside as soon as they walked into the room. Before the actual spanking, we always had a little question-based talk. "Do you understand why I'm not happy with your actions?" I would ask. This is not a rhetorical question, which is why it is very important to be patient and listen to their response. I really wanted to know if they understood why the offense they committed was unacceptable. I would also say, "Do you understand that the purpose of a spanking is not to hurt you? It is to hopefully encourage you not to make the same mistake again." During these moments, it is very important to talk *with* your child, as opposed to just fussing at them.

For a child who has gotten themselves into this predicament, the time leading up to the actual spank is pure agony. Minutes seem like hours and they would do almost anything to undo whatever happened. These moments of contrition are worth their weight in gold in terms of creating what I like to call "a healthy respect" for the desired behavior. Note: Don't be in a hurry to deliver the actual spank. From a pure education standpoint, this is the ultimate learning opportunity for a child to understand the difference between what they did and what you would like them to do differently next time.

Of our two girls, my older child (Sarah) fretted the most. Just before the main event, she would ask, "How hard are you going to spank me?"

I would ask her back, "How hard do I need to spank, so that we won't have to deal with this situation again?" A few times, we talked about the intensity of the spank for several minutes, to the point that it was sometimes difficult to keep a straight face during these negotiations.

When delivered caringly, the actual spank is beside the

point. The real value of a spanking was that it created a focused opportunity for Laura or I to communicate that we were indeed serious about the need for change. These moments of worry also gave our daughters a chance to reflect on their behavior and express regret for their actions. Afterward, there was always a great sense of relief that the ordeal was over, which I assumed also meant there was a strong likelihood that this level of punishment would not be necessary in the future.

The few spankings that have occurred in the Freese house have had a remarkably lasting effect. Even now, when one of my daughters gets sideways about something, a simple reminder is all that's needed. "Do we need go upstairs and have a little attitude adjustment?"

"No, sir," is the right answer.

Don't Use Your Child's Name as a Spear

Here's anther no-no for parents who aren't thinking strategically about their disciplinary actions. You must never use your child's name as a spear. In almost any public venue where you find families, you will see a handful of out-of-control parents trying to reign in their kids by repeatedly shouting their child's first name. They're probably the same parents who make empty threats and fuss at their children as punishment.

The next time you go into the food court of a mall, listen to what's happening around you. Some nearby parent will be pleading with a child to behave, saying, "Michael. Mikey? Mike! Michael David, you listen to me!" What starts out as a sweet-toned request becomes a harsh command.

This phenomenon usually begins very early in a child's life when they are just learning to talk. Two of the first words they learn are their name and the word, "No." Oftentimes, these words are combined by new parents, who are quick to say, "Katie, no!" "Stuart, no!" "Kevin, no!"

One of the next words children learn is, "Bad."

"Susie, no! Bad girl."

Let's think about what this communicates to the child. People who train dogs for a living teach owners never to use the dog's name when scolding or redirecting their dogs. The theory behind this is you don't want your dog to associate their name with something negative. "Fido, no! Fido, bad!" Do this enough times and your dog Fido will start to cower when called. They're confused. When you say the name, "Fido," does that mean, "Fido come!", or, Fido bad!"

The same thing can happen when a toddler has a limited vocab and an unsuspecting parent relies too heavily on the phrase, "Kevin, no!" for correction. You risk having your child start to associate their first name with something negative. Does mom mean Kevin is bad?

Next Sunday morning in the narthex of your church, some indignant parent will be trying to get a child's attention, pleading, "Elizabeth? Liz! Lizzy? Sweetie, come on honey. Elizabeth Ann! Come here this instant!"

Nearby, other parents will likely be clamoring for their child's attention, by calling out names, "Ben? Benjamin! Benjamin James! Tyler? Tyler! Mallory? Mallory Jane! Mallory honey?"

To bring this closer to home, how often do you harp on your child's name in the morning when you are hurrying them to get ready for school?

If you are having difficulty getting your child's attention after calling them two or three times, the child either can't hear you, or they are choosing to ignore you. Because much of this "name dropping" occurs within close proximity, I believe that it's the latter. They've tuned you out. Hearing frustrated parents repeatedly call their children's name drives me insane. If your child's first name was given to them out of love, then it shouldn't be used as a spear when you are venting your frustration.

Laura and I both feel this way, which is the primary reason we developed the "Whee-hoo" method of calling to our children. From all the way across a soccer field, when either of our kids hears a "Whee-hoo" whistle, it means, "we need your attention for a moment." No name calling is needed, they know the signal. They also know to stop and look for us. If we actually need to talk with them, we will motion with our index finger for them to come over. Once you have a child's full attention, it's pretty easy to communicate whatever message you need to convey, which is very different than shouting at your kids from across the way.

Escalation Strategies for Good Discipline

Regarding discipline, it is critically important that you *say what you mean* and *mean what you say*. Every Parent's long term credibility in the eyes of their children is at stake every time they open their mouth. This is especially true during those times when children are going to test the system. If after enduring whatever punishment you've handed out, they think, "That wasn't so bad," then you instantly lose any deterrent against similar behavior in the future.

Let me offer a couple of suggestions about dishing out punishments. First, never issue a consequence that cannot be fulfilled. "Young man, you are grounded for the next three months," means very little to a teenager. In most cases, it can't be enforced. Your child knows you aren't going to keep them under house arrest for three full months. It's more likely that the tightness of your grip will loosen by the end of the week. Now you have created a management problem. Following through on an unrealistic punishment is just as unreasonable as the punishment itself. Likewise, not following through on your words will lessen your credibility. Thus, the parent who makes declarations that cannot be reasonably fulfilled paints themselves into a proverbial corner.

A similar problem exists if your primary disciplinary strategy revolves around the idea of taking away more and more of the child's privileges. "You can't play computer games for a week. No television either. And, you are not allowed to talk with friends on your cell phone. And, no dessert!" What happens when there is nothing left to take away from your child? When no more disincentives remain, you essentially lose any leverage to curb further undesirable behaviors.

Rather than taking privileges away as a primary source of punishment, I like to do the opposite. I've said before, I don't want to fuss at my girls, and I don't want them fussing at me. One of the reasons Laura and I don't like arguing with children is because it wastes so much time. Very little gets accomplished when people are bickering back and forth. So, when a consequence is needed, we avoid many of the arguments over "privilege removal" by simply adding to their responsibilities around the house.

The message is clear: "If you are going to waste our time during the week, then we are going to get some of that time back from you, probably on the weekend." Therefore, when Saturday morning rolls around, it's an easy thing to say, "Mary Claire, since we had a problem earlier in the week, I need your help in the yard today."

"For how long?" she might ask. I generally give a vague

response on purpose. There's no need to watch the clock in order to get back an equivalent amount of time from your kids. If my child wasn't worried about wasting my time bickering during in the week, then I don't mind asking for a couple of hours of their time on the weekend to help around the house.

"But Daaaad, that's not faaair!" Frankly, I'm not trying to be fair. My priority is to minimize mindless bickering. As it turns out, it's usually not even that severe a punishment, as we usually have fun raking leaves or running errands. Even so, there's no need to test me because both my daughters know that I can keep them busy for the entire weekend if that's what it takes to revitalize their perspective on mutual respect. By the way, if you keep a child busy around the house, there's much less time for them to fuss at you about not being able to watch television or play computer games.

Different Strokes for Different Folks

As we talk about the issue of discipline, I worry about the parent who might be searching for the quick fix or easy answer. Honestly, there's nothing magical or gimmicky about raising impressive children. Nonetheless, some people don't want to put much brain power into thinking strategically about their approach to discipline, so anything that requires a proactive mindset is probably going to seem too hard.

I also worry about parents who make excuses by saying, "Yes, but my children are different." I agree with the premise that all children are unique in some way. And, I would also be quick to add that no single parenting approach works with every child, all the time. But, that doesn't mean we parents shouldn't have a plan for dealing with some of most common disciplinary issues every parent will face as we shepherd our children from the infant and toddler stages all the way through those challenging teenage years. I would even argue that in today's social climate, how you choose to interact with your kids has a greater impact on their destiny and long-term success than ever before.

For example, what about the child who is so caught up in sports teams and special events that they don't have time to do extra chores around the house as a punishment? That's an easy one to solve. Have them phone their baseball coach or dance teacher at home to apologize for missing this coming Saturday's game (or recital) because they will be working in the yard as a consequence for making a poor decision. It only takes one of those calls for a child to understand you are serious about being willing to practice what you preach.

What does this mean for parents? It means you might miss out on one of your kid's sporting events, too. It also means that you might end up having to expend some time and effort managing the situation, which could eat into your free time on the weekend as well. I encourage you to make the investment. You don't have to give up all your weekends. But, you do have to demonstrate to your son or daughter that you are prepared to mean what you say.

While there are lots of different perspectives on parenting, there are more similarities that differences. For the purposes of the question-based parent, let's focus our energy on those areas where it's easy to find common ground. For example, I believe that the primary purpose of discipline is to prevent undesirable behavior in the future, as opposed to seeking retribution for the past. Can we agree on that point? I also believe that a parent's frustration or anger at the time of an offense should play no role in whatever disciplinary action you choose to enact. An angry parent can neither be fair, objective, or consistent. Do you concur? Lastly, I believe that there is an implicit opportunity for parents to listen to their children, and to even ask for their input with regard to the expectations being established, and any consequences that need to be handed out. You might be surprised at your child's reaction when you say, "Can you coach me on something? I need to think of a consequence that is fair, but will also cause us not to have a recurrence of this situation in the future. What would you suggest?" I made the point earlier in the book that every ship needs a captain, but it's also true that every captain needs a crew who is willing to respect them as their leader.

Once again, the common thread shared by all question-based parents is a built-in need to understand the situation, rather than just issuing off-the-cuff punishments. Wouldn't you agree there is a big difference between a first offense when a child doesn't know better, and a recurring problem that needs to be dealt with in a more serious manner? That's why effective communication is so important, because there is a big difference between how you might respond to a one-time accident and dealing with deceptive or malicious intent.

If there was a magic formula for parental discipline, it would simply be this: Your resolve as a parent to achieve the longer-term result must exceed the impulsive rationale of a child who is only thinking of satisfying their next desire.

Chapter 6

Gold Medals & German Shepherds

"I go fishing in Maine every summer," Dale Carnegie wrote in the mid-1930s. "Personally, I am very fond of strawberries and cream, but I find that for some strange reason, fish prefer worms. So, when I go fishing, I don't think about what I want. I think about what they want. I don't bait the hook with strawberries and cream. I dangle a worm or a grasshopper in front of the fish and say, 'Wouldn't you like to have that?'" Why not use the same common sense when motivating our children?
—Dale Carnegie

When I teach salespeople, one of the most important topics we cover in the classroom is buyer motivation. It is very important for salespeople to understand that different types of customers tend to have different goals, objectives, concerns, desires, personalities, and buying motivations that influence their decision making and purchasing behavior. Understanding how someone is motivated, therefore, is one of the keys to effectively communicating with them, which in the professional world, means working with potential customers toward a mutually desirable result.

You see, human nature dictates that decision makers are ultimately motivated by two things: either the potential for receiving some positive reward, or an aversion to negative consequences. Every action that a person takes and every decision we make is influenced either by some desire to achieve something positive, or an equally powerful desire to avoid some potential negative. Did you eat lunch today? If so, the reason you selected whatever it was that you chose to eat was one of two things: either you wanted to reap some positive benefit like enjoying a delicious meal, or you were hoping to avoid something negative—eating light, for example, to avoid calories, or eating well enough to avoid feeling hungry later.

The metaphor we use in Question Based Selling to characterize these two distinct motivations originated back in 1996 when the Summer Olympics were being hosted in my home city of Atlanta. As everyone watched the world's greatest athletes perform in their respective events, I remember wondering what motivated them to compete so fiercely at the highest levels. On the surface, it seemed logical to assume these top athletes were probably driven by all of the positive rewards that a champion would receive— fame, admiration, money, and of course, winning the gold medal. After training most of their adult lives, who wouldn't want to experience the *thrill of victory*?

As we watched these games unfold, however, it occurred to me that while some athletes were undoubtedly motivated by positive rewards, I bet many others were trying to avoid the *agony of defeat*—not wanting to give into the pain or the competition. Suddenly it became clear. While some people are motivated to run fast toward *Gold Medals*, many other people run even faster from *German Shepherds*.

Rather than thinking of all the accolades that might come from success, some of these athletes were motivated to run even faster and jump even higher because they were trying to avoid an undesirable outcome.

Tapping into Your Target Audience

When watching commercials on television, you can actually see companies making a conscious effort to tap into these unique *Gold Medal* and *German Shepherd* motivations in the way they position products to their respective target audiences. For example, why do people reach for Johnson's Baby Shampoo? Some people choose it because it's gentle on the baby's hair (Gold Medal benefit). Other people buy Johnson's Baby Shampoo because it won't sting your baby's eyes (German Shepherd). Remember the slogan? "No more tears." Let's do another one. Why do people buy Miller Beer? Some people buy it because it "tastes great" (Gold Medal). Other people buy Miller Lite because it's "less filling" (German Shepherd).

Take Volvo automobiles—some people like the stylish elegance of a sports sedan, SUV, or wagon (Gold Medals), while others are motivated more by a desire to have maximum protection for their families in the event of an accident (German Shepherds). Both of these motivations can significantly influence a potential customer's purchasing behavior.

Corporations tend to put a great deal of focus on the positive benefits of their products and services without thinking too much about the German Shepherd aspects. The problem with this approach is that negative implications generally tap into an entirely different range of buyer emotions. Ironically, parents tend to have the opposite problem. We focus so much attention on trying to motivate children with discipline and punishment (German Shepherds), that we sometimes forget to create enough positive incentives (Gold Medals) to appropriately reinforce desirable behavior.

Does your child have any upside incentives that motivate them to keep their room clean, or are they just punished if they don't? What's the incentive for your child to be on-time and ready for school every morning? What kind of affirmations does your child receive when they confidently speak to adults other than their parents?

I am not suggesting you should reward your kids with candy, money, or prizes every time they do something properly. But, let's not ignore the fact that people (including children) are motivated by positive rewards as well as the inherent desire to avoid a negative consequence. The reward doesn't even have to be elaborate. It can be as simple as a thumbs-up, an approving nod, or a gentle smile. Just think what some kids would give to hear their own parents say something like, "Thank you," "Please," or, "Great job!"

Motivating children through positive reinforcement, in addition to discipline and punishment, seems logical, doesn't it? Most of the parents I know would much rather praise their children for their successes than beat them for their shortcomings. The challenge is, it's so much easier for most of us parents to be disappointed with a child's misconduct or inappropriate behavior, than it is to be impressed by their positive attitude or genuine unselfishness. Why is it easier to focus on the negative? Much of it has to do with us taking our kids' good-doings for granted.

Taking Good Manners for Granted

Have you ever noticed that disobedient children tend to garner significantly more attention from a parent than their well-mannered siblings? What do you suppose causes this to happen? Mostly, it happens because a child who is behaving poorly needs to be dealt with in the moment, and sometimes disciplined. That pulls the parent away. Meanwhile, other children in the family who are doing everything right tend to get far less attention. Do parents mean to neglect the child who is exhibiting desirable behavior? No, but children who are autonomous and self-sufficient typically don't need the same level of oversight and correction.

We could rationalize these situations by assuming that our attention should be allocated to where it is needed most. I'm sure you've heard an exasperated parent say something like, "That little Jimmy is a pistol. I can't let him out of my sight for one minute." Maybe it's just our nature, which would explain why you might see a greater police presence in the seedier parts of town than you would normally find in a peaceful upstanding neighborhood.

What a strange incentive program! Those who are defiant and rebellious get more attention than other children who politely conform? What message does this send to our kids? On some level, it's true that all children want to be the focus of their parent's attention. But, if a child actually receives *more* attention for behaving poorly, let's not be surprised when this results in a self-fulfilling prophecy where kids who naturally crave attention tend to exhibit more unacceptable behavior.

What if we turned the tables on our children and made a conscious effort to reinforce desirable behavior? In your house, for example, how often does someone say something like, "Charlie, you were extremely well mannered this evening. Thank you. You are certainly a pleasure to be around." I bet you already know the answer to this question. In many households, the number of corrections and directives is far more frequent than the number of times a parent hands out praise. Unless you are up for a parent-of-the-year award, it's easy to gloss over or forget to affirm positive behaviors. "Maggie, I really love your outfit today. Did you pick it out yourself?"

In our defense, we parents have a lot to think about, and we incur lots of daily stress worrying about things that our children cannot possibly comprehend. Kids don't have to worry about the instability of the economy or the ongoing ebb and flow of office politics at work. From a child's perspective, a clogged sink will somehow get fixed, the family car seems to maintain itself, and there's always food in the fridge. The next time you go on a family vacation, notice that your kids don't have to struggle through planning the logistics of the trip, and they certainly aren't worried about paying the bill.

Because we are living an increasingly complex world, it's easy for us parents to feel drained at the end of a long day. After devoting lots of energy to our career and other responsibilities that we may have volunteered for, we often have limited time and patience when it comes to dealing with those we love the most. This is another strange phenomenon. After spending countless hours battling the various fires that arise throughout the day, we bring our frustrations home, and then, we quickly run short on patience when one of our children wants just a few minutes of our time and attention to admire their most recent art project. I am just as guilty as the next person. But for some strange reason, we always seem to have enough energy to get upset at, argue with, or discipline a disobedient child. Something about this formula doesn't make sense.

Using Both Carrots and Sticks

I'm sure it's apparent by now that my wife Laura and I have relatively high expectations for our two daughters, which is one of the reasons we both support the idea of proper discipline. Believe me when I say that we want our kids to be highly motivated to avoid any negative consequences that come as the result of inconsiderate behavior or poor judgment. Part of our responsibility as parents includes teaching these lessons early on, so our children won't have to learn them the hard way later in life.

We must realize, however, that negative consequences are only one of two ways to motivate a child. The other way is through positive reinforcement.

It's long been thought that one of the world's most stubborn animals is the donkey or jackass. If you talk to a donkey farmer, they will tell you that there are ultimately two ways to motivate a jackass. (Sorry, but I just like saying the word jackass!) One way is to get behind the animal and whack them with a stick on their hind quarters. The other way to motivate the world's most stubborn animal is to get in front of the donkey and lead them with a carrot.

Doesn't that sound familiar? As we discussed in the previous chapter, there are times when popping a child on the back side might be an appropriate disciplinary action (albeit not with a stick). There are plenty of other times, however, where leading them with a carrot actually works much better.

Verbal affirmations are the simplest and most common form of the proverbial carrot. Everyone loves to be on the receiving end of a nice compliment. The problem is, some parents aren't very good at complimenting their children. It's probably because it's easy to take desirable behavior for granted. When so much attention is focused on punishment and discipline, we sometimes forget to reinforce positive behaviors. "Why should I compliment good table manners," parents think. "Kids are *supposed* to have good table manners."

That's true. Kids are supposed to mind their manners. Olympic runners are "supposed" to run fast enough to win the race, too. But, guess what? When they do win the race, they are appropriately rewarded with a shiny Gold Medal. Let me put it this way. Why shouldn't we, as parents, coaches, and mentors, pause to recognize our children's earnest efforts and show appreciation for their positive results?

As it turns out, a heartfelt compliment is one of the most valuable gifts a parent can give to a child. The best part is, verbal affirmations cost you nothing and they are always available to be freely given out. You don't even have to wait for something monumental to happen. Just identify a positive quality in your child, and make a specific point of praising them for it. It's easy once you realize that you can compliment your children for simple things like having patience, showing perseverance, or for offering encouragement to one of their friends at school.

I would, however, recommend against combining your compliments with other teaching moments. Because we want the best for our children, there is a tendency among parents to add the word "but" to the end of a compliment in order to add a few words of constructive feedback. "That was a great race Natalie," an enthusiastic parent might say, "but next time you might want to try running faster at the start." This type of feedback is *not* a compliment. That's a parent saying that it would have been a great race if Natalie had only done something differently, which negates the affirmation. If you want to raise impressive kids, then there is a lot to be gained (and nothing to lose) from showing your children that you are truly impressed by the good things they do.

Get Down to the Child's Level

One of the best ways to communicate with a child is to come all the way down to their level. Not their grade level. I'm talking about getting down to eye level. When I stand up straight, I extend to a full six feet, six inches tall. But I have found that most kids aren't necessarily comfortable when it comes to communicating into the upper atmosphere. So, back when I taught the first graders in Sunday school, we began every class with everyone (children and teachers) sitting in a circle on the floor. That put me more on par with them, and I have found that young people tend to act very differently when everyone in the group is on the same level.

Laura and I both use a similar technique when talking with our children. Instead of shouting instructions from across a room, I would much rather signal to them using my index finger or our trusty "whee-hoo" whistle, and then meet them part way. If I need to correct their behavior in some way, I don't stand over my daughters wagging my finger. I don't need the extra height advantage to maintain authority. Instead, I bend all the way down to their level and then we talk quietly—one-on-one, and face to face. There is nothing to be gained from embarrassing your children in front of their friends, family, or peers. Once I am on their level, we tend to communicate in a much more open dialogue. The reason is sample, as I said earlier. If you show respect to your kids, you increase the likelihood that they will reciprocate the same level of respect back to you.

You can use a similar strategy when delivering compliments. Until we had a teenager in the house, I didn't realize that you can actually embarrass someone by complimenting them in front of their friends. Don't be put off from complimenting your children, because even teenagers are motivated by Gold Medals *and* German Shepherds. But, you might get more mileage out of your compliments by delivering them privately—one-on-one. The next time you catch your child doing something good, tell them a lowered voice where no one else can hear that you were impressed by what you observed. For emphasis, give them a little private wink afterward. Then watch their face light up and their little self-esteem meters rise through the roof. The key is to communicate on their level, rather than yours.

Another technique you can use to get down to a young person's level is to ask them for advice. An adult asking for a kid's advice is a huge compliment to the child. For best results, mix their advice in with a compliment. For example, "Patrick, I was really impressed with how you led the conversation during the youth meeting today. What's your secret?" Of course, you have to adjust to be age appropriate. With a younger child, you might say something as simple as, "Wow, that's a really cool picture. Can you show me how to draw a horse like yours?" Show a little interest in a child's abilities, and it's amazing how quickly you can become the coolest parent on the block!

Are Boys Different than Girls?

One of the strangest questions I have ever been asked was posed during a recent media interview to discuss this book, where the program host asked, "Tom, in your opinion, are boys different than girls?" The very first thought that popped into my head was, "Yes."

In addition to the obvious physical differences between girls and boys, experts say there are measurable developmental differences as well. I am not in a very good position to compare and contrast these differences because my own personal experience revolves around a household environment complete with my wife, two daughters, and a female dog. Sometimes I feel like I'm swimming in an estrogen ocean. Therefore, I am relatively unfamiliar with what life might be like wrestling with a house full of boys.

I must caution you against associating the concepts presented in this book to either gender; however, as I would argue that *The Question Based Parent* is gender independent.

To solidify the point, let me ask you a few simple questions. Can a girl be motivated by positive rewards, in addition to negative consequences? If you don't live in a girl-house, take my word for it, the answer is clearly yes. Can boys also be motivated by Gold Medals and be averse to German Shepherds? Yes, again. The actual reward or consequence that ends up motivating your child could be affected by gender, but it can also depend on age, ability, history, and circumstance.

My kids are different from your kids, who are just as unique and different as someone else's children. Therefore, I reject any notion that a parent's responsibility can be simplified down into a step-by-step formula that tells us how to deal with every possible scenario or situation. At the same time, there are many more similarities than differences when dealing with different types of children. For example, universal qualities like love, respect, consistency, fairness, decency, self-esteem, independence, joy, reliability, and trust are common threads in the foundation of each and every successful parent-child relationship, no matter which gender you are dealing with.

To my fellow dads out there, I will offer this one piece of advice regarding gender. If you have sons, be sure to tell your boys how proud you are of them. Tell them often! Boys need to know that they measure up to their father's expectations. If you have daughters, tell them often how beautiful they are, inside and out. A daughter's impression of herself is often a reflection of what they think their father sees in them. These simple affirmations can provide a sense of security and confidence that can last for generations.

Being a Kid Should Also Be Fun!

Speaking of positive reinforcement, what steps are you taking to make your child's life a more enjoyable experience? Most of the parents I know (including us) fall into the trap of focusing so heavily on the logistics of a child's schedule and obligations, that we sometimes lose track of what makes life fun. "Jimmy, please take out the trash! Feed the dog! Clean your room! Do your homework! Mind your manners!" At some point, your child's responsibilities need to be counterbalanced by a certain amount of lighthearted amusement. I'm not talking about taking your kids to Disney World once a year. I'm talking about the little things you could be doing to enhance your child's experience this week.

Laura is much better at this than me. She is constantly inventing new games to play and neat little competitions that challenge our children. Notice how much I use the word little. Fun things often come in small packages, and

Laura is a master at creating little contests. This morning, for example, everyone was in the car, ready to pull away and take the kids to school, when my youngest, Mary Claire, remembered that she forgot to pack her gym shoes. A frustrated parent's first reaction may have been to nag, nag, nag. "Go upstairs and get your shoes!" might have been the first thought. "And, hurry!" Instead, Laura turned MC's oversight into something positive, simply by asking, "Mary Claire, do you want me to time you to see how fast you can get your shoes and make it back downstairs?"

How's that for being question-based? In a flash, Mary Claire was gone. Not only did she return in record time, she was smiling from ear to ear. If you don't already have a watch with a second hand, I recommend putting that on your Christmas list. You will be amazed how eagerly children will complete an otherwise undesirable task if it's "for the record."

Laura also implemented the red plate at dinner time. Do you have a red plate in your family? If not, just type the words "red plate" into your favorite Internet search engine, and you will get a long list of purchasing options.

The red plate is a standard sized dinner plate. But, it is very different from the rest of our china because it is candy-apple red and has the words, "You are special today" graphically imprinted in big white letters across the face of the plate. When the red plate has been substituted for one of the place settings on the dinner table, you can't miss it. Especially if the red plate is in front of your chair that day, you can't help but feel good about yourself.

It has always been a standard practice to put the red plate out for birthday dinners. A few years ago, however, Laura figured out that the red plate was also a great way to recognize noteworthy accomplishments, like a successful piano recital, a new personal best on swim team, or scoring an impressive grade on a test at school. Of course, using this type of reward too often would diminish its significance. But there's nothing wrong with looking for opportunities to bring it out two or three times a month. Just be creative and make it fun. We have even been known to slip the red plate through the back door of a restaurant, so the chef can prepare and serve one girl's favorite meal in an extra special way.

My last piece of advice with regard to the lighter side of parenting is to loosen up and be silly once in a while. When was the last time your kids saw you whoop and holler, wave your hands in the air, or dance around the room? If it has been a while, then I recommend that you make it a point to embarrass yourself a few times in front of your kids. Do it on purpose. Allow your children to see your silly side. Laughing together as a family creates all kinds of wonderful bonding experiences, and it's also an opportunity for you to communicate with your children on their level. Being silly is a welcome relief for your kids as well, especially during those difficult teenage years when social pressures tend to take over and everything they do feels awkward. Put it this way: My kids are forever comforted by the knowledge that no matter how awkward they may be feeling inside, at least they don't act as goofy as their dad.

Let Your Kids Make Some Decisions

When your family goes out for dinner, who chooses the restaurant? Or, on a trip to the mall, who decides which store to visit first? Who was it that selected the paint color in your child's bedroom?

There are some pretty big decisions that parents need to make regarding the overall health and welfare of the family.

I made the point earlier that every ship needs a captain, and one of the responsibilities of the captain is to make important decisions. But, on a daily and sometimes hourly basis, there are tons of little decisions that just aren't a big deal.

Next time you drive up to the corner to buy gasoline, ask your ten-year-old which of the two gas stations you should buy gas from, and why they feel that way? After they regain consciousness (having fainted because a parent actually asked for their opinion), you will get a surprisingly thoughtful opinion from a young person who all of a sudden feels a little bit more grown up. Then, heed their advice and pull into the gas station they suggested. So what if the gas is five cents more per gallon? What is your child's confidence and self-esteem worth per gallon?

If you are planning to take the family out to dinner, why not let one of your kids choose the restaurant? But don't just let them choose their favorite place. Instead, ask them to pick a restaurant the family hasn't been to previously. Or, make a game of it. Let them reach into a hat and choose from the pieces of paper you created in advance, listing different types of cuisine—seafood, barbecue, Asian, steakhouse, pizza parlor, burger joint, etc. If they pull out the slip that says seafood, open the yellow pages and give them a choice between three different seafood restaurants in the area. Whichever one they choose is the one you go to that night. Then, next time you go out to dinner, a different child gets to select the venue. Changing the selection process makes it even more exciting! You might even let your kids think of a new way to choose.

Involving your kids in the decision process promotes a collaborative culture within the family. Believe me; a collaborative environment is something every question-based parent wants because it fosters team spirit and an increased sense of cooperation down the road. Ultimately, we want to teach our children to have a sense of self-reliance and independence. The most difficult part of this training is letting go and trusting that they will, in fact, make reasonable decisions. The only way a child can learn to make good decisions is for you to afford them some opportunities to sink or swim on their own. It's easiest to start small and let your kids earn your confidence. The question-based parent might even ask, "Can I trust you to make a decision that is good for everyone?" This can become a self-fulfilling prophecy within the household, where showing some confidence in a child's ability to make independent decisions may, in fact, cause them to make better decisions.

Passing Time with Your Children

"Our calendar is so full," a parent laments. "One of our kids goes to soccer practice three times a week and the other starts baseball next month." Having children participate in organized sports or social activities is fine. My question is, what are you doing with your child on the way to soccer practice?

Whoever invented the Game Boy should be shot. The people who put DVD systems into cars and invented the iPod should be equally nervous. Before all of this individualized entertainment, riding in the car used to represent quality time where families could talk and enjoy each other's company. What would they talk about? Oh, just little things, like their plans, goals, and dreams for the future. Sometimes, they would talk about what happened at school, or whatever was going on that week. Nowadays, it's like pulling teeth to initiate a conversation with a child whose thumb is just itching to push the power button on an electronic device as soon as you finish your sentence.

We solved part of this problem by banning handheld portable electronics in the car. On long trips, it's a different story. If we are going to be driving for more than an hour, we allow usage for reasonable lengths of time. But I can tell you that a funny thing happened when the electronic equipment was turned off. Although we don't require our kids to converse, it turns out that conversation is much more enjoyable to them than just staring out the window. But, parents can still do things to make your conversations more interactive and enjoyable.

Laura is great at thinking up conversational games. She will say, "Let's go around the car and take turns thinking of an object that starts with the letter A, then B, then C, and so on all the way through the alphabet." If you have older children and that sounds too simplistic, it's easy to adjust the degree of difficulty. Try going around the car and naming foreign countries that begin with the letters A to Z, or naming celebrities. If someone is feeling overconfident, you can always raise the bar by switching the category to renaissance artists, or chemical compounds.

Especially on long trips, we like to play the "Looking Game." That's a game I invented where the driver of the car (usually me) thinks of two or three objects to "put in play," which the riders in the car then must visually identify. For example, I might say, "We're looking for a triangular sign, a green license plate, and a water vehicle." If the driver spots an item first, it is automatically out of play for the other riders. If one of the riders in the car spots an item, they get a point. But, each sighting must be verified by someone else in the car. None of this, "I saw it back there," stuff. On a recent trip to the beach, I put a silver bus in play, and my kids (and wife) looked for that thing for the better part of three hours. Playing verbal games with the surrounding scenery can make an otherwise lengthy trip much, much shorter.

Or, you can just as easily play, Star. I don't know how this game got its name, but one of my daughters will call out the first letter in each word of a movie title, and everyone else in the car (or at the dinner table) tries to guess the movie. Laura's favorite movie is T.S.O.M. (The Sound of Music). One of Sarah's favorite choices is the single letter S., which could stand for Shrek, Superman, Spiderman, or Scarface, depending on the mood she's in.

Most kids love to participate in thinking games. They also love to compete. There doesn't even have to be a prize. In fact, it's usually best not to have winners and losers. The pure fact that you are creating opportunities to enjoy each other's company and share the time you have together makes everyone in the family a winner. Note to parents: Some of the games kids like to play are incredibly unstimulating for a parent. That's okay. Finding ways to connect with your kids, which is the objective, provides a Gold Medal benefit that far outweighs everything else.

Be Careful Living Vicariously Through Your Kids

Speaking of sports, I was *very* excited when my daughter started playing pee-wee soccer, at least, until I attended her first game. She looked so cute in her little purple uniform. We made our way toward the designated area on the sidelines to stand with the other parents. Everyone was snapping the perfunctory child-athlete photos before the event. Sarah's team name was the

Sharks, although they may have been more appropriately named the Minnows.

The first thing that happens at a youth soccer game is the warm up. Parents all mill around and talk amongst themselves while the kids run through various drills they learned in practice. I discovered later that the warm up period before the game is much more important for the parents than the children, as parents were warming up their vocal chords for what was about to happen.

The pee-wees on both teams took their positions on the field and when the whistle blew, both the game and the parents started with the first kick of the ball at center-field. "C'mon Lindsay, kick the ball! Not over there! Jessica, get it! Run! Watch out Kelsey! Go! Not like that! Run Carolyn! Go!"

At any point during a soccer game, there are twenty-two kids on the field, eleven per team. But, there were twice as many parents on the sidelines yelling *at* their kids to perform better. "Hanna, where are you going? Turn around! Kick it! Get back in position!" The amount of instruction coming from the sidelines from overzealous parents was mind-boggling. Forget about the kids hearing any of the instruction the coaches were trying to convey.

I'm sure that most of the parents who attend youth soccer games have good intentions. I'm just not sure they can hear themselves as they live vicariously through their children. Let me put it bluntly. An obscenely obese, disheveled-looking parent doesn't have much room to stand on the sidelines of a soccer game yelling at their child to try harder.

One of the dads in our parenting Sunday school class shared a personal account of his son's wrestling match from the previous week. Todd, the father, is a mild-mannered, all-around terrific guy. Daniel, his eleven-year-old son, was an athletic kid by nature who took the mat to wrestle another similarly-aged boy in his weight class. Daniel and his dad both expected a tough match that day. Todd described the scene, where he was in the gymnasium bleachers cheering as loudly as he could for his son throughout the match. When the wrestling match ended, Daniel came off the floor with tears streaming down both cheeks.

"Why are you crying?" the Dad asked. "You won!"

In a quiet voice, Daniel replied, "Because you were yelling at me even though I was doing my best." Ouch! Once Todd heard that, he started thinking about how what he assumed was just supportive enthusiasm must have sounded to his son.

What messages are you sending your kids from the sidelines? Sporting events seem to be the worst venue in terms of parents losing control. Can you imagine a parent standing up in the middle of a high school play and shouting out, "C'mon Melanie, sing on key!"

As it turns out, there's a big difference between supporting your son or daughter and shouting at them to do better. If you are an avid sports fan or booster, I encourage you to listen to your words, for your child's sake. Cheering someone's effort by saying "nice shot" or "good job" is always a welcome compliment. But, please realize that shouting commands like, "Catch the ball" or, "Don't let those other players push you around," are words of correction that basically convey the message, "You are *not* performing well enough."

School projects are another cause for concern. Have you ever seen a young kid come to school with a project that looks like it was worked on by the entire graphics department of a Fortune 500 company? What does a child learn if their parent takes the project over completely? Your child might receive a better grade, but does it happen at the expense of your second or third-grader now thinking that their own work isn't good enough?

I am not suggesting that you shouldn't help your kids in school or root for them during sporting events. There is just a big difference between helping a child because they are stuck or faltering, and helping them because *you* want a more impressive result.

My wife has the perfect strategy for this. She recently took our oldest daughter to the library to do some research for a history project, and the first thing Sarah did when she arrived at the library was ask, "Mom, where are all the reference books?"

To her credit, Laura responded by saying, "It's not my project."

Going Overboard is a Problem

Some parents go overboard with consequences for bad behavior, using various punishments as the only form of motivation for their children. This is problematic because of the point we made earlier, that kids are motivated by both positive reward (Gold Medals) *and* negative aversion (German Shepherds). Therefore, focusing all your attention on being a strict disciplinarian is short-sighted and one-dimensional. As the old saying goes, "all work and no play makes Jack a dull boy"—and it creates a problem for Jill as well.

Other parents go overboard the other way, doling out lavish incentives to reward a child's good behavior. I like the idea of acknowledging desirable conduct with a gesture of appreciation or even surprising a child with a treat as a positive accolade for some significant accomplishment. But how nice does the gift have to be to motivate your kid to do the right thing?

One of my daughter's classmates in the seventh grade was a straight A student, supposedly because her parents started paying her twenty-five dollars for every "A" she brought home from school. Two years later, this child is making "C's and "D's" and struggling just to stay in school.

My other daughter has an acquaintance from the pool whose parents chartered a private jet to take the child and three friends to Disney World for his sixth birthday. I understand that some folks enjoy a different socio-economic level than the rest of us can fathom. But, I wonder what those parents will have to do next year to impress their child on his seventh birthday, or his sixteenth?

Offering rewards that are overly lavish makes it difficult to meet the child's expectations in the future. Plus, if a child already has everything they could possibly want, what incentive is there for them to do better?

Would you agree that the most important part of any motivation, incentive, or award is the actual thought behind the gift? If you think about it, a Gold Medal is simply a token of appreciation that conveys the message, "Good job." The sentiment behind the reward is what kids want most anyway, starting with their parent's approval and our respect. Such positive affirmations from parent to child do not need to be wrapped in increasingly indulgent packages, however.

Do you remember your child's very first Christmas? The one where the baby was showered with gifts, but all he wanted to do was play with the wrapping paper and the pretty bows? The very next Christmas, even though you spent a bunch of money to purchase that year's coolest toy, I bet your child spent more time playing with the box the toy came in. Now let's fast forward fifteen years. I know several people who have given their child a car for their sixteenth birthday. I often ask what led them to decide to purchase a brand new automobile for their new driver. Some parents have no idea. Others confess that they wanted to provide their son or daughter with the vehicle they never got when they were sixteen.

Honestly, it would have been great if my parents had coughed up new car when I was a teenager. But they didn't. Years later, I am a better person as a result of having to earn my own way. I am very much in favor of rewarding children for working hard and having good grades, but does the reward have to be a brand new Lexus? Again, if you gratify a child's every whim and desire, what do they have left to look forward to?

Buying every high-schooler their very own automobile is especially crazy as far as I'm concerned. My oldest daughter is on the verge of getting her driver's license, and I know that she already has visions of what life will be like behind the wheel. But, she also knows that we will not be buying her a car any time soon. Granted, she will probably have an opportunity to use one of the family vehicles, but I can tell you right now that driving is more of a privilege than an entitlement in the Freese house. I will add that maintaining one's full driving privileges will be one of those ongoing incentives to exercise good judgment and be a cooperative part of the family.

Perhaps Sarah or Mary Claire will put their entrepreneurial spirit to good use and earn enough money to purchase their own vehicle. That would definitely be impressive. It's funny how kids tend to have a greater appreciation for those things they have worked hard to purchase for themselves anyway. Wouldn't that feeling of satisfaction be a nice reward?

I just don't like the idea of giving a child too much too soon. Instead, I'm a big proponent of fostering parent-child partnerships. Here's the deal I plan to make with each of our girls. Because all of our cars are in my name, I have the right to know where my vehicles are and who is riding in them at all times. I am even willing to share in the operating expenses, but I expect my investment to be reciprocated with honest and responsible behavior from whoever gets behind the wheel. At that point, my daughter's good judgment will be rewarded with all kinds of Gold Medal privileges. If, however, either of my girls ever wants to test to see whether or not I'm really serious, she would be free to ponder that thought while riding the bus.

The Ultimate Lesson: Do the Right Thing

As we've said, one way to teach kids the difference between right and wrong is to issue punishments for unacceptable behavior. With any luck, these consequences or *German Shepherds* will serve as an ongoing deterrent against similar lapses in judgment down the road. Another option is to reward the child with positive incentives or *Gold Medals* that affirm and reinforce desirable behavior.

Parents must never lose sight of the larger goal, however. Punishments and accolades are just teaching aids to help kids learn the difference between right and wrong. One of these days, mommy and daddy won't be there to look over your child's shoulder. And when that day comes, and your child is enticed by some evil temptation or is suddenly faced with a moral dilemma, they will have to stand on their own two feet and decide for themselves which path to choose. But in these cases, their decision to walk away from a precarious situation won't just be driven by the motivation to avoid a parent's wrath. Rather, the child will hopefully turn away because some little voice in their head is telling them that *it's just not the right thing.*

Think about it this way. I didn't rob my neighbor's house today. Do you want to know why not? One reason is because I didn't want to run the risk of getting caught and being arrested. The consequence of sitting in jail and losing my family is a powerful deterrent for me. But, that wasn't the only reason I didn't rob my neighbor's house. The main reason was because it's inherently wrong to intrude upon or steal someone else's property.

Similarly, I tried to do several nice things today. I held a door for a lady walking into a hospital on the way to visiting my mother who recently had ankle surgery. I also extended a pleasant greeting to several people I didn't know along the way. Later, I helped my wife unload the groceries from her car. I didn't do any of these things in order to receive a tangible reward. Rather, I did them because I felt like it was the *right thing* at the time.

We try very hard in our house to avoid dictating orders to our children and then justifying those commands using the old-fashioned phrase, "Because I said so!" To me, that thought invites kids to believe that the only reason to do something (or avoid something) is because the parent says so. In reality, our culture is interspersed with a set of universal rights and wrongs that apply whether a parent says so, or not. Consequently, Laura and I concluded a long time ago that it makes more sense to replace the aforementioned logic with a more reasonable rationale, simply by saying, "Because it *is* the right thing to do," or, "Because it's *not* the right thing."

As they continue grow and mature, we want our kids to naturally gravitate toward making good decisions and exhibiting desirable behavior, but not just because they might receive some tangible reward or avoid a negative consequence. We want them to sense in their minds and in their hearts that they should participate when it's the right thing to do, and they should also avoid other things that are inherently wrong. Throughout the entire developmental process, this is one of the most important lessons you can teach your children. It's also where your parental guidance and consistency over time will ultimately transform itself into a lifetime of willpower and self-control within your child.

Chapter 7

Mismatching: A Contradiction in Terms

Mismatching is a natural human phenomenon. It is the instinctive tendency of individuals to respond in a contrarian manner. In addition to increasing the number of arguments, mismatching also tends to escalate tension within the household, and it chips away at the very foundation of the relationship you are working so hard to build.

—Thomas A. Freese

The only thing I hate worse than arguing with someone is contradiction. To me, the "is too, is not" type of bickering with other people is totally unproductive, and can be corrosive to any relationship. Contradiction is just disagreeing with someone for the sake of argument. While there's nothing wrong with having an open dialogue when people have differing viewpoints, constant bickering is a divisive force that is destructive to the family unit.

To minimize conflict in our household, we try very hard to have open communication. In addition to one-on-one discussions with our kids, we have periodic family meetings that serve as an open forum for us to talk about issues or concerns that need to be addressed. We also decided a long time ago to set expectations for how everyone in the family was going to treat each other.

Although we aren't perfect by any stretch, Laura and I have worked hard to create an environment that reinforces positive behavior, yet also imposes consequences when a little "attitudinal redirection" is required. Nonetheless, there will always be some amount of disagreement whenever an eclectic group of individuals is living together under the same roof.

After many years of practical research and teaching, however, I have discovered that much of the day-to-day squabbling between people (or, in this case, between parents, children, and siblings) is fueled more by emotional reflex than by conscious disagreement. Meaning, the person on the other side of the argument may actually be picking at you more as a defense mechanism to compensate for their own insecurities. Sounds strange, but the offender may not even disagree with you at all. This emotional reflex is a behavioral phenomenon that we call *mismatching*.

Have you ever had one of those experiences where another person in the conversation seems to take the opposite position on everything you say? Or, for some reason, you can't get all the way through a story because someone feels a need to jump in and clarify meaningless details along the way. These are common examples of mismatching. As you might imagine, this behavior is very frustrating for those involved and often puts a damper on further interaction.

For the sake of explanation, let me give you an easy analogy. Most of you are aware that the body has certain physical reflexes. Blinking is a good example. If I were to flick my fist toward your eyes, you would blink. You can't help it, blinking is an instinctive physical response. As my hand approached, you would not have time to evaluate the situation, nor would you make a conscious decision to contract your eyelid muscles. Reflexes would just take over, and you would instinctively close your eyes.

Blinking is a physical reflex. Mismatching, on the other hand, is more of an emotional reflex, but it works much the same way. Mismatching is the instinctive tendency of individuals to resist, push back, or rebel in a contrarian manner. In many households, this reflex is often the catalyst for much of the arguing and contradiction during the course of a normal day.

To witness a real-life example of mismatching for yourself, here's a simple experiment you should try. Next time you attend a dinner party in the neighborhood or you find yourself in the bleachers at your child's basketball game, turn to the person sitting next to you and make an innocent comment like, *"I hear it's supposed to be nice this weekend."* Don't be surprised if their knee-jerk reaction is to the contrary—something like, *"I heard that it's supposed to rain,"* or be *"too hot,"* or *"too windy,"* or *"too humid."* They may contend that the weekend is *"too far away,"* or, *"too close,"* Maybe the person will just lament that they have to *"clean the garage"* this weekend. If you listen carefully to how people respond, you will be surprised how easy it is for people to take the opposite position, *mismatching* your original supposition that the weekend is supposed to be nice.

Do people mismatch every time? Of course they don't. Mismatching is not a programmed response, it's a behavioral tendency. But, if it is so easy for adults to respond this way to each other, don't you think it's conceivable that we may also have a tendency to mismatch our children? And, because mismatching is such a natural tendency, children are also just as quick to mismatch their parents and siblings. With all the challenges we already face as parents, anything you can do to reduce the level of contentiousness between parents and children, or between siblings, may help restore the harmony within your household.

Satisfying the Need to Feel Valuable

The typical parent-child relationship endures a wide variety of emotions. I bet you've seen this where a child's mood suddenly shifts from joyful laughter into tears of dejection because someone's terse remark crossed the line and their feelings got hurt. If there is one thing I've learned from living in a house full of girls, it's that a young person's self-esteem is one of their most important and fragile possessions, and it needs to be protected at all costs.

I mean, don't most of us want to feel smart? We want to be respected by our peers, children, parents, and siblings, all of which is part of an instinctive desire to prop-up our own self-image. We also have a need for social acceptance. Behavioral psychologists characterize this feeling as the need to self-actualize.

During everyday conversations, this need to self-actualize often manifests itself into a desire to contribute something valuable to the dialogue. Therein lies the rub. People who want to feel that they are making a valuable contribution in conversations usually don't just smile and nod in agreement. As an example, if Jim were to say, *"The ceilings in this room are very tall,"* and Bill were to respond by saying, *"I agree,"* Bill may not feel as though he has actually added much to the conversation.

Don't get me wrong, being agreeable with others is a wonderful attribute. Amiable people tend to be quite likable and fun to be around. But, silently nodding in agreement generally doesn't satisfy our natural need to add value in a conversation. In order to satisfy this need, we tend to look for ways to inject our own perspective into the discussion, in the hopes of contributing some valuable nugget of information the other person hasn't yet considered. This mechanism is the genesis of most mismatched responses. As a result, mismatches are usually more of an attempt to satisfy our own emotional needs than to present an opposing viewpoint on the subject being discussed. If we refer to the earlier example, the need to contribute something to the conversation is most likely the catalyst that caused the mismatcher to respond with a suggestion that the upcoming weekend would be something other than *nice.*

While amicable agreement is certainly an attractive human quality, it doesn't always satisfy one's own instinctive desire to feel valuable.

Kids are People, Too

How receptive are your children to being on the receiving end of parental advice? Have you ever had a great idea that you wanted to pass on to one of your children, but the child wasn't open to listening to it? In fact, it probably isn't much different now than it was for our parents when we were kids. Hence, if you sometimes feel like you are talking to a wall, join the club. It's easy to strategize about the advisory role of a parent, but in order to provide any real sense of direction to your children, you must first have a receptive audience.

Wouldn't it be nice if every time we wanted to mentor our kids, they perked up and listened intently to whatever we had to say, and then pleasantly nodded in agreement? Sir, wake up, you must be dreaming! Those pleasantly nodding children must be someone else's kids—because yours have opinions and ideas of their own, and they would also like to contribute something valuable to the dialogue if given the chance.

If you think about conversations you have with your children from their perspective, kids are in a tough position. They have an emotional need to feel valuable, just like you and I do, but in most conversations with adults, they can't compete on the same intellectual level. As a result, it's common for children to withdraw around unfamiliar adults and only speak when spoken to. You can see this when you take little Johnny to meet the teacher on the first day of school. Johnny would rather hide under a desk than stand up tall and look his new teacher in the eye.

Teenagers do the same thing. During a youth gathering, for example, there will be all sorts of monkey business happening until an unfamiliar adult walks into the room, and then everyone stops talking and looks away.

Don't be fooled by the quiet, though. Most kids are very observant, and even if they aren't actively participating in a conversation, they are keenly aware of what is being said. Younger children in particular are quick to point out discrepancies in a conversation, either by asking a question about something they didn't understand, or more overtly by mismatching—contradicting some piece of information that has been communicated.

Our younger daughter Mary Claire set the world record for asking the most questions before the age of seven. She wanted to know why the grass was green and she wondered why we couldn't fly like birds. She also wanted to know why orange juice was really yellow, how cars were made, and why we can't see God. Why? Why? Why? She asked about everything. As the result of her questions, Laura and I discovered that we were not as smart as we thought, because we often didn't have a good answer for the questions she posed.

I like to encourage my kids to be observant and ask lots of questions. I want them to have great curiosity about the world, and I would much rather they feel comfortable enough to step up and ask, rather than just cower away feeling insignificant. The only thing I want in return is for them to think about what the answer might be before they ask. Often, I will toss one of her questions back over the fence, asking, "Mary Claire, why do *you* think the water coming out of the tap is clear?" Asking questions without really wanting to know the answer is a bad habit for a child or an adult.

As children learn to absorb information at a rapid pace, accuracy starts to become very important to them. That's because they are constantly processing all of the information they hear and see against a developing data bank inside their heads, as a way to try and make sense of the world. Most kids have tremendous computing power for their size, which enables them to sense discrepancies between the data that has already been received and new information coming in. These discrepancies then raise further questions, and the cycle continues.

In addition to being curious and asking lots of questions, both of my children are also great content editors. Whenever Laura or I finish telling a story at the dinner table, for example, it has become somewhat of a sport for our kids to listen for and point out any conflicting facts. One of my daughters might say, *"That happened when I was five years old, not six."* The other will jump in and say, *"And it happened while we were eating lunch, not dinner."* *"And, Dad you didn't drive to the hospital, mom drove."* As precise as children sometimes are when correcting us parents, we often wonder why they can't be more articulate when completing their homework assignments for school. Hmmm.

Because this type of nit-picking is the purest form of contradiction, it can have a destructive influence on inter-personal communication. On the surface, one could argue that it is disrespectful for a child to openly contradict their parents. But, if you think about what's happening deep down beneath the surface, the child's natural inclination to spot discrepancies is likely driven more by their own intrinsic need to feel valuable and be correct, as opposed to just putting someone else down.

That's the point I am trying to make. Mismatching is the instinctive tendency to respond in a contrarian manner, driven by one's own need to feel valuable. To minimize the negative aspects of this behavior, however, we must first understand what causes this reflexive tendency to occur.

Different Forms of Mismatching

Since we are talking about a behavioral reflex, it's safe to say that virtually everyone mismatches, albeit to varying degrees. In fact, it's so natural that when I explain mismatching to *live* audiences, I can usually see the expressions on the faces of people change as they recognize their own behavior in some of my examples.

I hope you are getting the picture that delivering a mismatched response doesn't equate to having malicious intent. As I said, mismatching is a common and instinctive response behavior. In fact, it's true that some of the most well-intentioned people are also some of the most fervent mismatchers. The real question is, how can you recognize mismatching when it occurs in order to minimize any negative impact on family relationships or in your everyday conversations?

This behavior I am describing actually manifests itself in several different forms, which are easily recognizable either in a child's behavior or in our own, once explained. The five most common mismatch responses include:

I. Pure Contradiction

Telling someone that they are wrong is one of the fastest ways to shut down a conversation. But that's exactly what happens whenever you or someone else contradicts what another person is saying. Pure contradiction is the first and most common form of mismatching.

A contradiction is typically a knee-jerk response, where one person takes the opposing position on a comment that is made or idea being discussed. Our earlier example about whether the upcoming weekend was supposed to be "nice" is a classic example of contradiction. One person's assertion about the quality of the upcoming weekend can easily be contradicted by someone else who takes the opposite position, citing some reason why it's *not* going to be "nice."

Sibling to sibling contradictions are especially common. Brothers and sisters tend to pick at each other, as if it's a way to secure their position within the family hierarchy. Maybe it's just a power thing, where one child assumes that the easiest way to raise themselves up in the pecking order is to prove that they are correct. Another way to try and raise oneself up is to show that the other person is wrong.

Contradiction provides a vehicle for a mismatcher to achieve both of these hidden objectives in one fell swoop. While this form of communication is very common, it can actually be quite destructive to relationships. Constantly communicating that someone else is wrong tends to chip away at their self-esteem. This, in turn, creates a desire on the other person's part to fire back. With kids, the ultimate contradiction example is one of those "am too," "am not" arguments. Where does it end? Your kids will eventually grow up, but the scars of battle often linger and may even get passed onto future generations.

II. Unnecessary Clarification

An enthusiastic fourth grader bursts through the kitchen door, having just gotten off the bus, and says, *"Hey mom, guess what happened at school today?"*

"What?" the mother inquires.

"Well, in the first period of the day we had our math test," the child begins, *"...and then..."*

"I thought you had math during second period?" the mom interjects.

"Oh yeah, it was second period. That's right. Anyway, just before the test started, Mr. Lenhart made an announcement, and...," the child continues.

"I thought Mrs. Jones was your math teacher," the mother interrupts.

"She is. Mr. Lenhart was just making an announcement over the intercom. Anyway, Mrs. Jones went to the chalk board in the front of the room, and...," again, the child gets interrupted.

"Honey, the board in your class is a dry erase board."

Dear moms and dads of the world, please let your kids

finish their sentences and paragraphs. They simply cannot think as quickly or as clearly as you can, and their little minds are trying very hard to organize their thoughts, and impress you whatever story they are trying to share.

Chronic mismatchers have a need to clarify or restate everything that's said, rather than listen to the essence of what is being communicated. Does it really matter whether the board in front of the classroom was chalk or dry erase? For that matter, does it matter whether math was held during first period or second period? What I would want to know in this parable is what the child was so excited about. Most parents can be good detectives, and as such, you will have plenty of time to clarify any bits of conflicting information (like the teacher's name) after your child finishes telling their story.

Needless to say, interrupting someone just to point out the inaccuracies of whatever they are saying is destructive to the other person's self-concept. It's the same with adults, as well. When someone continuously interrupts me in the middle of a thought, I might ask them, *"Would you like me to continue?"* While a certain amount of detail is needed, there's a point at which clarifying unnecessarily is detrimental to your communication.

The same sentiment applies to those people who have a need to finish other people's sentences. I can probably name a dozen people off the top of my head who are unrelenting sentence-finishers. For example, as part of a normal conversation with someone, I might say something like, *"Last Thursday, when my flight finally arrived in Atlanta, it was...."*

"...raining. Yes, we had terrible weather that night!" The other person jumps in and finishes my thought. But, how do they know I wasn't about to say, *"it was...eleven o'clock, and I just caught the ending of one of the best football games ever!"*

This quirky behavior of finishing another person's sentences is usually not driven by malicious intent. It's more likely that people who do this are attempting to demonstrate that they are indeed listening intently, and are very interested what you are saying. Intentions aside, interrupting someone unnecessarily is counterproductive to the exchange and destructive to the larger objective of effective communication. As slowly as kids sometimes tell stories, there is often a great temptation to hurry them along by completing their sentences. However, part of our responsibility as question-based parents is to be patient enough to actually listen to what our children want to say.

There's an easy solution to this problem of always finishing someone else's sentences. You simply talk when it's your turn and listen when it's not.

III. One-Upsmanship

One-upsmanship is the third type of mismatched response. You often see this when kids are playing in a school-yard or sitting around a campfire verbally trying to out-do each other. One person makes a comment or tells a story, and someone else who yurns to make an even bigger impact in the conversation, says something like, *"The same thing happened to me, only worse! I had to have twelve stitches."*

This response is a mismatch because of what it communicates. Instead of acknowledging the value of another person's contribution to the conversation, one-upsmanship reduces the significance of what the other person is saying by essentially suggesting that, *"I'm better than you."*

Do you really want to send your children a message that says "I'm better than you?" I bet you don't. But, that's the message that comes through loud and clear if you compete with them, story for story. You might say this type of mismatch is a boomerang that almost always comes back.

Think about it this way, if you treat your child's stories as the most fantastic and awesome you have ever heard, they will likely show significantly more interest in whatever you want to share with them. Conversely, if you are always one-upping your children, lamenting about the old days and telling about how difficult life used to be when you were a kid, a pathological mismatcher probably won't be able to garner much of an audience.

IV. Saying "I Know"

The dreaded "I know" response is yet another form of mismatching, which is a slight variation of one-upsmanship. Perhaps you've noticed that some people are not very open-minded when it comes to taking advice. Take college kids. For some reason, they already seem to know everything. Just try offering some constructive feedback to a college freshman, and you will see what I mean. They think they have been out in the world and know it all already. It's not just young adults, either. Just a few years ago, after only three weeks of school, my five-year-old said, *"I know, Dad, I'm in kindergarten now."* It takes most parents twenty years to raise a child, and we finished in five. Wow!

It's not that people are averse to improvement. It's just that most of us have an instinctive need to protect ourselves against feeling inadequate. Once again, the underlying intent of the mismatcher is generally not malicious and often different than the message they actually communicate. For example, the phrase, *"I know"* is often intended to mean the same as, *"I agree."* To your child, however, just saying, *"I know"* could sound more like, *"I'm already aware of that, so buzz off."* Of course, this type of defensive reaction tends to close off conversations and degrade the value of the other person at the same time—a double whammy. Your intent may have been pure, but in the end, there's a big difference between, *"I agree"* and *"buzz off,"* don't you think?

V. Sarcasm is a Double-Edged Sword

What comes to mind when you think of the word sarcasm? Is it a good thing or a bad thing? Did you know that sarcasm can actually be a valuable conversational tool, like when it is used to emphasize a point you want to make? Sarcasm can also be a "verbal condiment" that makes humorous comments even funnier if the tone of the remark is properly embedded into a sentence. But, sarcasm is best known for its destructive qualities, especially when communicated in the form of a mismatch to point out someone else's inadequacies.

"Are you going to Grandma's house?" sister Jane says to her brother.

"No, I'm going to stay home and celebrate Christmas all by myself!" her brother Joe says sarcastically. "Of course, I'm going to Grandma's house!"

Well, which is it, Joe? Are you going to grandmother's house or not? Just by listening to Joe's harsh tone, sister Jane could probably tell he was being sarcastic. But, think about what Joe actually said. He first suggested that he was not going to go, primarily just to make his sister feel stupid for having asked. What an odd response? Someone who cares about Joe asks a valid question, and he rewards her by making her feel stupid. I bet this never happens at your house!

The rule of thumb is this. If something you say sarcastically isn't ha-ha funny, then there is a good likelihood that it is demeaning to the person in which the sarcastic remark was directed. Like most mismatches, sarcasm is more often used as a defense mechanism than a personal attack. Nonetheless, communicating with people by purposely saying something different than you mean is a high-risk strategy for building long-term relationships.

Telling is Not Selling

In my business career, I travel all over the world delivering strategic sales training that is foundationed on this simple premise: The harder you push, the harder your customers will push back. Furthermore, it is very difficult to build relationships with, or sell to, people who are feeling defensive or holding you off at arm's length.

The realization that prospects and customers *are* going to push back comes as a rude awakening for many companies. There's an old saying that *telling is not selling*. Though most customers love to make purchase decisions, very few prospects want to be told and even fewer want to be "sold." Buyers in today's business climate don't want to be pushed, persuaded, or otherwise convinced, and nobody wants to feel as if they are being forced or manipulated into making the wrong decision. As a result, trying to push customers harder and harder tends to increase buyer resistance, which actually reduces your chances of making a sale. Even if you have a terrific solution or great idea, you must still have a receptive audience. Otherwise, whatever information you are trying to convey will likely fall on deaf ears.

This brings us to another parallel between the business world and parenting. Like customers, children are often just as quick to put up their defenses when a parent wants to offer advice. And, no matter how good your advice is, pushing harder and harder to give it doesn't usually cause people (or in this case, children) to suddenly open up and become more receptive. If anything, *forcing* a child to listen could further dampen their enthusiasm or even cause them to rebel. That's why it's so important for parents to understand and deal with this concept of mismatching, because it is an early form of rebellion.

Three Strategies to Reduce Your Risk

The fact that mismatching is an instinctive tendency does not mean you have to let this behavior negatively affect your relationships. Parents and children alike have feelings. As such, no one wants to be contradicted, corrected, one-upped, and we especially don't want someone else to make us feel inadequate. Similarly, just because someone is a habitual mismatcher doesn't mean we should banish them from the family or write them off as a friend. Some of the people you care about the most might be natural mismatchers.

The good news is, *habitual mismatching* is relatively easy to change. And, when the behavior stops, you will see an immediate improvement in the quality of your interactions. You just have to remember that most of the mismatching that occurs is a defensive reaction to satisfy one's own subconscious need to feel valuable. With that in mind, let's put some thought into ways in which we can be proactive strategy to reduce this type of defense mechanism, or eliminate the reaction altogether.

The secret to creating a less defensive and more receptive audience lies in your ability to do something that causes listeners to want to share openly with you, and conversely, listen open-mindedly to you. Is there a magic bullet that will make this happen perfectly every time? As you might guess, the answer is no. But, I can give you three very specific question-based communication techniques will enable you to reduce the frequency and negative impact of mismatching within your circle of friends and family.

1.) Use More Questions and Less Statements

The ability to minimize the mismatching reflex starts with prevention. If you can avoid certain things that cause people to mismatch, then you might be able to modify your approach in a way that avoids the reaction altogether.

The primary culprit that generates a high frequency of mismatched reactions is the declarative statement. Since most statements are absolute, they are easily mismatched. When someone makes a declaration, it's natural for people to challenge a definitive viewpoint. Why? It's because we have an instinctive need to be insightful as opposed to just being dictated to.

Earlier, I suggested you try an experiment—to make the casual comment to someone that, "I heard it's supposed to be nice this weekend." See for yourself how they respond. If you actually try the experiment, I bet you will be surprised how quickly this type of innocent statement gets immediately mismatched by someone, saying, *"I heard it's going to be hot, windy, rainy...,"* or some other response that contradicts the original supposition. It's virtually impossible to make a statement that cannot be contradicted, clarified, one-upped, or interpreted in some defensive way. In fact, the more definitive your statements are, the greater the likelihood that they will be mismatched.

While statements are easily mismatched, questions are not. That's because the conversational dynamics of a question actually help diffuse the emotional triggers that otherwise fuel another person's need to respond in a contrarian manner. In essence, it's virtually impossible to disagree with a question. Think about it. Instead of stating that it's going to be nice this weekend, what if you had asked, *"What's the weather supposed be like this weekend?"* How can someone disagree with that? You haven't taken a definitive position, so there's nothing to disagree with. In fact, asking questions as opposed to making statements has a double benefit. One, it reduces the probability of a contradiction, and two, it satisfies the other person's need to add value by actually inviting them to offer their opinion.

Here's a practical application of this idea, one that I wish every parent would pass onto their children. Social awkwardness is one of the biggest challenges most every child will face at some point during their formative years. Walking into a room full of other kids or adults, for example, tends to make most kids feel a little awkward. Children aren't always eager to strike up a conversation with someone they don't know. (Starting conversations can be just as difficult for adults.)

Sometimes, people try and break the ice in these conversations with a statement like, *"This sure is a nice party."* While this initial salvo will no doubt generate some type of response, it may just be a single word or grunt.

"Yep," or *"Uh huh,"* doesn't get you very far in a conversation.

Perhaps, your child will take another shot, saying something like, *"I think most of the kids here are from other schools."*

"Um hmm," replies the other conversationally-challenged kid. Who knows, the dialogue could take off from there; but I doubt it, since a statement-based conversation, coupled with a series of mismatched responses, is a bad formula for long-lasting interaction.

Therefore, I encourage you to seize this opportunity to teach your kids how to initiate small-talk conversations with questions, rather than tossing out random declarations and hoping for the best. The child in the analogy above, for example, could just as easily have asked, *"What do you think of this party?"* From there, it would have been natural to follow up by asking, *"How many of these kids do you think are from Wentworth High?"*

The difference between statements and questions in everyday conversation is monumental. For one, asking questions greatly reduces the mismatching reflex. How can you disagree with someone who is interested in your opinion? More importantly, asking questions is a selfless act. The asker is intentionally showing interest in the other person's point of view by asking, "What do you think about…?" Do people like it when you are truly interested in their opinion? The answer to this question is clearly, yes.

Challenge your child to give it a try in the next day or two. All they have to do is pick a topic someone might be interested in and ask, *"Hi Bobby, how's soccer going this season? Jennifer…how is the high school play coming along? Steven…how was the field trip yesterday?"* Basically, saying, *"I care about your opinion,"* is a great conversation starter with just about anyone.

One more point on this. If you are going to teach your children how to initiate a conversation with questions, be sure to encourage them to also listen for the answers. If they ask a question about the field trip, for example, and the other person responds by saying, *"The field trip was lots of fun,"* it's easy to further engage the other person just by asking the next logical question, something like: *"What was your favorite part? Who did you sit next to on the bus? What time did you get home?"*

The questions your child asks don't have to be complex or sophisticated; the secret is just showing interest. Most people, young and old, are quick to become interested in others who show even the slightest amount of interest in them. If we as parents don't invest the time to explain this to our children, who will?

2.) Be Impressed with Your Children

Why is it so easy to take the people we love most for granted? Just before dinner, little Sally comes into the kitchen and says, "Mom, look at this cool leaf I found outside." Unbeknownst to Sally, mom has been having a rotten day. The PTA meeting at school was a bust, her doctor appointment got rescheduled at the last minute, and she just discovered that the vegetables she was planning to serve for dinner are no longer fresh.

"Sally, can't you see I'm busy?" the busy mother replies, without even turning around.

As a parent myself, I understand that we sometimes feel like our emotions are running on empty. In those cases, even the smallest thing can grate on your last nerve. But, I would like to suggest that this type of distraction, where all your child wants is a little attention from one or both parents, may just be a simple matter of perspective.

For example, let's suppose you just received word (God forbid) that your child was involved in some freak accident. A terrible head injury has left your little Sally unconscious, and, after a few days, she lapses into a comatose state. What would you give at that point to have your child back, even if she was interrupting as you were preparing dinner?

If we take this example a little further, suppose after many long nights in the hospital, with your entire family holding twenty-four hour bedside vigils, your little girl (or boy) suddenly opened her eyes and softly said, "Momma." Through the tears you would hug the child and kiss them ceaselessly, and then maybe even dance around the room in celebration. I imagine this would probably be one of the happiest moments of your life.

Throughout their recovery process, you would demonstrate extra patience and caring in order to fulfill the pact you made with your God when your child was lying in the hospital bed on life-support. You would also be ready and willing to support your child during every stage of their recovery. And, you would go out of your way to outwardly express how impressed you were that they could do simple rehabilitative tasks things like holding a cup in their hand, or drawing a circle with a crayon.

With this image fresh in your mind, let me ask, were you "impressed" by anything your children said or did today? This is a difficult question because the concept of being impressed connotes out-of-the-ordinary acts. To a mom who has seen thousands of leaves in her lifetime, being interrupted to look at a leaf that her daughter brought home is hardly out of the ordinary. That's where one's perspective comes into play. For little Sally, that leaf she wanted to show her mother may have been extraordinary.

The mistake we parents often make is judging the value of something before we truly understand what is being presented. Our analytical brains receive information, and we process that information against our adult perspective to decide whether something is relevant and valuable or not.

I remember misjudging a similar situation several years ago when our younger daughter, who was four-years old at the time, approached me right before dinner and said, *"Daddy, what do you think of my picture?"*

"That's nice, honey," I said, essentially brushing her

aside. I was busy. Out the corner of my eye, I could tell that my response had taken the wind out of my daughter's sails, but honestly, her drawing was just a bunch of shapes scribbled onto the paper with a crayon.

My wife Laura, who is often much wiser than me, whispered, "Why don't you ask her what it's a picture of?"

Ugggggh! How long is this going to take, I wondered? But I asked, "Mary Claire, does your picture tell a story?"

Instantly, the twinkle came back into her eyes. "Yes," she said as she climbed up onto the bar stool next to mine. "This is a picture of me in my bed, dreaming of all of the things I want to be when I grow up. And, these stars in the sky are fairies that will watch over me and help me do things." To my surprise, every star had a fairy, and every fairy had a purpose. There was a school fairy, and a fairy to watch over our family, one to talk with God, and even one to watch over our dog. Imagine my chagrin. I thought she just wanted to show me an ordinary four year-old's crayon sketch. Instead, my daughter was offering me a front-row seat to her innermost thoughts and dreams.

Do you let your child finish their sentences? Do you eagerly respond to their questions even if they are asking something that seems obvious to a seasoned adult? Do you show interest in their activities and their opinions by asking questions about them? Do you tell your child how impressed you are with ordinary things they do, like having good posture or picking up their shoes without being asked? Do you tell your children how much they mean to you? Or, was today just another ordinary day, where mismatching abounded all day long at the office, and then again at the dinner table?

I was once told by someone that you are either giving energy to other people in your conversations with them, or you are taking it away. If you had the option, wouldn't you want to energize your kids by letting them know you admire and respect them? If so, here's a little secret. Demonstrating to your kids that you are truly impressed by who they are and what they can do is one of the surest ways to end up with truly impressive kids.

3.) *Use Curiosity to Eliminate the Mismatching Reflex*

As a defense mechanism, mismatching is an expression of emotional reluctance, as we have discussed. The opposite of reluctance is intrigue and curiosity. After investing a significant research effort into understanding what causes customers to want to spend lots of time with some sales-people, while completely avoiding others, it became clear to me that it is impossible to be reluctant and curious at the same time. We also discovered that when someone becomes intrigued, they also become very curious, thus making it possible to engage them in fruitful conversation.

Whether you want to share a cool idea with your child or offer constructive feedback, just because you want to talk with them doesn't necessarily mean you will get a receptive audience. Furthermore, the messages you convey are only as valuable as your child's desire to receive the information being offered. Couple this with the natural inclination to mismatch, and it's amazing that we parents are able to communicate with our kids at all! In fact, one of the biggest challenges for parents is that the information we want to convey is often very different than the messages being heard by our children. This creates a communication barrier that I like to call Charlie Brown's Teacher Syndrome.

You remember Charlie Brown, the popular cartoon character many of us first encountered back when we were kids? Although it has been a while since Charles Schulz created the original Peanuts comic strip, most people still remember Linus, Lucy, Snoopy, Schroeder, and the gang. But, do you remember Charlie Brown's teacher? We never actually see an adult in the cartoon, but we did hear the muffled nasal sound of a nagging teacher's voice, saying: "wah, wa, wah...wa, wah...wa...wah."

Unfortunately, that's how we, as parents, sometimes sound to our kids. Especially if a parent is in the middle of a tirade, whatever you think you are saying becomes irrelevant, if all the child actually hears is some version of, "wah, wa, wah...wa, wah...wa...wah." Ironically, it turns out that talking *at* your children with lots of words is one of the quickest ways to cause them to tune out. While ranting and raving might make the parent feel better, you won't accomplish much if your child doesn't absorb the message.

Instead of fussing at your kids in a way that brings on Charlie Brown's Teacher Syndrome, the alternative is being question-based. It's basically a two-step process, where the first objective is to get your child's attention, and only then, to communicate your message. I discovered this idea by participating in committee meetings at our church.

Church meetings can be quite tedious, especially when each participant on the committee feels a need to reiterate what has already been said. Unfortunately, I am not always as patient as I should be in these situations. I tend to be an analytical person who wants to get to the bottom line. When I think of something that I believe is a good idea, my mouth immediately wants to blurt it out. *"Why don't we just do this, that, and the other?"* I will suggest, in an attempt to move the conversation forward.

After having many of my ideas fall on deaf ears, I decided to try a different approach. When I thought of something, instead of just blurting it out, I waited for an appropriate moment to say, *"I have an idea that I think might help us a lot."* Then, I would pause. This type of comment generally stops everyone in their tracks. Once you have everyone's full attention, it is a lot easier to share ideas and gain consensus. When the audience you are dealing with is receptive to whatever you have to say, you are in a position to truly be heard, as opposed to sounding like... wah...wa...wah...wa.

The key ingredient, I discovered, was *curiosity.* People who are curious will *want to* listen to what you have to say, while those people who are not the least bit curious, won't. The question-based parent can use this technique to their advantage, in a way that causes children to be more receptive to their input or feedback. Basically, all you have to do is preface your comment with a curiosity-inducing question, like, *"Can I make a comment about your plans for the weekend?"* It's okay if your child (especially a teenager) doesn't dance around the room, excited about receiving parental advice. It's more likely that they might roll their eyes in your direction. But, if they are even the slightest bit curious about what you are about to say, at least you have their attention. That's the first step on the way to communicating an effective message.

Averting a Downward Spiral

It's important to note that mismatching also poses a silent risk. Rather than being confrontational, some children will silently grit their teeth, because they would rather disagree quietly than have to contend with the unbridled ego of a defensive parent who senses their authority slipping away.

Whether it's verbalized or silent, mismatched responses foster discord and dissension within the household. That dissension slowly chips away at the relationships you are trying to build. While it's true that people in close quarters are sometimes going to have conflict, we should do everything in our power (as parents) to break down barriers that could otherwise inhibit or dampen communication.

You might as well deal with this issue early in your pilgrimage as a mother or father, because your ongoing credibility as a parent is at stake. While mismatching is a natural reflexive tendency, it is also a sign of disrespect. With younger children, it's common for parents to respond to this behavior with some combination of anger, frustration, and punishment. This may curb the symptoms for a time, but one must wonder, what are the longer-term implications of a parent squashing a child's spirit? Don't get me wrong. I am not opposed to proper discipline when needed. We already gave that subject a good look. But, the issue of mismatching is a different animal.

Early mismatching is actually the first stage of rebellion. You may be able to force children to do lots of things when they are young, but you will not be able to force them to respect you later in life. And, the more you try and force a child to conform, the greater the likelihood is that they will want to rebel.

We must remember that the tendency to mismatch is usually driven by the need to feel valuable. I'm no psycho-analyst, but it's pretty clear to me that squashing a child's spirit won't do much to bolster their self-esteem. Now we are engaged in a circular problem, where low self-esteem leads to increased mismatching, mismatching shows disrespect for parental authority, this disrespect causes parents to pull the reigns even tighter, and around we go. The net result is often a downward spiral, where bad behavior leads to a harsh response from the parent, and those harsh responses from a hard-line parent cause even worse behavior in the future.

Could the antidote to this problem be as simple as changing punctuation? Could transforming your sentences from statement into questions be the key to more open and more productive communication? The short answer is yes. While this may seem like a small adjustment in strategy, becoming question-based will instantly improve the way you interact with your children and your spouse, as well as your neighbors, co-workers, and friends. More importantly, it will also change the way they all interact with you. Wouldn't that be impressive?

Chapter 8

A Quick Course in Listening

"Listening, not imitation, may be the sincerest form
of flattery."
                                    —Dr. Joyce Brothers

Most parents love their children with all their hearts.
Perhaps that goes without saying. But, how much you love
your child may not be the critical success factor when it
comes to effectively communicating with them. There are
plenty of times when parents who love their children find
themselves at odds with said child over something, and
sincere attempts to communicate with them either escalate
the argument or make the initial problem even worse.

Last fall, I attended my wife's class reunion at a recep-
tion hall in a small town in North Georgia. As the spouse of
a graduate, I was several steps removed from the nostalgic
reminiscences of Laura's high school class, so I spent much
of the evening congregated in the corner with several other
similarly orphaned spouses. Kate, the spouse of one of
Laura's high school buddies, and I were having a casual chat
when I happened to mention that I was in the middle of
writing this book. Apparently, my ideas struck a chord with

her, because she started telling me about an ongoing predicament she was facing with one of her two daughters. Since I have two daughters myself, my ears were cocked and I was very interested in her story.

Kate explained that she often found herself in a no-win situation. The daughter, who was suffering from some of the same anxieties every teenager faces, often turned to her mother for comfort and advice, although I suspect it was more for comfort. Kate painted a verbal picture of the daughter droning on and on about whatever was 'the crisis of the day.' Can we agree that teenage catastrophes don't always sound as bad to an adult as they seem to your son or daughter, especially if your child's hormones are working overtime that day?

Kate, being the caring mother that she is, tried to offer advice for how the daughter could deal with the issues being presented. But, according to Kate, offering advice just seemed to upset the daughter, as she didn't want mom to actually help fix the problem. When Kate tried the opposite approach, by just listening quietly and giving understanding looks and nods, this created a problem as well. Apparently whenever Kate remained silent, the daughter just assumed her mother wasn't really interested in what she was saying. It sounded like a classic, "Darned if you do, darned if you don't..." scenario.

I made the comment earlier that most metropolitan areas are full of counselors—marriage counselors and family counselors. Do you remember what the chief complaint is that these counselors hear from clients every day? The most common grievance usually involves communication issues between people who love each other. But, when you look more closely at the facts, people who are frustrated by a lack of communication generally aren't worried about their own ability to run off at the mouth. Instead, frustrated clients are usually most concerned about someone else's inability to listen.

For children and adults, both, it is in our nature that we want to share our feelings and experiences with people who will listen attentively. More importantly, we want those who mean the most to us to "want to" listen, because we want them to be emotionally involved in things we care deeply about. There's nothing particularly earth shattering about this notion. People being attentive and listening carefully serves as validation, especially since we want others to find what we have to say important and valuable.

Attentive listening is also a way to show respect. When someone doesn't feel appropriately listened to, they tend to feel disrespected. That brings us back to a familiar theme with regard to the question-based parent. It is critical for kids to respect their parents. This includes children listening to what their parents need to say, and also the stories you have to share. It is equally important for parents to listen to their children. As it turns out, bidirectional listening is an expression of mutual respect. Kids feel appreciated by a parent who invests the time to listen carefully. On the flipside, those who don't feel appropriately listened to are the ones who will likely need counseling at some point in the future.

What we need to realize is, there's a difference between listening and hearing. My hearing, for example, is pretty good. I can always tell who's home and what they are doing just by gauging the various noises I hear throughout the house. But, my wife and kids would quickly tell you that I am not always the best listener. And, they are correct.

Usually, it works best for me to deflect responsibility for this by blaming something else, like being preoccupied with problems at work. Sometimes, I blame the television or claim that I was distracted by our dog Sandy. But when the dust settles in the conversation, it usually comes down to a simple matter of priority. What's more important, the television, the dog, something at work, or whatever your child or spouse wants to share with you? Sadly, I have missed the boat on this more times than I would like to admit.

During the time that I was developing the QBS methodology, it occurred to me that there must be a way to become a better listener. In the process, I also found the solution to my friend Kate's predicament with her daughter. It all boils down to exercising a question-based listening skill we call *active listening*.

Active vs. Passive Listening

Have you ever attended a listening skills course? When I first started in sales, one of my early managers thought the entire organization would benefit from a half-day seminar designed to teach proper listening skills. I was skeptical. "I already know how to listen," I thought. What in the world is a listening skills class going to teach me? Are they going to make us cock our heads to one side like a dog, in order to improve our hearing?

Sure enough, that listening skills class turned out to be a valuable experience. And, as often happens, the concepts I learned in the course applied to many things outside the traditional work environment. In fact, the most impactful thing I took away from the class was the realization that there are actually two different kinds of listening—active listening and passive listening.

Passive listening is the physical act of hearing. Passive listening is what husbands do. Sorry to let the cat out of the bag, guys, but the phrase, "Yes, dear," really means, "Whatever you just said isn't very important to me." Similarly, looking away while grunting, "Uh hum," in the general direction of your children basically means you are either not interested at all, or this is not a good time. Mothers do the same thing, only it sounds nicer when they use their soft voices to say, "Uh hum."

Not surprisingly, passive listening does little to perpetuate conversation or build relationships with your children or your spouse. In fact, there is an interesting correlation between depth of relationship and listening, where the closer the relationship, the less inclined we are to pay close attention. I have observed this phenomenon throughout my life. When I was a young boy, I remember noticing that my grandparents were barely listening to each other by the time they reached the age of seventy. For some strange reason, they could hear me perfectly well, just not each other. And, the funny part is, they were often yelling back and forth, but neither one was really listening.

In business, I am a terrific listener. With clients, I make a point of listening carefully and I will try to examine every nuance of information they share. As a result, clients tend to openly share lots of information with me. When I get home from work, however, my ears have a bad habit of turning off. Laura usually wants to tell me about her day and the kids like to share the latest news from school, but if I succumb to natural forces, I often hear and retain only some fraction of what is being communicated. Again, it's easy to blame fatigue or business concerns for being distracted. Do you ever feel this way? If so, then it's definitely time to listen up, or I can pretty much guarantee that it will cost you later in other ways.

One of the best pieces of advice I ever received about

listening came one day years ago when I met an older gentleman at a church retreat. He wisely suggested that I try asking people who are in the twilight of their lives, what wisdom or ideas they might pass on to younger person like myself who was hoping to get ahead in life. So, over the past twenty years or so, I have posed this question to many of my elders. Invariably, the responses I receive always seem to convey the same sentiment. An elderly person will always tell you that life is short, and the time you spend with your family is precious and fleeting. A young person thinks that they will live forever, and they simply can't imagine not being surrounded by loved ones. I wish now that I had understood this concept better when I first started asking the question.

My daughters are now nine and fifteen, and although I think we have done a decent job as parents thus far, I have admittedly missed some things along the way. Likewise, my wife and I have been married eighteen years, and during that time, I have actively participated in only some fraction of the conversations we've had. With every day that goes by, however, I try to miss less and less. Can we ever be perfect listeners? The probable answer is no. No matter how hard you try, life always seems to get in the way. But, you can become a much better listener almost overnight, just by doing one simple thing. Instead of just hearing the words that someone else is saying, the secret to being a successful communicator is becoming an *active* listener.

Active listening is completely different than passive listening. Rather than just hearing the words that are being spoken, active listening is the act of participating in what's actually being said. How can you be more engaged in what someone else is saying? Simple—by demonstrating a high level of interest in others as they communicate with you.

What's the best way to show someone you are truly interested? That's where questions come in handy. Isn't that strange? One of the most effective listening skills one can have is the ability to ask insightful questions that will take the conversation deeper.

Do children like it when their mother or father is genuinely interested in what they have to say? The answer is, absolutely! Listening intently is a subtle, yet powerful, way to show your children that you love and respect them. So, if your child is sharing something that happened at school, don't just sit there with a blank look on your face or grunt an acknowledgement toward their end of the table. Ask who they sat with during lunch, or find out more about what happened in science class. Your questions don't have to be sophisticated to create the desired effect. Just pick some part of the child's story that can easily be expanded and fire away.

Once you peel back the shell and examine the anatomy of human interaction, you will find that good listeners are also usually great question askers. These two conversational skills go hand in hand, and the process of becoming a question-based parent will automatically make you a better listener. You get the best of both worlds.

Use Global Questions

If you pay attention to your interpersonal communications, you will discover that most people share only some fraction of their total thoughts, feelings, and concerns. Hence, there are lots of opportunities during the course of a normal conversation to say, "Tell me more." But, since I would rather be question-based than command-oriented, I use the simple conversational technique of asking global questions to further expand my conversations.

For example, if I am home for dinner during a normal work week, at the dinner table I usually ask, "Girls, how was school today?"

"Fine," is a typical response.

"What did you do after school?" I might follow up.

The likely answer is, "Nothing."

It's not just me. As I deliver QBS training all over the globe, it turns out that kids in Europe and China provide these same minimal responses to their parents, too.

You could try wagging your finger in your child's face as a way to force them to tell you what happened after school. But, that only works when children are very young, and have not tested you to see what might happen if they totally clam up. Because I don't like the idea of using force as a strategy to communicate with my wife, kids, friends, co-workers, or clients, I naturally gravitate to using *global* questions.

A global question contains no subject. It is simply a communicative device you can use to say, "Tell me more." But, rather than ordering someone to tell you, it is much more productive (and respectful) to ask a global question like, *Can you tell me more? ...And then what happened?* Or, you can simply raise your eyebrows and ask...*How so?*

I can tell you that the single most productive question I used to ask as a salesperson, still works very well for me today...as a father, husband, neighbor, and friend. It is a global question that contains the following four words, "How do you mean?"

Try this experiment. The next time someone makes a comment to you or asks you a question, simply respond by saying, "How do you mean?" For example, suppose your ten-year-old bursts through the kitchen door saying, "The boys down the street were playing too rough."

You can easily respond by asking, "How do you mean?", and then watch the words tumble out. Don't be surprised if this one question causes you to receive two, three, four, or even five paragraphs of additional information about the situation. Trading four simple words for a waterfall of information is a pretty good return on your investment, don't you think? If you want to know the full story about whatever is happening in your child's life, asking global questions can make a parent's job much easier.

If someone asks something as simple as, "What's your favorite show on television?" you can easily respond the same way. Saying, "How do you mean?", will likely produce tons of additional insight and conversation.

Sometimes people think the syntax of this question is grammatically challenged. Instead, they ask, *What do you mean?*

The English language is a funny thing. When you ask someone, "What do you mean?", they generally go backwards in the conversation and restate what they just said. I usually don't want to go backward in a conversation because I heard what the other person already said. Asking, "What do you mean?", also tends to elicit a defensive reaction, as if you are challenging whatever the person is trying to communicate. If the other person happens to be your child, you don't want to put them on the defensive. We know what happens when children get defensive. They pull away and share less information with you, rather than more.

Asking, "How do you mean?", has the opposite effect. It invites people to share the next level of detail about whatever they originally said or asked. Here's why you don't have to worry about grammar. By asking, "How do you mean?", you essentially communicate the following: "I am really interested in what you just said (or asked), could you please tell me more?" Do people like it when we show interest in what they are trying to communicate? Bingo!

Global questions are fantastic active listening tools. You don't even have to think of a sophisticated question. All you have to do is repeat the subject of the previous question or statement, and then lift your voice to phrase it as a question. For example, the next time your child says something like, "My stomach hurts," a question-based parent could respond by simply asking, "Your stomach hurts?" Or, if my child said, "I'm going to put my homework off until later," they might get a response from me saying, "Did you say you're going to put your homework off?"

Keep in mind that asking global questions is not some kind of conversational gimmick or sales trick. Rather it's a proven way to bolster communication throughout the family, which should be every parent's goal.

Clarify Vague-O-Nyms

Would you agree that miscommunication is the root cause of many conflicts and arguments within families? These lapses in communication aren't always someone's fault, however. In fact, one of the leading causes of miscommunication is the fact that the English language is highly interpretable. As a result, what you think someone is saying may be very different than what they actually mean. That's why it's so important for the question-based parent to clarify what I like to call *vague-o-nyms*.

What's a vague-o-nym? Do you remember learning about synonyms back in high school English? Synonyms are different words that have the same meaning, like big and large. Homonyms are words that sound the same but have different meanings, such as hair and hare. Antonyms are opposites, like up and down. So, what's a vague-o-nym? A vague-o-nym is a label we use in QBS to characterize a word or phrase that, without any additional information or context, is too vague to understand what the other person actually means.

Clarifying vague-o-nyms when they come up in your conversations is a valuable listening skill. Once again, people want you to be interested in what they are saying and you also want to understand what they mean. That way, everybody wins.

Suppose you call your child at the neighbor's house and ask, "When are you planning to come home?" The child says, "Soon." What do you suppose the word "soon" might mean? You might assume that the child will probably be on their way in a few minutes. But to a child, especially one without a wrist watch, the word "soon" could mean an hour, or whenever we finish this fun game. Of course, when a kid rolls in thirty minutes after the parent expects them to be home, it's easy for a frustrated parent to light into the child, saying, "I thought you said soon!"

Or, how about this scenario? When your child starts driving a car, beware of the phrase, "Dad, it's just down the street." California is just down the street. It's more likely that your new freedom-seeker is wanting to drive to a place that is somewhere between a reasonable distance away and California.

"How much television are you planning to watch?" a parent might ask.

"A little bit," the child responds.

With vague-o-nyms, you don't get enough information to know what the other person is really saying. There's no need to get frustrated with your kids. We all say things that can be interpreted different ways. The key is to seize the opportunity to clarify vague-o-nyms as they arise.

A frustrated child, lamenting to a parent, might say, "Everybody else has nicer clothes than me." When I hear something like this from my child, the first thought that pops into my head is a question. When she says, "everybody else," does she mean all the other kids at school? I might also wonder what she meant by the word, "nicer." Is my daughter really worried about fashion trends like color and style, or might she be down on herself for some other reason?

The objective here is not to pick apart or diminish what someone else is saying. In fact, this technique of clarifying vague-o-nyms seeks to achieve the opposite goal, which is to truly understand what your children, spouse, friends, and neighbors are trying to communicate.

Clarifying vague-o-nyms is easy for the question-based parent. For example, if my child says, "I will be home in a little while," it would be easy for me to ask, "When you say a little while, do you mean a few minutes or an hour or two?" Note: asking your child to clarify what they mean does not give them free reign to do whatever they wish, by any means. In fact, that's why I'm asking. If for some reason we are not on the same page relative to what is reasonable, I would much rather have an opportunity to reset expectations, than be at odds with my child over an issue that was ultimately caused by miscommunication.

Be a Conversational Detective

Listening carefully to your children can be hard work. It is especially difficult to listen intently if you have to pretend to be interested in what the child is saying. If your child has a problem, the natural instinct for most parents is to jump in and try to fix it. But kids don't always want parents to offer suggestions. Sometimes they just want to talk. And talk they do—often droning on and on without concern for their audience's stamina, or for how much detail is too much. I'm sure most parents, at some point, have wanted to run away screaming when they were halfway through a preteen's account of the he-said/she-said bickering that happened in the school lunchroom that day. Nonetheless, our kids need our support, and that means caring enough to listen.

Truth be known, kids can always tell when you aren't really interested in what they're saying. That leaves us parents in somewhat of a dilemma. We want to give our kids the support they need and deserve, but it is still very difficult to listen intently, especially if time is of the essence and your mind isn't tuned into whatever they are sharing.

If you sometimes face this dilemma with your own children, I have good news. The solution to this problem lies in the ability of the listening party (you) to become a better listener. When I teach salespeople about listening, I challenge students to enter into detective mode, essentially listening for clues that tell you what is really being communicated, which goes far beyond just hearing the words.

Do you remember Columbo? Even as one of the most famous television detectives, Columbo was never fortunate enough to meet criminals who would just spill the beans. Instead, he spent the entire sixty minutes of the show piecing together clues from the various conversations he had with different characters in the episode that ultimately enabled Columbo to solve the crime.

Are *you* able to recognize the various clues that surface in your daily conversations? Ironically, experts say that seventy-five percent of all human communication is non-verbal. And, it's often the combination of the words along with hand-gestures, facial expressions, body language, and tone of voice that reveal the true story about what's really being communicated. If you have a teenager in your house, you must also watch out for the dreaded eye-roll, the deep sigh, and the demonstrative exhale/grunt combination.

I live in a house full of girls. Consequently, I have had to learn the hard way that there is often a lot more to the story than just listening to the words. I have also discovered that how words are being communicated is just as important as the actual meaning of the words by themselves. For example, I might come home from work and ask my wife, "Hi honey, how was your day?"

"Fine," she says. "How was yours?"

A few minutes later, when one of my daughters appears, I might greet her with the same question, "How was your day?"

"Fine!" she snaps. But her tone of voice and the accompanying frown instantly tells me that something is not fine.

People (especially children) use non-verbal gestures and voice-tone to communicate that there is more happening than they are able to convey with just words. Trust me, the information is in there. You just have to do the detective work to unveil the full picture—in this case, using questions that will open the floodgates of information.

Being the question-based parent that I am, my instincts tends to launch me into detective mode very naturally. Without saying a word, I visually scan the room for clues. Is there a book bag lying open, revealing a large amount of homework or an impending exam? A quick glace at Laura's expression might tell me if the two of them have had a spat, or if Laura even knows what's wrong. And, having grown up watching detectives on television, I know that the next thing Columbo would do is focus his attention on the person of interest, and innocently ask, "Is something wrong?"

Don't be put off if your child's first reaction is negative. You may get a smart retort, like, "Well, duh. What do *you* think!?" Be patient. The child is obviously upset about something, and it may take a couple of passes to tear down the walls built by frustration. Kids need to know that you are truly interested in their innermost feelings and concerns. So, try again—only this time, raise your eyebrows. Give them a non-verbal signal that demonstrates you care enough to be interested in knowing the full story. And men, don't offer to fix it. Just offer to understand, by saying, "Can you please tell me more?"

A funny thing always seems to happen in a question-based conversation. Showing interest in other people, by asking questions, invites them to share more openly, and they generally share more accurately as well. Asking questions also causes the questioner (you) to become a better listener, because you are actively participating in what is being communicated. Going into detective mode simply makes you more curious, which increases your level of interest in what the other person is saying. And, your interest in the other person tends to increase the value and relevance of the information being communicated. When this chain reaction occurs, the job of listening suddenly becomes easy and interesting as opposed to boring and arduous.

Reflective Listening

Reflective listening is another listening technique that works well when communicating with children, or with your spouse. I said earlier that the chief complaint families have when it comes to effective communication is the feeling that nobody cares, and that others don't recognize or acknowledge that what you are saying is valuable. In these scenarios, conversations rapidly turn into confrontations, and communications with your child or spouse quickly breakdown into point/counterpoint debates.

My first question is: Does what your children or spouse have to say really matter to you? Of course, the politically correct answer is, yes. But, are you sure? Does what other people have to offer in conversations matter enough for you to listen intently, or intentionally, for that matter? You might think, "Yes, I am a very good listener." Well, let's see.

One way to find out how good a listener you are is to take note of what happens immediately after the other person in a conversation (with you) ends their sentence. Do you pause for a moment to consider what they have said? Do you sometimes ask a question that shows you are truly interested in what they have shared? Or, do you change the subject? Perhaps you mismatch, by one-upping them with a story of your own, or offering a contradictory point of view.

An objective way to measure your level of interest in what someone else is sharing is to time yourself. After they finish a sentence, how long does it take for you to jump in and offer your own point of view? Oftentimes, the response is reflexive. Our egos make us so quick to want to jump in and present our own perspective regarding whatever topic is being discussed. I'm pretty sure we all do this to some degree. But, what does jumping into the conversation with your own perspective say about how much you value the other person's point of view? That's where reflective listening comes in.

Can we agree that in most conversations, there's generally enough give and take that you will have a chance to share your thoughts at some point? The other person will surely pause to take a breath, giving you a window of opportunity to talk. But there is a tradeoff. If you want others to listen to you whatever you want to say, then it is incumbent on you to listen carefully to them. How do you demonstrate to someone that you are indeed paying attention and value their input? One way is to reflect back to them what you heard. This is an active listening technique called reflective listening.

After a child shares their account of a problem that occurred at school, for example, the parent can show that they were intently listening by verbally reflecting back to the child the essence of the story. Don't just restate the words, however. The objective is to summarize key points in order to confirm that you understand the real meaning of what they are trying to communicate.

"If I understand what you just said," the parent may summarize, "you completed the assignment and turned it in to Mrs. Graham on time. And, because you got an A+, you don't have to take the exam on Friday. Is that right?" In addition to reflecting what I heard, I often ask a question or two to verify that my understanding of the situation is clear and accurate.

Sometimes, the additional depth of conversation causes me to discover that I have missed the point entirely. (Remember, I have two daughters.) As a result, my interpretation of what the other person said may be skewed or incorrect. When this occurs, my children especially are quick to put me back on course. That's good, because I wouldn't want to form an impression or judgment that is based on a miscommunication. When my perception of the facts is accurate, everybody benefits. The other person feels respected, what they wanted to share has been appropriately heard, and I now have enough information about the situation to respond intelligently.

One could argue that reflective listening is difficult and requires a lot of extra time. It is and it does, but what's harder and takes even more time is the investment required to repair a damaged or broken relationship within the family because people aren't able to communicate effectively. I would ague that reflective listening is a valuable investment because it helps prevent misunderstandings in a way that promotes mutual respect.

Ask Your Child for Advice

If you are in a curious mood, try asking your kids for their advice on how they might handle a certain situation. Once the shoe is on the other foot, you can demonstrate (to them) how to listen attentively when someone is giving advice. Soliciting a young person's opinion is one of the easiest and most impactful things a parent can do to raise a child's self-image. Who knows, you might even get some valuable perspective and input on sensitive topics that otherwise would have not been considered.

All you have to say is, "What advice would you offer someone like me in this situation?" Of course, there is more than one way for the question-based parent to ask for advice. You could say, "Son, what would you do if you were in my shoes?" Or, "Do you have an opinion on the best way to handle this?" The common thread between each of these requests is that the parent is willing to admit that he or she doesn't know everything. With kids, it's funny. The sooner you acknowledge that you don't have all the answers, the quicker the communications with your children will open up.

When we talked about discipline back in Chapter 5, I made the point I sometimes ask my kids for input on how they should be punished. After discussing my concerns with the offender, and it's clear that a reasonable consequence is appropriate for whatever happened, I often ask, "Can you help me think of a consequence that will ensure that we won't have to have this conversation again?"

Don't just ask for your child's input or opinions when they are in trouble, however. In fact, there's a reason I make a point of asking my children for advice. If you listen carefully to how they respond, they will pretty much tell you how much more parental intervention is needed (if any) to complete a task or accomplish a certain goal.

I have come to realize that when I give a young person the chance to demonstrate their capabilities, they end up surprising me much of the time. Sometimes, when I ask my fifteen year-old for her input, I am delighted when she responds with the maturity and insight of someone much older. Of course, that doesn't always happen, but those little glimpses of adulthood are worth their weight in gold. Put it this way, there is a good chance that one of your children will be looking after you someday when you're old and frail, so it is to your advantage to establish an open exchange of ideas early on, because these communication skills may very well help them now, and you later.

As an added bonus, when you do receive a kernel of wisdom from one of your children, ask them this question. "Is there anything else you would recommend that might be valuable?" Their next idea may be even better!

One last point on not being perfect. If you make a mistake, which you will, try asking your son or daughter to forgive you. *Are you kidding? I don't have to ask my child to forgive me!* That's right, you don't. However, if you feel this way, I encourage you to try it just once. If for some reason you fail, blame me for the fallout and you can feel justified that you were right...again. Something magical seems to happen when a parent who generally has the power in the relationship, is a big enough person to allow themselves to ask a child for forgiveness. The first thing you will experience is an instantaneous release of any pent up stress, anger, or frustration that either of you may be harboring. Those vibes will then quickly be replaced by feelings of goodwill and reconciliation.

As an added bonus, being asked for forgiveness is tremendously empowering for a child. "Wow," they think. "My dad is willing to admit his mistake and ask for my forgiveness. Cool!" The only question that remains is, do you want to be "cool" in the eyes of your children?

Pass it On

Are you a good listener already? You might be. But, are you a great listener? If you are indeed a great listener, the next question is: Are your children great listeners? Who knows, your family may be well ahead of the curve. I bet many of the parents reading this book would agree that there is still work to be done in this area. In either case, the ideas being introduced in this book can help tremendously if you are open to improving your interpersonal skills.

How exactly does a child in today's day and age learn the finer points of listening? Well, how did you learn to listen? Did an over-zealous Catholic nun rap you on the hand a few times for not paying attention? Did you end up digging ditches in the military because some drill sergeant in boot camp wanted to send a message to the rest of the platoon? Or, did you learn to listen like the rest of us, through your daily experiences of trial and error?

Bad habits are often passed on by parents to their children, from generation to generation. Using this logic, I assume that it must be possible to pass along good habits as well. Therefore, it is a fair question to ask: What are you doing to pass effective listening skills on to your children? How are you teaching them so they can avoid making some of the mistakes we made over the last thirty or forty years? There must be a way, don't you think?

By this point in the book you have either learned something new about communication or you haven't. Hopefully, you have. But, I want to take this opportunity to point out that every idea I wrote about in this book can easily be passed along to someone else, whether it be to a neighbor, friend, relative, spouse, or co-worker. Specific to this chapter on listening skills, I very much want to encourage you to share this information with your kids. This is not just a book about making parents more effective. It is also a resource that is full of ideas that parents can pass on to their children.

One of the most valuable ideas we parents can pass along to our children is the difference between active listening and passive listening. This includes investing the time to show your kids how to develop social skills using conversational techniques like global questions and reflective listening. Let them know the value of asking someone for their advice, and the benefits of having conversational objectives like being respectful, showing interest in other people, and gathering complete information before making judgments.

I encourage you to start by making sure that your kids listen to you. Of course, when you say things, there is some responsibility on your part to mean it. And, if you mean what you say, then it is incumbent on your child to listen with respect. What if one of your children doesn't listen, especially if they are being disrespectful? Frankly, creating a cooperative household may require some discipline to get your child's attention if you don't already have it. Some discipline may also be required on your part as well, to be sure that you do mean what you say and then follow through on your convictions. This might include cutting down on the number of commands you dish out on a daily basis, because you simply cannot let a child just refuse to listen to their parents.

Active listening is a great communication strategy, and one that should involve the entire family. Sharing these skills with your kids may just give them the boost in self-confidence they need to stand tall and proud in social situations, as opposed to wanting to slink away to the nearest corner of the room. As parents and life coaches, we at least owe our children the benefit of our experiential wisdom, because I can pretty much guarantee that they aren't going to learn any of these skills in the classroom.

Better Listening Means Better Decisions

There is a practical side to developing effective communication skills as well. Being question-based puts you in a better position not only to have more in-depth conversations, but also to elicit more accurate information, which will enable you to make better and more informed decisions.

I sometimes get frustrated with my girls because they tend to be creatures of habit. "Where do you want to go for dinner?" I might ask. There must be a thousand restaurants in Atlanta, but my kids only want to consider about five of them—the five chain restaurants they are already familiar with.

"What about Joe's Crab Shack?" I might suggest.

"No, thanks," one of them will say. "We don't like it there."

"How do you know? You've never even been there," I challenge.

"We just know," is normally what I get back.

Either we are raising a couple of clairvoyants who have some mystical connection with the culinary world, or our two daughters aren't very open to new ideas. It's probably the latter. See, they've already made a decision about Joe's without knowing anything about it.

The ability to gather and assimilate information before jumping to conclusions or making a decision is a life skill. You don't walk into a doctor's office and tell him that your stomach hurts, and expect him to write a prescription. He doesn't yet have enough information. Your stomach could be hurting for any number of different reasons. Frankly, your stomach may not be the problem at all. Doctors have been trained to fully understand the problem, in order to then make a proper diagnosis and recommendations. Asking questions and listening carefully to the responses, therefore, is part of the normal diagnostic process.

Suppose, then, that your son or daughter comes home crying after a brief visit to a friend's house. The initial sob story might make you want to stomp down to the neighbor's house with a raised fist. "Can you believe the nerve of that other kid!" you might presume. "How could the other parent be so ignorant?" It may be wise to take a deep breath before reacting, however, because there's usually more to every story. During most conflicts, each of the involved parties generally has their own version of what happened, and the truth often lies somewhere in between.

The first thing a parent should do in these situations is find out, "What happened?" Uncovering the total picture is better than reacting on impulse or just responding to your child's first report. After everyone calms down and you make sure your child is unhurt (other than their feelings, of course), the question-based parent goes into "active listening mode" to understand the full extent of what occurred.

For an active listener, more information is *always* better. How else can you know how best to proceed? Gaining a complete perspective isn't always as easy as it sounds, however. Even if you are a good listener, sometimes the other person is not very focused and they skip around, sending the conversation off on tangents. For example, next time you attend a dinner party, listen to how often one of your adult friends changes the subject during the course of a conversation, because they aren't really listening to what is being communicated.

Someone will say, "My Uncle Herb drove his brand new red BMW off the road last weekend into a ditch."

"My father almost bought me a red car when I was in college," another person interjects.

"Where did you go to college?" someone asks.

"The University of South Florida," is the response.

"My family used to vacation in South Florida when I was a kid!" someone else chimes in.

Pardon me for interrupting this stream of "unconsciousness," but doesn't anyone care about poor Uncle Herb? The man drove his car into a ditch. Within a few seconds, for some reason, the conversation has randomly transitioned from Herb wrecking his BMW all the way to spring break! These people aren't really listening. Instead, they are simply looking for an opportunity to associate with something that is being said in order to jump into the conversation. At a neighborhood gathering, this type of small talk might be fine. But, if mutual respect is going to be the foundation for a long term relationship with your spouse or children, random and superficial conversation isn't going to help you much.

The guy who cuts my hair (Bart the barber) is a world-class listener. He has been cutting my hair for many years, and like any good bartender, Bart understands that there is some obligation on the part of a barber to listen to a customer's off-color jokes, bizarre stories, and general lamentations about their day. Bart is also a terrific sympathetic grunter, as he offers encouragement to his customers with innocuous comments like, "Oh no," "Ah hah," "Um hum," "Jeepers", and "Holy Cow!" Needless to say, a trip to Bart's chair can be very therapeutic at the end of a long week. Why else would a full slate of nearly bald men schedule a haircut appointment every other Friday?

I also know from experience that Bart is a world class question asker. When a topic arises that really interests him, Bart switches gears and his passive grunts quickly turn into a series of inquisitive questions. Either way, "Bart the barber" knows how to make people feel that what they have to say is both important and valuable. In large part, making people feel good about themselves is how he makes a living. Bart's communication style causes me to wonder, what are we doing to show our children that what they say and share is important and valuable? It's a fair question, and one that probably deserves an answer, don't you think?

Listening attentively and being willing to proactively participate in conversations with your children is definitely important, but it's only half the battle. The other critical piece to this puzzle regarding effective communication is the topic of the *conversational dynamics,* which includes having the ability to cause other people to "want to" open up and share important information with you.

That's what we will talk about next in Chapter 9.

Chapter 9

Conversational Dynamics

"The types of questions you choose to ask your children, and how those questions are delivered, might be more important than what you could ever say."
—Thomas A. Freese

Becoming a question-based parent is a choice. It doesn't matter how you were raised, or how your mother and father were treated by their parents in the previous generation. Your relationship with your own children is unique and special, and it will largely be shaped by the choices you make with regard to how you interact with them.

Ironically, becoming question-based does not limit you to only asking questions. Have you noticed that this book, just like most normal conversations, is loaded with statements in addition to question marks? Being question-based refers more to a style of communication that is ultimately based on the way you choose to communicate and deal with people you care about.

Many of the conversational choices we face are fairly simple ones. For example, do you want to show interest in what other people (particularly your children) are trying to communicate? Do you want to know the whole story (the total picture) before forming an initial impression; or, before making a decision, issuing a punishment, or offering advice? Do you want your children to feel important and have the confidence that comes from feeling respected by their own parents? Would you want to know how you are doing as a parent? From a parent's perspective, the answers to all of these questions are fairly obvious. Perhaps the more important question is, how do your children feel?

Now there's an interesting concept! How a child *feels* about their parents or how they feel about themselves is very important, but how someone *feels* is not something that can be empirically measured. I can assure you, though, that how your children end up feeling will be directly impacted by their daily interactions with friends, teachers, siblings, and you, their parents. In many cases, we find that it's not the words that have the biggest impact, either. Instead, it's the way those words are being delivered (and interpreted) that ends up being either uplifting or disheartening.

We parents can only control half the conversation, however. You cannot control what someone else chooses to communicate nor can you control how they might respond to what you say. You can only control your side of the conversation. Everything else is up for interpretation. That's the challenge with interpersonal communication. What you actually meant to say isn't necessarily the same as how someone might interpret your comments, and vise-versa. Particularly when different personalities coexist under the same roof, these conversational dynamics become critical if you aspire to communicate more effectively within your family.

Is it wrong to be proactive and think about managing the relationships you have with your husband, wife, or children? I would never suggest that you should try to control other people. The fact is, you can't. Your family, friends, and colleagues all have minds of their own, and most people don't want to be controlled anyway. But, given that people are always forming their impressions based on things you say and do, it's not too much of a stretch to conclude that the choices we make in terms of how we communicate with other people, will have a direct impact on their perception of us.

So, let me ask, who's in control of the statements you make and the questions you ask? That's right, you are! Hence, by controlling your end of the conversation, you put yourself in a stronger position to manage the overall relationship.

Being a question-based parent is not about using force or manipulation tactics to accomplish your parental objectives. Rather, it's about becoming aware of the cause and effect relationship that exists between your intentions and other people's perceptions, and then using specific conversational devices and techniques to improve the quality and value of the interactions you have with your children. As I said before, you may be able to force a child to do certain things when they are very young, but you will not be able to force them to respect you as they mature into young adults.

Kids Need to Think for Themselves

Wouldn't you agree that part of our responsibility as parents is to nurture children toward their own independence? Well, in large part, that means helping them learn how to think for themselves.

It's always sweet to see a new mother coddling a newborn baby. Moms and dads have to do virtually everything for newborns because they simply cannot do for themselves. But, with any luck, your babies will at some point begin to flap their wings, and over time, they will hopefully learn to fly on their own before completely venturing out of the nest.

Some kids can thrive in almost any environment, especially if they are naturally independent. Other children will develop a lasting dependence on their mothers and fathers who either aren't willing to let go or don't see the value in teaching a child to fend for themselves. Granted, the process of letting go should be gradual. You don't just turn a kid loose and hope that they make it on their own when they are four or five. But, it has always been my belief that independence is a learned behavior that can only be achieved if you are willing to give your child an opportunity to experience success on their own, and also, some of the difficult lessons that can only be learned from the school of hard knocks.

What can you do to help your children learn to think for themselves? Well, as a mentor, coach, counselor, and parent (who presumably will play an advisory role throughout much of their development), you basically have two options with regard to the guidance you provide. You can either communicate with your kids by making statements, or by asking questions.

To a large extent, teaching kids to think for themselves is becoming a lost art. I suppose it has something to do with the pace of life and the fact that it's just faster to tell a young person what they need to do rather than letting them figure something out for themselves. Just listen to your neighbors, friends, or extended family members who have children. Doesn't it always seem like there is so much to be accomplished, but so little time? As a result, we tend to live in the world of tell, tell, tell.

"Johnny, you need to hurry up and get ready," mom yells from another room.

"And, don't forget to feed the dog," dad chimes in.

"Samantha, be sure to pick out a clean shirt," mother calls out.

"Matthew, you also need to empty the trash before we leave," father says, not wanting to miss a turn.

In this type of environment, the list of commands could go on and on:

> *"Everybody put on your coats. We're have to go!"*
> *"You need hats and gloves."*
> *"It's time to get in the car."*
> *"Remember to bring your backpack."*
> *"Close the back door!"*
> *"Buckle your seatbelts."*
> *"Please, don't everyone talk at once."*
> *"Leave your sister alone!"*

Here's the funny part. Parents who constantly dictate to their children often issue the same commands day after day. On Monday, the parent tells their child to feed the dog. At almost the exact moment on Tuesday morning, the same parent once again issues the "feed the dog" instruction. Wednesday, Thursday, and Friday, the parent nags their child with the usual series of "do this" or "do that" commands. Come on now. Are your kids really so incapable that they need to be told over and over when and how to complete every task? If your style of communication is causing them to develop a dependence on you, in order to know what to do and when to do it, then you might be undermining your own efforts by not teaching your children how to think for themselves.

Most kids I know are actually pretty smart. They're also fairly observant. Hence, if you find yourself saying the same things over and over, it's probably time to step back and make a few changes in your own approach. Rather than just blaming the child for not being attentive or responsible, it's more likely that the parent is the one who needs to make some adjustments—in this case, to help the child develop a sense of personal accountability and independence.

Some behaviors are extremely difficult to change. As a result, they require a huge personal commitment in time and energy, which can sometimes make new ideas quite painful to implement. Other adjustments are easy. Good news, this change is an easy one to make.

The simplest way to foster independence and create autonomy in your children is to use questions to subtly reveal the status of an undone task, rather than just issuing direct commands. Look at the contrast below as I replay the statements from before, only this time, from the question-based parent's point of view.

> *"Johnny, how long before you are completely ready?"*
> *"Did you remember to feed the dog?"*
> *"Samantha, honey, do you have a clean shirt to wear?"*
> *"Matthew, when are you planning to empty the trash?"*
> *"Does everyone have a coat?"*
> *"How about hats and gloves?"*
> *"Does everyone have their homework?"*
> *"Could someone please close the back door?"*

You may be wondering what the difference is between saying, *"Everybody put on your coats,"* and asking, *"Does everyone have a coat?"* On the surface, one could argue that the statement-based parent and a question-based parent are essentially addressing the same issue. That may be true, but the conversational dynamics are such that the question-based approach conveys the message in very different terms. Consider this: Do you really want to spend eighteen years giving your children step-by-step instructions for every-thing they *need* to do? The statement-based philosophy implies that commands are necessary because your kids either are not smart enough, aware enough, or capable enough to think for themselves. Are you sure you want to communicate those messages to your children? I don't.

It is not by accident that I would rather use a question to ask, *"Does everyone have a coat?"* When asking a question, most kids love to answer correctly. It makes them feel smart and grown up. You watch, if your child already has their coat on, they will pipe right up and say, "Got it!" If you happen to have a straggler in the family, a child who always seems to be a half step behind the rest of the gang, asking the question gives them a chance to think, "Oh yeah, I'd better get my coat." In that case, they can be correct, too.

The pure act of asking for a child's input is empowering for them. We have already talked about this a couple times. For example, it would be very unusual for me to *tell* one of our kids "not to forget" their homework. Instead, I would much rather ask if they "remembered" it. We are not just talking about semantics here. The psychology of asking questions is very different from that of issuing commands. If you think about it, children don't like being hounded any more than you or I. Do this! Do that! Now, do this! How would that make you feel if your supervisor at work did that to you? Asking for a response, on the other hand, presumes a certain amount of intellect and capability, where just telling a child to do this or do that assumes the opposite-a level of incompetence.

Furthermore, issuing a bunch of orders doesn't provide parents with any feedback or information. Seriously, wouldn't you want to first know if the dog has already been fed *before* you bark that order in your child's direction?

Similarly, wouldn't you want know if your kids have already thought to buckle their seatbelts, rather than saying it every time you get in the car? It really comes down to this: given the choice, would you want your children to try and impress you by doing things the right way before you even have a chance to correct them? If so, then you will probably be very successful using question-based techniques.

One of my personal objectives within our family is to foster a certain team spirit, where each of our daughters is able to handle age-appropriate responsibilities independent of parental supervision. I believe you should be able to count on an eight-year-old child to brush her own teeth everyday without being told. Even before that, kids can learn to wash their hands before meals, and at some point, they should be able to complete their homework on time, without being hounded. Don't worry, there will be plenty of times when your independent little minions will need to be reminded, sometimes for the hundred and fiftieth time. In those cases, using questions gives you (the parent) an opportunity to offer gentle reminders for tasks like feeding the dog, brushing teeth, or emptying the trash. "Have you already brushed your teeth?" is a good way to help a child remember without having to indict them for being forgetful or irresponsible.

Asking questions also provides you with an opportunity to explore a situation further if there seems to be a recurring problem. If Johnny, for example, seems to always be running late, the parent once again has two choices—either to issue more (and more severe) commands, or to ask some well-placed questions to try and understand the root cause of the problem. If my child was always running late, I might try to preempt the situation one morning, long before it came time to rush out the door, perhaps by asking a few proactive questions like:

> *"Do you think you will be ready on time today?"*
> *"What can we do to avoid a last minute rush?"*
> *"Is there anything I can do to make sure we aren't late?"*

This style of communication may require some patience on your part, which in the hustle and bustle of today's hectic pace, isn't always easy to accommodate. But, if you invest the time and energy to communicate more effectively with little Johnny, you may discover that he is distracted for some reason, or he may be organizationally challenged. If either is true, then just issuing orders to "hurry up" won't address the actual problem. Let me put it their way: addressing the root cause of a problem once is exponentially easier and way more efficient than fussing at your kids repeatedly for the same request.

Getting it Right Next Time

Critics of this approach could argue that a question-based parent gives their children too much latitude by asking instead of telling. Ironically, that's the beauty of opting for a question-based approach. The proficiency and effectiveness of your communications can increase without compromising your parental authority.

If everyone in the family is running late one morning, for example, there may not be time for an in-depth strategy session with your kids. That's true. But, I would counter that there is always time to ask a quick question like, "How long before you are ready to walk out the door?" before you just start harping on your children to hurry up. Moreover, I would assert that asking the right questions, instead of relying solely on parental commands, actually speeds up the process. Why? Because someone who *wants to* hurry will almost always outperform someone who feels that they are being harassed or pressured. That person silently wishes the parent would "get off my case." It's also worth noting that these silent wishes will only remain silent until a child becomes tall enough to look you in the eye.

When a child does forget to do something as simple as brushing their teeth, it's easy for one or the other parent to blast them for being absent-minded or forgetful. Hold onto your hats, however. We made the point earlier in the book that good training is a forward-looking proposition. Fussing at a child for what they didn't do correctly doesn't guarantee that things will be any different in the future. That's another reason I would much rather use questions. If my child forgets to bring their homework home from school two days in a row, for example, it would be easy for me to ask, "Is something causing you to forget your homework, or would you call this an accidental oversight?" Let them answer. If there is an issue brewing, I would like to know about it. If your child has simply made an honest mistake, rather than verbally dressing them down, you could just as easily ask, "After today, do you think you will be able to write down your assignments and remember to bring your work home from school?" If they agree, we now have a binding verbal contract.

Once again, I don't use rhetorical questions to shame my children, and you shouldn't either. For example, you will never see me wag a finger in my child's face asking, "What do you have to say for yourself?" Likewise, there's no point in asking cliché questions like, "Do you think money just grows on trees?" If you really want to know your child's thoughts, then you have to make it okay for them to *want to* share that information. In fact, I would be more likely to thank our kids for sharing the whole story, because it gives me an opportunity to work through any concerns or issues that come to light.

While I was in the midst of writing this book, my own father made an interesting point. He said that if a child reaches their hand up toward a hot stove, you may not have time to be question-based—you don't want kids to learn about the dangers of boiling water by making an unexpected trip to the emergency room. He's right. In dangerous situations, there usually isn't time to be thoughtful or strategic. In those cases, you may have to act first and talk later. Fortunately for most of us, these emergency situations represent a very small portion of the daily interactions we have with our children.

But, if your child does happen to put themselves in a dangerous situation, wouldn't you want to talk with them about it afterwards? If you are like me, you would want to have what the military calls a debriefing. You would you want them to understand that you were very concerned about their safety. I assume you would also want to convey a sense of seriousness in order to prevent similar risks or accidents from happening in the future.

And, when you talked with your child after the incident, what exactly would you say to them? Well, you once again have a choice, either to use a bunch of statements or ask a few insightful questions. Not surprisingly, I choose to be question-based. In fact, I might start by asking, "Do you understand why I pulled your hand away from the hot stove?" Then, I would listen for the answer. In the case of a dangerous situation, I would *absolutely* want to know what my child was thinking. Were they being careless, funny, or was the child unaware that the stove was hot? Finding out what really happened is the only way a parent can know whether the child needs additional guidance or a consequence for demonstrating poor judgment. By the way, it doesn't make sense to punish a child who didn't know better or for some reason wasn't aware of the danger. My goal in these conversations is very simple—to make sure my child has a clear appreciation for why I am concerned, and to prevent similar incidents from happening again in the future.

What's the alternative? I suppose you could just fuss at your child until you bring them to tears, which might sound something like, "Lindsay, you know better than to reach your hand up to a hot stove. You could burn your hand or start a fire! Don't you let me catch you doing something like...*wah, wa, wah, wa, wah...*" By, the second punctuation mark, the child probably is no longer listening, and more likely it's your authority that has "gone up in smoke."

Someone once said to me, "Tom, you can't hold this type of thoughtful conversation with a two year-old." Good point! *The Question Based Parent* is a communication strategy, and it only works when you are dealing with someone who can actually communicate. But, I encourage you not to underestimate the power of a question-based approach, even with a toddler. It is still much easier to engage a preschooler with questions than to continually barrage them with commands.

Advanced Questioning Strategies

We talked about the importance of asking good questions and we have also talked about the importance of listening to the child's response. But, still, just because we parents want to ask a bunch of questions, doesn't necessarily mean our kids will open up and share their innermost thoughts and feelings. How do you cause a child to *want to* respond openly to your questions?

With interpersonal communication, there is definitely some element of chemistry (or dynamics) that causes people to either bond together or drift apart. I can tell you from raising two children myself that certain people make them feel relatively comfortable, while others make them very nervous. That's probably consistent with what we experience as adults. Some people you meet are easy to converse with and others, for whatever reason, cause us to be much more cautious and reserved. I make the point because some things in life you can't control, like human chemistry. Different strokes for different folks, as they say.

However, there are some very specific communication techniques we can use to inspire the bonding process during a conversation, thus causing our children to feel more comfortable and respond more openly to the questions we ask. These techniques have more to do with *how* you ask the question, than the actual substance of the question itself.

We all know that it's possible to phrase questions harshly. And, for some strange reason, we are sometimes harshest toward the people we love the most—our children. When you ask a question harshly, what do you suppose happens? The person you posed the question to often clams up. Their defensive shields go on full alert and you get minimal responses, if they even respond at all.

Perhaps we should explore the opposite approach— asking questions in a way that actually defuses tension, makes people feel more comfortable, and generates a much more thoughtful response. If that sounds good, let me introduce several advanced questioning techniques that I have been teaching (salespeople) for the last ten years that might help you immensely when interacting with your children.

Soften Your Questions With Permission

The first sales course I ever attended was the old Xerox sales school. One of the big things they taught in this course was the importance of asking open-ended questions. The thought was, if you want to *open* a dialogue, then you need to ask lots of open-ended questions. Like a good soldier, I went back to my sales territory and started asking open-ended questions; like, "Mr. Customer, what are your goals and objectives for the next five years?", or "Ms. Customer, what's the biggest issue you currently face?"

I was eager to be successful, but things were not going as well as I expected. Even though I was taught that open-ended questions were the best way to open a dialogue, I quickly discovered that lots of prospects weren't necessarily open or willing to sharing information with me.

Years later, in Question Based Selling, we now teach the opposite strategy. I agree that open-ended questions can be valuable conversational tools, but only if the other person *wants* to share information with you. Asking probative questions can also put people on the defensive, as asking for too much, too soon usually feels quite invasive. While it sounded logical at first, it turns out that asking open-ended questions is not always the best way to open a dialogue.

Fortunately, I happened across another useful kernel of wisdom that has been around for centuries. Have you ever heard the saying, *sometimes you must learn to walk, before you run*? One way to put this logic into practice in your daily conversations is to ask permission first, before just beating someone over the head with your questions.

For example, I might say to one of my daughters, *"Do you mind if I ask about your plans for this weekend?"* Or, I could have just as easily said, *"Can I ask you a couple specifics about the dance on Saturday night?"* You might even choose to phrase it like this: *"Would it be okay if I inquired about..."*

Technically, the parent in these examples is asking permission "to ask" about a certain topic. Critics of this approach could argue that as a parent, you don't have to seek a child's permission to ask them questions. That may be true. I am not saying that parents are *required* to seek a child's permission. I am merely suggesting that softening your questions increases the likelihood that you will get a more thoughtful and accurate response.

To master this technique, you must understand the psychology behind asking permission to ask questions. For example, when I say to one of my girls, *"Can I ask you a couple specifics about the dance on Saturday?"* they usually respond by saying, "Sure, go ahead." The dynamics of the conversation have suddenly changed. Instead of me feeling like the Spanish inquisition, I have now been invited to ask about the topic at hand. This is significant because once someone invites you to ask them questions, you tend to have a more productive dialogue with a more accurate exchange of information. This greatly reduces my risk of sounding nosy and their tendency to be standoffish.

Do I always seek permission before asking a question? Frankly, I don't "always" do anything. But, particularly when it's clear that the conversation is entering a sensitive area, it's much easier to invest a few seconds to soften your approach as a sign of mutual respect, than to just rely on force or obligation.

Whenever I talk to audiences about this technique, this question always finds a way to come up. "How do you handle a belligerent child who simply refuses to answer?" For example, what if you say, *"Do you mind if I ask about your plans for the weekend?"*, and the child gives you a smart-mouthed retort (essentially transforming your token of respect into what they might perceive as a sign of weakness)? First of all, I would tell the question-based parent not to worry. If this ever happened in the Freese house, I would be shocked to the point where the paramedics would have to revive me with paddles. I suppose that's because we have already established a pattern of mutual respect for how we communicate with each other. It's one thing if your child is being playful or even sarcastic, but sheer belligerence is unacceptable. In my household, that would signal that it was time to have a heart-to-heart about the first three points outlined in the *Freese Family Rules* from Chapter 2.

Listen for the Question Behind the Question

When a child asks about something that we think we know the answer to, parents sometimes have a bad habit of jumping in and responding too quickly. After all, *as the authority figure, we must heed the responsibility to do whatever is in the best interest of ...yada, yada, yada.*

Earlier, we talked about how important it is to listen carefully to your children. Everyone wants to be heard! And, when your child asks a question, it's equally important to truly understand what they are *really* asking, and why. Too often, parents respond to what we presume is being asked, only to discover later that some other motivation was actually driving the question.

Perhaps you've heard the story about the father who was relaxing in a backyard hammock when his ten year-old walked up and asked, "Daddy, what is sex?" Fumbling for a response, the father looked deeply into the innocent eyes of his young son and decided it was time to explain the facts of life. Although he had always hoped this would be the mother's responsibility, the dad hoisted the young lad up into the hammock and began to explain the differences between boys and girls. The lecture culminated with a detailed explanation about sex and where babies come from.

The son listened intently as his father concluded his eloquent speech. "Uh, thanks, dad," the boy said as he hopped down from the hammock.

Curious, the father turned to him and asked, "What made you want to know about sex?"

"Gym class," he replied. "On the parent permission slip, there's a box that reads…Sex: M or F?"

The father in this story answered the question that was asked, which was, "What is sex?" And he did a fine job explaining the birds and the bees. What he didn't do, however, was take the time to understand why the question was being asked. In your daily conversations, very few questions are so well articulated that they cannot be further explored or clarified to gain more insight into what the person is really wanting to know, and why.

Laura and I faced a similar circumstance years ago, back when our oldest daughter was in kindergarten. One evening at the dinner table, Sarah announced that some of the kids on the bus were using the "S-word." Then, she asked, "What should I do if they say it again?"

Upon hearing this, the little hairs on the back of my wife's neck stood straight up. She's no prude, but come on…does a five-year old really need to be exposed to the "S-word" while riding the school bus? Instantly, her mothering instincts kicked in and Laura readied herself to deal with the issue. I jumped in and asked, "Excuse me, Sarah, but what exactly was the S-word they used?"

"Stupid," Sarah whispered.

Whew! Laura and I both breathed a sigh of relief. I can tell you this—it's a lot easier to offer advice about how to handle something as simple as the "S-word" once you know exactly which S-word you are talking about.

Neutralize Your Questions to Solicit Accurate Feedback

If you listen carefully to the type of questions people ask, you will find that most people have a tendency to ask hopeful questions. Nobody likes to hear bad news. As a result, we tend to ask questions with a certain positive hopeful tone. Hopeful questions are delivered in a way that says, "This is going to be good news, right?" For example, child gets home from school and the parent asks, "Did you score well on your science quiz today?"

What answer do you suppose this parent wants to hear? Of course, every parent wants to hear that their child earned a good grade, don't you think? What parent wouldn't? The question is, do you think your kids are aware that you are hoping to hear good news? If your children are old enough to get a report card, then I can pretty much guarantee they understand that you have high aspirations for them. But, what if your child did not score well on his or her science quiz? To the person being asked, it becomes much more difficult to honestly respond when the truth isn't necessarily what the parent would want to hear.

Let me give you a different example to further the point. Suppose you got invited to a friend's house for dinner. After serving a five-course meal, your friend Linda, who was obviously bursting with pride having cooked a fancy meal, asks, "How was your dinner?" Let's suppose in this example that it was the worst food you ever put in your mouth. Would you tell her? Of course, you wouldn't tell her it was terrible. Why not? Because in our culture, it is easier to sidestep the truth (or even tell a little fib) than it is to share information that the other person obviously would *not* want to hear.

What if a child returns home from a swim meet, and an enthusiastic parent asks a hopeful question like, "Did you win your race today?" If the child actually won a ribbon for first place, everyone whoo-woos and celebrates. Hooray! But, what if your child didn't win? It's possible that this level of hopefulness can make a young person feel like they're not living up to a parent's expectations. Some parents try to make it okay with supportive comments like, "You'll get 'em next time." Other parents who don't realize the impact of their words, rather than being supportive, react negatively when their child shares bad news. Like when reporting a poor grade, some parents go berserk. Do you think this type of reaction will cause the child to share more openly in the future?

Speaking of grades, have you ever thought about how difficult it must be for a young person to come to their parents and admit that they are having a problem in school? You and I probably weren't that forthright when we were kids. Imagine the scene from the child's point of view. They see a parent eagerly awaiting good news after asking a hope-filled question like, "Did you get a good score on the science quiz today?" If a problem is brewing, just like you with your friend Linda, it is easier (for a child) to sidestep the truth or even tell a little fib than to share information that a hopeful parent wouldn't neces-sarily welcome.

I am not suggesting that you shouldn't ask your child about their grades, or about how they fared at a recent sporting event. But, you may want to pay attention to the conversational dynamics that are in play when you deliver these questions. Ultimately, you want the truth, the whole truth, and nothing but the truth, right? If some problem is lurking, you *do* want to know about it. And, if there is good news to report, you want to know about that, too. The challenge is, kids are naturally reluctant to share bad news with their parents, and parents aren't particularly good at asking for it.

To solicit more accurate information, I encourage you to neutralize the disposition of your questions. What does this mean? Well, every question you ask has a certain disposi-tion, or tone—either positive, negative, or neutral. Positive questions are very common in everyday communication, mostly because they are easy to ask. Think about it. When you see one of your neighbors in the morning, you might say, "Hello, Harry. How's life treating you these days?" At that point, you are just being cordial and friendly. But just being cordial and friendly doesn't always cause people to share their true thoughts, feelings, and concerns. Even if your neighbor Harry was having a terrible week, there's a good chance he would still respond by saying, "Fine, fine. How's everything with you?"

There's nothing wrong with asking hopeful questions. We are cordial and friendly to people on a regular basis. But, if you begin to think in terms of managing healthy long-term relationships with your children, the quality and depth of your communications needs to go far beyond just being friendly.

If you want people to open up and share more accurate information with you, then try neutralizing the disposition of your questions. In layman's terms, simply remove the hopeful tone. The practical application of this technique is actually quite easy. Just ask something like, "Was the science quiz easy, or harder than you expected?" Or, "How did everyone fare at the sleepover last night?" Notice that the parent in these examples isn't asking if the child received a "good" grade, or if the sleep over went "well." These questions are phrased in a completely neutral tone. Instead of lacing the question with a built-in expectation that hopes for any certain answer, the parent in these examples just wants to know the *real* answer.

With most people, it is assumed that good news is always welcome. Therefore, one of the secrets to asking effective questions is to invite the other person to open up and share any problems, issues, or concerns they might otherwise have. Do parents want to be on the receiving end of bad news? I don't. But, if there is a problem or issue brewing that involves my child, I definitely want her to feel like she can share it with me.

The easiest way to neutralize a question is to add four letters, O-R-N-O. "Would next Tuesday be a good day to meet with your guidance counselor at school, *or no*?" You can adapt this to your own personal style just by tweaking the verbiage. For example, "Would next Tuesday be a good opportunity to meet with your teachers, or do you need more time to prepare?"

A question-based parent is not afraid of hearing bad news, and they don't ask questions with a positive tone in hopes of generating a more favorable response. Instead, they would much rather become aware of any issues and then deal with them in a forthright manner, as opposed to beating around the bush with a less direct approach.

Preface Your Questions with Humbling Disclaimers

A parent who wishes to govern by force may not want to ask *any* questions, holding on to the belief that they can just give orders and expect their children to comply, or else. Likewise, a parent who doesn't really care about the opinions, emotional state, or self-confidence of their kids probably won't be interested enough to inquire as to what their children are really thinking or feeling. As for me, I would much rather strive to build relationships within my family that are based on strong two-way communication, than depend on whatever temporary authority I may have as a parent.

Making the shift from statement-based commands to a question-based philosophy is the obvious first step. The next order of business is to realize that when asking questions, some questions are softer and less forceful than others. Once again, the dynamics of the conversation is just as important as the substance.

What makes a question forceful? Probably the best way to answer this is to say that forceful questions generally rely on having authority or power over someone. As a result, a person who uses their position of authority to put others on the defensive generally has trouble getting them to open up. Moreover, if you make someone uncomfortable to the point where they choose not to share at all, then it doesn't matter what questions you ask.

For parents, if we are doing something that causes our children to be less forthright, then our actions may be in direct conflict with the goal of fostering open communication. The opposite of forcefulness is humility, which turns out to be a very attractive human quality. To me, being respectful and humble at the same time is a winning combination. And, you don't have to forfeit your authority to be humble toward your children.

Back in Chapter 4, we talked about the concept of delivering bad news gracefully. You might remember, that's when we first introduced the idea of humbling disclaimers. A humbling disclaimer is a question-based communication technique that purposefully injects a small dose of humility into the inquiry in order to lower the other person's natural defense mechanisms. Humbling disclaimers are very effective conversational devices that can be used when interacting with your children, spouse, friends, coworkers, or even your customers in a business setting. In QBS, we use humbling disclaimers to defuse customer skepticism. This same technique is a very effective way for parents to defuse much of the pressure or anxiety a child might otherwise feel from the questions you might want to pose. Essentially, humbling disclaimers are another way to neutralize your questions in order to cause children to share more openly and more accurately.

Let me give you give you some real life examples of humbling disclaimers in action:

Parent: *"I realize that it's a sensitive subject, but do you mind if I ask… how have things been going since you and your best friend had that big argument?"*

"I don't want to be forceful, but I need to ask…what are your plans for straightening your room this weekend?"

"At the risk of asking a tacky question, were you the last person in the bathroom?"

"I don't want to step out of bounds, but do you mind if I ask...how much make-up is reasonable for a girl your age?"

Critics of this technique could argue that you are giving the child an *out*. God forbid that a parent would relinquish their authority and give a child the option not to answer. But, that's the beauty of this technique. Using force or pressure to cause children (or adults) to respond is one of the quickest ways to actually cause them to clam up and not share with you. Fortunately, the opposite is also true. To appreciate the significance of this technique, please allow me to make the following observation about human nature. If you are respectful of the other person's right *not* to share with you, it is amazing how much more information you will receive. In fact, in an ironic twist, humbling disclaimers actually make it easier to be more forthright in your conversations, enabling you to softly and caringly address sensitive topics that might otherwise feel very uncomfortable to your children.

The use of humbling disclaimers, again, does require some presumption that a child is old enough to communicate. Humbling disclaimers have little impact and infants or toddlers, for example. But, don't think this technique is only reserved for teenagers and above. By the time kids reach the age of five or six, they can definitely sense the tone of your questions, and you might be surprised about how easy it is to cause an otherwise guarded child to suddenly open up.

Silence is a Parent's Best Friend

Parents must always remember that after delivering whatever questions you choose to ask, there is some responsibility on your part to give your kids an opportunity to respond. This includes allowing them enough time to organize and present their thoughts, which generally takes longer than it does for your adult colleagues during the course of a normal work day.

That being the case, a period of uncomfortable silence often follows a question that get posed by a parent to their children. This is very common and quite natural. Too often, parents cave in to this silence and feel that they must fill the void with words. That's a mistake. If you have asked a legitimate question, then you must show some confidence in your child's ability to provide a legitimate response. Be advised that this window of silence, though short, is equally uncomfortable for both parties. Even if there is a significant pause after your questions, once a child figures out you are patient enough to give them an opportunity to respond, they generally will. To those parents who are habitual about jumping in and filling the silence, your children might surprise you if you just give them a chance.

Basically, there are two dynamics that cause kids to share information with adults. One is obligation. If a parent, teacher, neighbor, pastor, or some other authority figure in your child's life asks them a direct question, there is some obligation on your son or daughter's part to respond. Predictably, these obligatory questions tend to be accompanied by quite a bit of pressure, which can cause even the most secure children to stiffen up. Fortunately for us, force is not the only way to compel a child to respond to questions. It's not even the best way. The other dynamic that causes children to respond openly with adults is feeling comfortable. When kids are comfortable with you and your conversational style, they will want to open up and share more information about their thoughts, feelings, and concerns. This is an important distinction. A child who *wants to* share is significantly more forthcoming and thoughtful with their responses than the same child who is responding simply because they have to.

Chapter 10

How to Become a Question Based Parent

"You are where you are today because you stand on somebody's shoulders. And wherever you are heading, you cannot get there by yourself. If you stand on the shoulders of others, you have a reciprocal responsibility to live your life so that others may stand on your shoulders. It's the quid pro quo of life. We exist temporarily through what we take, but we live forever through what we give."

—Vernon Jordan

Have you thought about what kind of parents you want your children to be when they grow up and have kids of their own? Let me ask the question a different way. Have you ever thought about what kind of parents you want your future grandchildren to have? Would you want your grandchildren to be communicated with in a respectful and loving manner, or would you want them to be on the receiving end of a continuous stream of dictatorial commands? Do you want your future grandchildren to understand the difference between earning a privilege and being given a consequence? Would you want them to feel secure and confident enough to easily engage in comfortable and productive dialogue with their parents (currently your own children)?

My overall goal as a parent is to simply raise our two daughters in a way that prepares them to become productive, responsible, caring, self-reliant adults. Once we realize, however, that how we choose to parent our children will leave a lasting impression that will likely influence how they deal with subsequent generations, our awesome responsibility takes on a multitude of longer-term implications.

As a member of the NSDAR (National Society, Daughters of the American Revolution), my wife has the ability to track her family genealogy back 200+ years. I, on the other hand, know very little about my ancestry prior to my grandparents. The contrast of my limited knowledge of my own heritage versus my wife's confirms for me the importance of my own legacy. We are only here for an instant in time. And the legacy that is being created on a daily basis will outlive all of us by many generations. Though the actual impression I end up leaving on my children and the lasting impact of our decisions is largely undetermined at this point, I am keenly aware that my role as a parent is still a work in progress. I mean, it's almost spooky how quickly time passes and how little we realize about the ramifications our current actions will have on events down the road.

Most people's approach to parenting is heavily influenced by how they were parented when they were kids. Whether you desire to mirror those things you feel your parents did well or you want to compensate for mistakes you feel they made along the way, there is no question that your current parenting style has been strongly impacted and shaped by how you were raised. With so much at stake, however, it's no longer enough to rely solely on your own personal upbringing or experience for guidance.

This brings up an interesting philosophical question. Should someone who was treated harshly by one or both parents when they were young, go totally in the opposite direction and be extra lenient with their own children as a result? On the other hand, should a person who was raised without boundaries revert to being overly strict with their children, to hopefully prevent them from straying down a similarly over-indulgent path?

There are so many different variables and nuances that affect how you deal with children that it is simply *not* possible to write an all-encompassing book on the art of parenting. The good news is, you don't really have to know all the answers to be an effective parent. In fact, it is this author's opinion that your effectiveness has more to do with the questions you ask your children, and the questions you cause your kids to ask themselves, as opposed to any declarations you may have already made or will make in the future.

If you agree that your legacy as a parent ultimately rests upon the quality of your daily interactions with your children, then perhaps it's time to pay attention and make a decision as to whether or not you are ready to become a question-based parent. For me, this has been an easy choice. Years from now, I would like to be known as the best father my kids could have had. This doesn't necessarily translate into being their best friend or giving in to their every request. I realize that I am *not* the most popular person in the household when one of my kids needs to be reeled back in for an attitude adjustment. My kids don't like to be disciplined any more than your children. But, it's the longer-term objective that takes precedent in our house, as opposed to satisfying the whim of the moment, whether it be mine or theirs.

Children are very smart, and they are watching us all the time, learning not only how to act as a child, but also absorbing information that will shape their values and forever influence how they treat their friends and family, as well as their own children ten, twenty, or thirty years from now. As for me, I can tell you right now what kind of grandchildren I look forward to having. I hope they end up being impressive young people, being raised by impressive parents who continue to build on a well-established legacy of open communication, mutual respect, and unconditional love. I also hope that future generations will look back and see this book as a collection of truths that will be just as relevant and applicable a hundred years from now as they are today. That alone would be an impressive and remarkable accomplishment. Let's call everything else a bonus.

Change is Often Difficult

It's easy to agree with the overriding philosophies presented in this book. Who wouldn't want to raise their children to be impressive individuals, grounded by a value system that is based on love and mutual respect? What's difficult is being committed to the actual implementation of these ideas. Implementation requires change and change is sometimes difficult, especially when the habitual grooves that have been worn into our psyche over time are deeply engrained.

People are naturally averse to change, anyway. Most of us are set in our ways, myself included. We do things in a certain way because we have always done them that way, and it feels right to us. Similarly, we tend to avoid things that are unfamiliar, often because we aren't as comfortable doing unfamiliar things. Some of this is just a function of human nature—people naturally gravitate to whatever is most familiar, which by definition, is whatever you did last week. Consequently, you may be most comfortable with raising your kids in the way you were raised by your own parents, because that's what is most familiar in terms of the parenting style you obviously know best.

Therefore, it's decision time. The well-being of our children is too important to base your parenting style on whatever happens to be most familiar. In fact, what may have worked for previous generations may not even apply today, given the rapidly changing social and economic environment to which our kids are now being exposed.

The sheer volume of material presented in this book is another challenge. Too many ideas (even good ones) can be overwhelming and cause a sincere implementation efforts to seem random or scattered. Therefore, I would like to take this opportunity to help you organize the different strategies presented in *The Question Based Parent* into five simple, straightforward, and salient points. Basically, to become a question-based parent, you need to have a recipe for implementation—one that can be tested, followed, and then reinforced. To be successful, the parent must clearly understand the cause and effect relationship between the tactics proposed and the desired result.

During live seminars, I often make the point that there is an interesting parallel between raising kids and baking cakes. Baking a cake is easy if you have a good recipe. Just carefully follow the instructions and you will end up with a perfect cake every time. Of course, the opposite is true. If the recipe you rely on is flawed, you might end up with a mess.

The strategic nature of the question-based parent is such that your family's cohesiveness will largely be influenced by the effectiveness of your parenting strategy. Just like baking a cake, if the choices you make while raising children are both sound and consistent, the principles of cause and effect would suggest that your efforts will produce desirable results. That's sounds a bit odd, doesn't it—to think of raising impressive children in terms of achieving a desirable result? Nonetheless, it's true. The opposite can also be true, where an inconsistent or flawed strategy for dealing with children can just as easily create a big mess, both in the short-term and down the road.

As we review, you may want to go back and reread previous chapters to pick up additional details, but I can tell you right now if you are able to master each of the following five ingredients, the manner in which you interact with your kids will change forever. More importantly, successfully implementing a question-based approach will positively change the way your children choose to interact with you.

Ingredient #1: Telling is Not Selling

Parental authority is like a fine kitchen knife. Used properly, it can be a useful and productive tool. But, once a parent begins to abuse their authority or take it for granted, their ability to exercise power quickly becomes a double-edged blade that unfortunately cuts both ways. Those who rely solely on parental authority may be able to force their kids to do things on command for a while, but you will not be able to *force* them to respect you as they get older.

Younger children don't have much choice. They must yield to their parent's authority as they are totally dependent on the parent for food, shelter, clothing, and pretty much everything else. But, I can tell you with certainty that the day is coming when your children are going to mature to the point where they will pull away from parental authority and start calling their own shots. At that time, whatever power you may have held over them will begin to wane. Some kids reach the point where they simply decide not to follow parental requests because they are fed up with being on the receiving end of a long list of instructions. A rebellious child may even choose to go the other direction just because they are no longer willing to be *told* what to do.

It turns out that dictating orders to your children yields only short-term gains anyway. That's because most people (children and adults) don't want to be under someone else's control. In the business world, even though bosses have the power to hire and fire employees, exercising that power in a irresponsible manner will lead to low employee morale and create an unmotivated workforce full of people who are looking for a different boss.

Using this logic, we don't just *tell* our kids to take out the trash or order them to finish their homework. It's much easier and more effective to communicate these requests in the form of a question. "Sarah, would you please take the trash out after dinner?" It is just as easy to ask, "How much homework do you have today? When are you planning to knock that out?"

From my perspective, it's about mutual respect. As we discussed back in Chapter 1, you can invoke parental authority by dictating to your kids, or you can communicate in a way that causes them to want to participate, as opposed to feeling forced. For the skeptics who will cling to the notion that you can't get cooperation from a child without using force, I would encourage you to think about how you talk to your colleges at work, or your neighbors, or your friends, or your spouse. If that doesn't work, you may want to go back and re-read Chapters 2 and 3.

Ingredient #2: Always Gather the Facts Before Acting

I recently had lunch with a friend who shared an interesting situation he was experiencing regarding his sixteen year-old son. Earlier that morning, he had received a call on his cell phone from his spouse saying, "You're never going to believe what happened!"

From the kitchen on the ground floor, his wife could hear the water running in the upstairs bedroom, which generally signalled that her son was up, and getting ready for school—presumably brushing teeth and taking a shower.

When he didn't appear for breakfast at the usual time, she went upstairs to check on things. A gentle push on his bedroom door yielded the sight of the son lying asleep in bed…with the shower running. "Young man, you get out of bed this instant," the mother exclaimed. She was so angry, she literally lost her voice. Mostly, the mother felt she had been intentionally deceived, where the son had turned on the shower to make her think he was getting ready for school, which was obviously not the case.

"Tom, what would you do in this situation?" my friend asked. Keep in mind that this was a developing story. At this point, the boy was at school and the issue would surely come to a head later when my friend (the boy's father) arrived home from work.

Let me ask, what course of action would you take? There's no doubt it's easy for us parents to work ourselves into an emotional frenzy, especially when something happens that makes us feel disrespected or that we have been intentionally deceived. This tendency to let an undesirable situation rule our emotions is why gathering all the facts before acting on impulse is very important.

Here's how I answered my friend's question about the best way to respond. The first thing I would do is call the involved parties together, perhaps in a family meeting, probably after dinner. The dinner hour would give me a chance to take everyone's temperature and get a feel for my child's attitude and disposition. Guilty children usually reveal themselves to a patient parent. Once we sat down together to discuss the event in question, the first thing I would do is find out what happened. I might start by asking the son, "Why were you in the bed this morning with the shower running?" And, I would be very interested in hearing his response.

As I said earlier, there is a big difference between dealing with deceptive behavior and an honest mistake. It's possible that the son thought to himself, "I'm so tired I'll just lie back down for a moment and rest my eyes." The next thing he knows, the mother bursts through the door, and he's in big trouble.

Frankly, I spend very little time worrying about one-time offenses. If lying back down on the bed wasn't a very smart idea, let's hope this situation serves as one of those life experiences that provides valuable guidance at some point in the future…like when the child heads off to college and mom is no longer there to make sure he gets to school on time.

After listening to the son's explanation, if I could see that it was truly an honest mistake, I would probably ask, "What can we do to make sure this situation doesn't happen again?" Once again, I would be very interested in his response. If the child had a reasonable plan to prevent the situation from reoccurring in the future, as far as I am concerned the discussion would be over. There's no need to beat a minor issue to death. Plus, it's a good idea to conserve your parental power for when it is really needed.

My personal pet peeve is the repeat offense. Honest mistakes are one thing. But, when things start to happen in multiples, now you are dealing with either careless behavior or malicious intent, which is very different than simply making an honest mistake. For example, I don't worry about one bad test score. But, a trend of sub-par grades means it's time to probe further in order to uncover the root cause of the undesirable results. Even with repeat offenses, the same strategy applies—the question-based parent must first gather the facts before making a judgment in order to determine the best course of action.

Ingredient #3: Set and Communicate Clear Expectations

Our kids know where both my wife and I stand on most issues. They don't have to wonder about the difference between right and wrong and they know how to act when they are guests in someone else's house. Were they born with impeccable values? No. Every child comes into this world with a clean slate and much of what they learn and value, not to mention how they are shaped into young adults, is going to come from their parents.

Yes, we parents *do* have an awesome responsibility, particularly once we realize that we are far from perfect ourselves. That being the case, how much should a parent truly expect from their kids? Should you always demand perfection? Do you have a secret desire for your children to become robotic automatons, who do everything the way you want it done? Or, could you be satisfied if they adopted your core values, but still afford them a little flexibility and poetic license to be creative within the bounds of reason?

This idea of setting and communicating clear expectations for children is very important from my perspective. Your kids might as well understand from a young age that certain boundaries exist in every society, and while it's natural for young people to want to test the system, there comes a point where immaturity and innocence must be replaced by personal responsibility. You've heard the saying, *your right to punch me in the face ends where my nose begins.* But, how much latitude should you give a child to express themselves? I remember how my grandparents virtually "wigged out" when The Beatles came to America. They couldn't understand why young men would want to grow their hair out a couple of inches. You would have thought the world was coming to an end. We look back now and wish we were dealing with such simplistic challenges.

To uncomplicate things, there are actually three aspects to setting and communicating clear expectations with your children. The first and most obvious component is education. We talked about this at length back in Chapter 2. It is clearly our responsibility as parents to *Train up a child in the way he should go, and then later in life, he/she will not depart from it.* (Proverbs 22:6). A parent is the primary source of guidance for young people, and as we all know, there is much work to be done in order to teach a child everything they need to know about being successful in life.

Many of the values a child needs to learn must be acquired over time. This will require a fair amount of patience mixed with perseverance, along with some much needed love and support from their primary teacher (you).

As you know, old habits sometimes take time to break, and I can promise you that new habits take just as long to form. And, while there are definitely lessons that can be learned from a child's failures and mistakes, there are just as many lessons that can be learned from your child's successes. Therefore, my best advice for any parent is to be steadfast, patient, kind, and supportive, for the formation of these qualities over the long term will pay big dividends.

The second aspect of setting appropriate expectations is consistency. Who you are as a parent and what type of person you want your children to become should not change from day to day, or week to week. Fundamental values like honesty, integrity, and responsibility, are not something you turn on and off depending on the circumstance. These qualities are either important to you and your family or they are not. The idea of being consistent on core values over time is what has given us enduring documents like The United States Constitution and The Bill of Rights. A similar desire for consistency also produced the Freese House Rules (Chapter 2), an esteemed document which still hangs on the bulletin board in our breezeway. As young people become more autonomous and begin to develop their own belief systems, the decisions they make will largely be influenced by the core values that have been instilled and reinforced by the consistency of their parent's principles and actions over time.

The third aspect of setting reasonable expectations is accountability. If one of your little lambs wanders off course, some corrective action may be needed to guide them back into the flock. For some reason, corrective action usually translates into punishment, to the point where over-punishing children is becoming a larger and larger social problem within families. Punishing a child, for example, who had no way of knowing better is a bad strategy. If the parents aren't willing to invest the time and energy needed to educate their children, then perhaps they themselves should be punished. Oftentimes the best corrective action is facilitated by some good old-fashioned question-based communication. For example, "Jimmy, do you understand why such-and-such is a bad idea?" Granted, if you have already talked with little Jimmy once, twice, or three times, then you might have to move beyond simply communicating with your child into dishing out some good old-fashioned consequences.

Ingredient #4: There Must Be a Downside for Unacceptable Behavior

In any society, culture, or family unit, certain rules of decorum are required to maintain social decency and order. Kids not only need boundaries that are adequately defined and communicated, they need to know that you are serious about your convictions. They also need to understand that there will always be a downside for exhibiting poor judgment or unacceptable behavior.

Throughout this book, we have talked about discipline and consistency at length, and I myself, am consistent with regards to advocating the need for parental discipline. But, I am not a proponent of penalizing a child with harsher and harsher punishments as the primary vehicle for corrective action. There's an old saying that if your only tool is a hammer, then everything will start to look like a nail. Let me put it this way. You are in for a tumultuous ride if you plan to punish your kids every time they step out of bounds in some way.

Instead, it's a better idea to reserve the more severe consequences for more significant offenses. As we discussed in Chapter 5, the purpose of a consequence is not as much to punish the child, as it is to foster a learning opportunity that will prevent the same incident or offense from happening again the future.

Putting a child in *time-out* is a popular strategy among parents who wish to adjust a child's attitude or behavior. It would be easy for me, for example, to ask my child to sit in a designated time-out chair if they spoke sharply to me or their mother. How long the child needs to stay in time-out, of course, depends on the situation, but the purpose of the consequence is to create a downside that will hopefully cause the child to realize that being disrespectful to a parent is something that needs to be avoided in the future.

We also talked about the need for an escalation strategy when it comes to administrating consistent discipline within the household. If two minutes of time-out does not succeed in curbing the behavior, then perhaps you escalate to five minutes next time. If five minutes is not enough to make an impression, then I might combine some time-out with an increase in the child's responsibilities around the house. Or one of my favorites, turn their Saturday into a "work day for dad." It is critical your child understands that you are prepared to escalate the level of consequences until the undesirable behavior changes. I don't threaten my kids, and I'm not interested in participating in a game of, "let's see how far we can push dad before he backs down." If my child wants to play games by continuing to defy the expectations we have set, then I am going to get something out of it—an impeccably groomed yard, perhaps.

My mindset toward discipline is relatively simple. Basically, I don't want to fuss at my kids, and I darn sure don't want them fussing at me. I have found that the best way to accomplish this goal is to create enough of a downside early in the learning process, so that small bumps in the road don't become larger issues later on.

Last night, I happened to notice that my daughter's assignment book from school had no entries. The entire page was completely blank. The assignment book I am referring to is the daily planner students are expected to use to document homework assignments, projects, upcoming exams, quiz grades, etc. A blank assignment book generally indicates that something unusual happened that day. Either they had no classes, or my daughter took the day off from her responsibilities. As suspected, it was the latter.

When something is not right, you could easily get emotional and barrage your child with an intense verbal assault. I suppose that's one way to create a downside, but there are only so many times you can yell at a child before they stop listening. Let me say it like this. There's nothing you can say in a loud voice that you couldn't also communicate just as effectively in a calm, serious tone.

Sometimes, a well placed question (or two) is the best way to create a behavioral downside without losing your composure or your position as an authority figure. In the example from last night, I simply asked, "Why are there no entries in your assignment book for today?"

My daughter is pretty intelligent. So, she sometimes offers an innocuous answer to sidestep the question. "It was a hectic day," she said. But, since I know that the primary reason to ask a question is to get the real answer, I persisted, "What does that mean?" I'm thinking, it doesn't make sense that a busy day would yield fewer notes or *less* homework. If you can exercise a little patience, most kids quickly realize that the best way to end the conversation is to come clean and give the real answer. Last night, the real answer was that a temporary lapse in judgment took priority over her school work.

Sometimes, there is no good explanation for a child's erratic behavior. It's a safe bet that your children will likely participate in some brainless shenanigans, and they will surely make a few bad decisions on the way to becoming adults, just like you and I did when we were young. While youth does have certain advantages, one of them is not humility. It's often difficult for young people to admit they have erred. Frankly, saying, "I was wrong," is difficult for most grown ups as well. Coming to a mutual conclusion, therefore, that some adjustments need to be made creates a wonderful learning opportunity without having to formally 'penalize' the child. But, I can tell you this. Both of my daughters would rather tend to their responsibilities rather than have their dad in their rooms inquiring as to why something seems to be off-track. It is not the threat of punishment they fear. Rather, it's the downside associated with the heart-to-heart conversation that will end up happening with a question-based parent who is not afraid having to uncover the root cause of the problem.

As a litmus test for how you are doing, consider these questions. How many times do you have to ask your kids to do something before they actually do it? Are you the type of parent who asks a child to "come over here," or "be quiet" in church, but for some reason, the boy or girl completely ignores your request? How do you respond? If they ignore you, do you repeat yourself three or four times? Exasperated parents often blame their kids for not being good listeners. I'm here to tell you that the child in these cases is not the problem.

As a parent, you have to establish early on that there is a downside for unacceptable behavior (like not listening), so your children don't have to wonder whether or not you are serious when the time comes. If you ask a child to *come over* or *be quiet*, and they don't, it's your responsibility to create a downside significant enough to cause them to be more attentive next time. Start by having one of those "Uh oh, dad's got that look in his eye," conversations. If a defiant child really wants to test your resolve, they might have to miss a few soccer matches or birthday parties before the message completely sinks in. But, you must make sure that defiance does not get rewarded, and the easiest way to accomplish this is to make sure that there is a downside when it occurs.

Ingredient #5: Make it Your Goal to Foster Open Communication

Open and honest communication is one of the most important ingredients in any relationship, particularly between parents and children. By this point in the book, you understand that just because you want a child to openly share their thoughts, feelings, and concerns, doesn't mean they always will.

Causing kids to open up unfortunately is not as easy as just asking a bunch of questions. Is it possible to ask questions that will cause children to open up and share lots of important information? The answer is yes, it is absolutely possible. Is it also possible to ask questions that will cause a child to clam up or shut down completely? Unfortunately, the answer to that is yes, as well.

If you are a question-based parent, then you have a lot of control over the types of questions you ask, and how you choose to ask them. Exercising the strategic use of questions gives you the ability to be more effective when communicating with your kids. Otherwise, there are very few mechanisms in place to teach parents on how to ask more effective questions, which is why we spent the time in Chapters 8 and

9 talking about specific questioning techniques like *Active Listening, Global Questions,* and *Humbling Disclaimers.*

Think about questions as the fuel that drives a conversation. Here's a simple analogy that you can try. Sit down with someone you trust and try having a conversation where neither person is allowed to ask questions. No matter what, you cannot use a single question mark. See what happens. Besides feeling awkward and stiff, the conversation will stall out in less than thirty seconds. You simply cannot keep a two-way conversation going without someone "giving it a little gas" by asking questions.

A well placed question can also be a great relationship builder. Asking a friend, for example, how they are doing is one of the easiest ways to show interest in them. Do people like it when we are truly interested in them? Of course, they do! That's why when a husband, wife, or child returns home from work or school, it's always nice to hear, "How was your day?" The purpose of asking this question isn't necessarily to gather facts about someone's day. The reason people ask is to communicate, "I care about you a great deal, and I am very interested in what might be happening in your world." One caveat: be sure to listen to their responses, because you might just receive some important insight into what they might be thinking or how they might actually be feeling.

Too often, I have made the mistake of shutting down communication with my kids, without meaning to. Later I find myself apologizing and then having to work twice as hard to rekindle our relationship. Open communication is a rare and fragile commodity and one that must be treated with ultimate care and mutual respect. There's that familiar phrase again—mutual respect. Can we agree that relationships are a two-way street? A parent has to show respect in order to be respected. Even when you have good intentions, it's easy to say the wrong thing at the wrong time. That's why I spend less time worrying about what to say, and more time thinking about what to ask.

The question-based principles that foster effective communication do require some effort on the part of the parent, that's true. But the open lines of effective communication that will result are much more desirable than existing in an otherwise combative or non-nurturing environment.

Strategic Questioning is an Acquired Skill

Just talking about the importance of asking good questions is easy. By now, you must have a pretty good idea about the differences between being question-based and statement-based. However, developing your ability to be totally fluent in the strategic use of questions, and gaining the confidence that you will ask the right question at the right time is an acquired skill.

What does it mean to be *fluent* in the strategic use of questions? The concept of fluency is generally used to describe someone's ability to converse proficiently using a second language. Being fluent in a second language, for example, means that you can comfortably speak and understand the language. The true definition of fluency, however, is ability to actually "think" in terms of a certain language or communication style, as opposed to the mental gymnastics that would be required to translate back and forth between multiple different languages in your mind.

I studied Spanish in high school for two years. Even so, I honestly had no idea what other people were saying most of the time. Someone in the class would turn to me, and say,

"Como se llama?" Then, I would have to think to myself, "Oh my goodness, what does that mean? Let's see...como means *how*. Se yama...means *are you called*? I would eventually figure out that the other person was asking my name. I would then have to reverse my thinking to go from, I am called Tom Freese...to, "Me llamo Tomás." Whew!

Having to work this hard to translate an entire conversation in your mind makes it extremely difficult to communicate. Similarly, if a parent has to rack their brain to think of the right question at the right time in the conversation, then communicating with your spouse or kids becomes equally difficult. Fortunately, I can tell you that the opposite is true, where having the confidence to know you will ask the right question at the right time can be very empowering.

Here's a question I invite you to ponder: How much time have you spent thus far in your personal life (or professional career) conditioning yourself to become more fluent in the strategic use of questions? I bet we already know the answer. Nobody talks about conversational dynamics!

I understand that people are often set in their ways. It's natural to be averse to change, especially since some life changes can be quite difficult. If you would like to become more proficient in the strategic use of questions, then I have good news. Learning to become question-based is a skill that is easily acquired. It won't happen without some practice on your part, but if you are willing to invest just ten minutes per day for three consecutive days, you can do it. That's a small price to pay to develop a life skill that will change the way you interact with children.

Ten Questions Exercise

When delivering QBS Methodology Training to live audiences, we often use a simple exercise called "Ten Questions" to teach salespeople how to *think* in terms of question marks, rather than statements. This same exercise can work just as well for friends, neighbors, coworkers, and yes, even parents.

Of course, in order to facilitate an exercise about asking questions, we need to think of some possible topics to ask questions about. I encourage you not to think about specific situations at home or your daily routine. For now, let's just focus on the idea of becoming more proficient in the strategic use of questions.

The first time I facilitated this exercise in a corporate environment, I asked the audience to help me think of three obscure topics we could ask questions about. The suggested topics were: Sailing, Yugoslavia, and Nuclear Physics. Weird, huh? I wrote those three topics on the flipchart in front of the room. Next, I had everyone stand up and choose a partner. Then, I explained: the object of this exercise is simple—one person counts (on their fingers) while their other asks ten questions about the topic. Hence the name, *Ten Questions*.

How many questions do you suppose could possibly be asked about a topic like sailing? The exercise only calls for ten. Sounds easy, doesn't it?

There are a couple ground rules you must follow when playing Ten Questions. First, speed is important. If you want to condition yourself you to easily think of the right question at the right time in a conversation, then it is to your advantage to complete this exercise by asking the questions with a certain popcorn consistency. Your questions should come out with a certain steadiness that sounds like the *pop, pop, pop*…of popcorn popping.

Secondly, you want to train yourself to think outside the box of your assigned topic. If your topic is sailing, for example, it doesn't help to fixate on the topic word by asking questions like: Does your mother like *sailing*? Does your brother like *sailing*? Does your sister like *sailing*? Does your father like *sailing*? Your challenge is to think of questions that explore periphery ideas related to the topic, like asking about the history of boats, or the financial investment required to compete in the America's Cup race. Asking questions on the periphery of the main topic will help broaden your thought process. In fact, I usually tell students they cannot use the topic word in more than four of the ten questions being asked.

If a topic is chosen that someone in the class isn't very familiar with, people sometimes complain, "Photography! But, I don't know anything about photography!" Well, doesn't that mean you should have lots of questions? Plenty of things will happen in your child's world that you know little about, and your newfound ability to ask good questions might just be the bonding agent you need to have meaningful conversations in those areas.

Now it's time for *you* to try this exercise. If you are up to the challenge, I will assign a topic, and then I want you to put the book down, pause a few seconds to collect your thoughts, and then practice asking ten questions about the suggested topic. Be sure to count on your fingers so you know when you get all ten. Are you ready? Are you going to try it? Good! Your topic is: Bicycles. Go!

(Mark the page and complete the exercise.)

Did you make it to ten questions? If not, close the book now and really try it! Most people discover that what they thought was a simple exercise turns out to be quite challenging. For many, the brain goes blank after the first few questions and it can be surprisingly difficult to get back on track. Therein lies the opportunity to sharpen one's communication skills.

Completing this initial exercise of stringing together ten questions about a selected topic is just the tip of the iceberg. While some personal skills are difficult to master, becoming question-based is actually pretty easy, if you are willing to commit to ten minutes per day for three consecutive days. In ten minutes, you can easily run through this exercise three times, using different topics. No doubt, you will discover that thinking of ten questions about a selected topic becomes progressively easier each time through.

What topics might you choose when doing this exercise on your own? It doesn't matter. Get some suggestions from your local newspaper, or on your commute to work. You can ask ten questions about anything—violins, road signs, or fertilizer. If you happen to be in a funky mood, try asking ten questions about hair styles or leather sofas. What you are trying to do is develop the skill of thinking, not just reacting, which can then be applied to anything related to your daily routine.

People often ask, "Tom, how are you able to think of the right question at the right time?" The truth is I don't try to think of the "right" questions. Instead, I use this same technique to formulate a mental list of questions that *could* be asked. At that point, choosing the most relevant question from a mental list is relatively simple.

Once you become fluent in the strategic use of questions, you are in a strong position to apply all of the question-based techniques that have been presented in this book. Might it require going back and reviewing some of the material again? Perhaps. But, do you know what requires even more work? Things like dealing with conflict in the household, a lack of cooperation, disrespect for the rules, or just general bickering.

Doing "The Right Thing"

A few months ago, I was away on a business trip to London. Late one night, I called home to check in with the family. My wife Laura answered the telephone.

"Hi, Honey. How was your day?" I asked.

"Actually," she said, "we have had a very interesting evening."

"What exactly does that mean?" I inquired. *Interesting* is one of those words that people use to let you know that something unusual has occurred, and it might not be good. There's usually more to the story when I hear that word.

Apparently, my youngest daughter Mary Claire called a family meeting during dinner earlier that evening. In the Freese house, anybody can call a family meeting at any time, about whatever happens to be on their mind. In this case, Mary Claire felt that the other two (mom and big sister) were ganging up and "picking" on her in a hurtful way. Frankly, from the way my wife described the scenario, it sounded like one of those times where a little sarcastic humor escalated into a situation where someone's feelings got hurt. In this case, the hurt feelings belonged to my eight year-old daughter.

In the meeting, Mary Claire expressed her frustration and asked Sarah and Laura to please stop their teasing. She also asked for an apology, which they quickly gave. In less than five minutes, everything that needed to be said had been communicated and everyone felt better. After we talked, Laura handed the telephone to MC, and I said, "I heard you called a family meeting tonight?"

"Yes," she replied, "and everything is fine now."

When I hung up the telephone afterwards, I remember feeling very gratified. If my eight-year-old can call a meeting, and then openly convey her feelings to whoever is causing her a problem, in a way that resolves the issue in a matter of minutes, isn't that ninety percent of what it takes to be successful in life right there? You go, girl!

At some point, you must decide as a family how you want to interact with each other, and also, how you want to be interacted with. This decision is not something that can just be dictated to your children. Instead, part of your role as parent is to establish and communicate reasonable expectations for the family, and then deal with any differences in opinion as they arise.

Can I let you in on a secret? The more effective you are as a question-based parent, the less you will have to wield the sword of parental authority. How about this idea? Rather than just relying on the phrase, "Because I said so," why not base your parental logic on this idea; "Because it's the right thing to do." Or, when your child wants to do something that doesn't make sense, the opposing logic works just as well, "Because that's not the right thing." If you think about the actual message behind the phrase, "Because I said so," this phrase is ultimately being used to either encourage a child to do the right thing, or avoid something that is not the right thing.

"Mom, why do I have to take out the trash?" is a familiar complaint parents hear when a child feels unfairly put upon. And, yes, all children feel put upon when it comes to taking out the trash. How should the parent respond to this complaint? At some point, you have to explain, "Honey, we all have chores and responsibilities, and one of yours happens to be taking out the garbage once a week, or as needed. As the mother, I am expected to do certain things around the house, and you are expected to take on certain responsibilities as well. So, can you please take care of the trash before you go outside to play with your friends?"

What we are really talking about here are core values. Why should your child refuse to cheat on a test at school, even if the opportunity presents itself? The answer is, "because it's not the right thing" to cheat on a test. Why should a teenager say no to drugs? Ultimately, because experimenting with drugs and underage drinking is "not the right thing."

By the way, why does dad spend a Saturday every now and then to help build a Habitat Home? Or, why does mom sometimes prepare meals for families in the church who are experiencing hardship of some kind? Because it is absolutely "the right thing" to help others in their time of need.

Some day in the not too distant future, your children will be totally independent. At that point, they are going to have to make decisions for themselves. When that day arrives, in addition to being tempted by any number of life's indulgences, your kids will be exposed to levels of vulgarity that would make a sailor blush. They will also become privy to all kinds of short cuts for how to circumvent authority and cheat the system.

What path will your children take when these opportunities present themselves? There's no way to know for sure until the time comes. But, we do know that human nature dictates that people tend to gravitate to whatever feels most comfortable. With your child's future in mind, it is incumbent on parents, especially during the formative years, to demonstrate to children that the actions they take and the decisions they make should be based on doing the right thing, as opposed to parents just telling kids to do something, "Because I said so." Honestly, it's not difficult to teach kids the difference between right and wrong. The challenge is being consistent, especially during those times when kids who are testing their negotiation skills push to find out if you have true convictions with regard to upholding certain values, or if you are just going through the motions.

The Ultimate Question

The question-based parent has the ability to ask lots of questions, but they are careful not to ask too many at one time. The question-based parent also asks meaningful questions, and they are patient enough to give their children a chance to respond. And, though our primary focus throughout this book has been on how to be question-based, I want to close by giving you one of the most valuable questions a parent can ask their kids. Don't wait to implement this idea, however, because the answer to this question might just change your life.

Do you *really* want to know how you're doing as a parent? Would you also like some perspective on how your kids perceive you as a leader, mentor, coach, and confidant? If you are at all interested in hearing your child's opinion, I would strongly encourage you to take the following risk. The next time you experience one of those special moments when you have an opportunity for some quality conversation with your son or daughter, ask them the following question. *If our roles were reversed where you were the parent and I was the child, what would you be doing differently?* If you can open both your ears and your heart, you will receive some of the most valuable feedback a parent could ever wish for. Imagine that, parents sharing wisdom and guidance with their kids and their children sharing insight and perspective back with their parents. Maybe this family thing really is a team effort!

While you're at it, try asking your spouse a similar question. "Honey, if you were me, what would you be doing differently?" Now, you may have to give them a moment to get up off the floor, as spouses are not used to their partners asking for feedback. Again, you might be equally amazed by what you hear. Try asking your co-workers or subordinates, "If you were me, what would you be doing differently?" The information that will subsequently come your way is priceless, yet you would probably never hear it if you didn't directly ask for it.

Be sure to notice two things about the feedback you receive. First, I bet you will hear different versions of the same advice from multiple sources. This is a good way to identify and confirm certain behavioral trends (of yours) that need further evaluation. If you are an assertive person, for example, you might get some indication that you can sometimes be pushy, and you will hear this from multiple people. On the other hand, if you are the disorganized type person who often over-commits, you will hear that, too— again, from multiple sources.

Secondly, an honest request for constructive feedback like I am suggesting, is a terrific relationship builder. Why? Because people don't solicit advice from just anyone. Instead, we seek input from people we care about and trust, and whose opinions we value. Once again, your question creates the classic win/win scenario—you gain valuable insight and feedback on how to be a better friend, spouse, boss, co-worker, or parent, and the person you asked feels important and valuable because you respected their opinion enough to ask such a vulnerable question.

No More Business as Usual

At the outset of this book, I told you that much of what I have learned about dealing with people has come from my experiences as a salesperson, a sales trainer, a Sunday school teacher, and just having been around long enough now to have the frosted-hair look of someone in their mid-forties.

When the salespeople who attended my courses started telling me many years ago, "Hey, Tom, your question-based techniques have boosted my sales, but they have also helped me be a better husband, friend, wife, and parent," I was flattered. It took me a while, however, to realize how much value there was in applying question-based communication techniques outside of work. The truth is, being question-based is not something that you just turn off at the end of a business day. You either *are* interested in communicating effectively with other people, or you aren't.

Ironically, people who are now being exposed to these ideas for the very first time, either through this book or my work in speaking about *The Question Based Parent*, often come up to me saying, "Tom, these techniques have not only helped me to become a better parent and spouse, but your question-based approach has also empowered me to become much more effective at the office! One unsuspecting parent even went so far as to ask, "Have you ever thought about creating a seminar program for business people?"

Life is funny, isn't it?

Chapter Highlights

Chapter 1: *The Psychology of Questions vs. Statements*

1.1 While a parent may be able to control a young child with authority, the only way you will be able to influence your children as they get older is to earn their respect.

1.2 If you are willing to communicate in a way that is respectful to your children, you then have the moral authority to expect a reciprocal level of mutual respect in return.

1.3 Avoid rhetorical questions that have no purpose other than shaming your children. One of the keys to effective communication is being patient enough to give the child a legitimate opportunity to respond.

1.4 Asking thoughtful questions is one of the best ways to communicate that you are genuinely interested in someone's feelings and opinions.

1.5 Very simply, telling is not selling.

Chapter 2: *Train Up a Child*

2.1 Parents have a responsibility to teach children that there is an upside for doing things that are positive and helpful, and there is also a downside for behaving in ways that are detrimental to themselves or to others.

2.2 Affording a child unlimited access to privileges without an age-appropriate responsibility makes it easy for over-indulged children to take many of life's blessings for granted.

2.3 Hold regular family meetings to set expectations and discuss issues when they arise. Then you can formulate a plan that will adequately deal with issues and secure agreement from everyone involved.

2.4 Don't make idle threats to your kids. A question-based parent always tries to say what they mean, and mean what they say.

2.5 It usually takes a child longer to complete an assigned chore than if you just went ahead and finished it yourself. However, teaching children to stick with it and always do a quality job is an investment in time that will pay big dividends over the long run.

2.6 When you assign responsibilities, you must be ready to praise your kids for a job well done. Words of affirmation from parents to children are needed vitamins that nourish the soul.

Chapter 3: *The Art of Negotiation*

3.1 Do you want your kids to grow up to be good negotiators? Are you willing to let them practice on you?

3.2 For a child to get what they want, they need to make sure the parent also gets what they want in exchange.

3.3 You must not give into a child's demands in exchange for them to stop exhibiting unacceptable behavior. This will only escalate their tantrums in the future.

3.4 For kids, part of learning how to negotiate is understanding that you don't always get what you want.

3.5 The best way to teach kids the value of money is to let them run out a few times. If you bail a child out every time they run short, you are setting yourself up to be bailing them out for a very long time.

3.6 Resist the temptation to answer for your kids. Speaking confidently to adults other than a parent is an important life skill, one that can only be learned through practice.

Chapter 4: *Delivering Bad News Gracefully*

4.1 If your child makes an unreasonable request, the answer could still be "yes," if certain conditions are met that makes the request mutually beneficial.

4.2 When a child argues for something because "everyone else" is doing it, encourage them to consider all the kids in third-world countries who are significantly less fortunate that most of us.

4.3   Children should be expected to follow certain rules of the house, and parents should have the fortitude to stand behind them.

4.4   Use humbling disclaimers to have better conversations. If you are respectful of the other person's right not to share with you, it's amazing how much information you can get.

4.5   Some people are naturally good at always knowing how to say the right thing. The rest of us have to think about what we say and the messages that might get communicated as a result.

Chapter 5: *The Balancing Act of Discipline*

5.1   The purpose of discipline is education—teaching your kids the difference between right and wrong in a way that causes them to gravitate naturally toward reasonable behavior.

5.2   There has to be a downside for poor judgment. Kids won't understand the importance of respecting authority until they discover that there are consequences for crossing the line.

5.3   Before punishing a child, first understand the nature of the incident, because there is a big difference between an accident and intentionally disrespectful behavior.

5.4   The objective of a consequence is to deter the young person from making the same mistake in the future.

5.5   Self-discipline is that little voice inside your child's head that will cause them to ask, "What is the right thing to do in this situation?"

5.6   Avoid using your child's first name as a spear.

Chapter 6: *Gold Medals & German Shepherds*

6.1   While some people are motivated to run fast toward Gold Medals, many other people run even faster from German Shepherds.

6.2   If a child receives more attention by behaving poorly, let's not be surprised when that causes a child who craves attention to exhibit more unacceptable behavior.

6.3   A heartfelt compliment is one of the most valuable gifts a parent can give a child. They are always available to be given out, and they don't cost a thing.

6.4   Show a little interest in your child's abilities and it's amazing how quickly you can become the coolest parent on the block!

6.5   Tell your sons that you are proud of them. Let your daughters know that you think they are beautiful. A child's impression of themselves is often a reflection of what their parents see in them.

Chapter 7: *Mismatching: A Contradiction in Terms*

7.1   A younger person's self-esteem is one of their most important and fragile possessions, and it needs to be protected at all costs.

7.2   Mismatching is the instinctive tendency of individuals to respond in a contrarian manner, usually driven by one's own need to feel valuable.

7.3   Because mismatching is the purest form of contradiction, it can have a destructive influence on interpersonal communication.

7.4   If something you say sarcastically wasn't ha-ha funny, then it was probably demeaning to whoever the sarcastic remark was directed.

7.5   While declarative statements are easily mismatched, questions help to defuse the emotional triggers that otherwise fuel another person's need to respond adversely.

7.6   Demonstrating to your kids that you are truly impressed by who they are and what they can do is one of the surest ways to end up with impressive kids.

7.7   Mismatching is the early stage of rebellion.

Chapter 8: *A Quick Course in Listening*

8.1 Children and adults both have an innate desire to be heard. We want to share our opinions and our experiences, and we very much want other people to listen attentively.

8.2 One of the most effective listening skills is the ability to ask insightful questions that will expand what the other person is saying.

8.3 Good listeners tend to also be great question askers.

8.4 Seventy-five percent of human communication is non-verbal. Hence, there is a lot more to active listening than just hearing the words.

8.5 Ask your child for their opinion. The sooner you acknowledge that you don't have all the answers, the quicker the communications with your children will open up.

8.6 For parents, having more information is always better.

Chapter 9: *Conversational Dynamics*

9.1 Being question-based is a choice. The relationship you have with your children will largely be shaped by the choices you make with regard to how you interact with them.

9.2 Independence is a learned behavior that can only be achieved if you are willing to give your child an opportunity to experience the ups and downs of success and failure.

9.3 Understanding and then addressing the root cause of a problem is much easier than fussing at your kids repeatedly for the same offense.

9.4 If you ask a legitimate question, you must be patient enough to give your child an opportunity to provide a legitimate response.

9.5 Use humbling disclaimers to defuse any pressure or anxiety a child might otherwise feel from questions you pose.

Chapter 10: *How to Become a Question Based Parent*

10.1 Every ship needs a captain, but every captain also needs a willing and cooperative crew who respects their leadership.

10.2 A child comes into this world as a clean slate, and much of what they learn will come from their parents.

10.3 Kids need boundaries that are adequately defined and communicated. They also need to know that you are serious about your convictions, and that there will be a downside for poor judgment or unacceptable behavior.

10.4 There's nothing you can say in a loud voice that you couldn't also communicate just as effectively in a calm serious tone.

10.5 Open communication is a rare and fragile commodity and one that must be treated with ultimate care and mutual respect.

10.6 At some point, you must decide as a family how you want to interact with each other, and also, how you want to be interacted with. This decision is not something that can just be dictated to your children. Instead, part of your role as parent is to establish and communicate reasonable expectations for the family, and then deal with any differences in opinion as they arise.

10.7 The more effective you are as a question-based parent, the less you have to wield the sword of parental authority.

10.8 Ask this question, "If our roles were reversed and you were the parent and I was the child, what would you be doing differently?" If you can open your ears and your heart, you will receive some of the most valuable feedback a parent could ever wish for.

Secrets of Question Based Selling

Tom Freese's first book is a business block-buster. As the flagship in a best selling series, Secrets of Question Based Selling introduces a new and proven sales methodology (QBS) showing sales professionals how to dramatically increase their results without making customers feel pushed or pressured.

It Only Takes 1% to Have a Competitive Edge in Sales

Most sales are won or lost by very small margins. Consequently, salespeople need an edge, a differentiable advantage that sets them apart. That's what you will find in Tom Freese's second book—100 chapters, each designed to give you a one-percent advantage over your competitors. After all, it only takes 1% to have a competitive edge in sales.

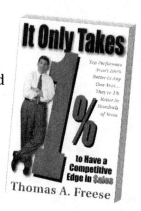

The New Era of Salesmanship

Sales gimmicks from twenty years ago won't benefit you in today's business environment. In this book, Tom Freese steps outside the box of traditional thinking to improve the performance of your entire organization. Positive change is eminent and there is no time to waste. A new era of salesmanship has definitely begun!

About the Author

As an expert in question-based communication techniques, Tom Freese is a dynamic public speaker and one of the leading trainers in corporate America. Drawing upon his own personal life experiences, Tom developed the QBS Methodology, which is now being used to teach business veterans all over the world how to build and manage effective long-term interpersonal relationships.

In *The Question Based Parent*, Tom Freese applies the same principles of human nature and mutual respect to the parent-child relationship, in order to show parents how to create a happier, healthier, and more cooperative household environment. After all, mentoring and interpersonal communication is what parents endeavor to do every day.

Tom and his wife Laura were married in 1989, and now live in Atlanta with their two daughters, Sarah and Mary Claire.

Contact Information:

QBS Research, Inc.
PO Box 922933
Atlanta, GA 30010-2933
Office: (770) 840-7640
www.thequestionbasedparent.com

"I hope that future generations will look back and see this book as a collection of truths that will be just as relevant and applicable to parents a hundred years from now as they are today. That alone would be an impressive and remarkable accomplishment. Let's call everything else a bonus."

—Thomas A. Freese